Charlotte Perkins Gilman's
The Yellow Wall-Paper

Charlotte Perkins Gilman's *The Yellow Wall-Paper* (1892) generated spirited debates in literary and political circles on both sides of the Atlantic when it was first published. Today this story of a young wife and mother succumbing to madness is hailed as both a feminist classic and a key text in the American literary canon.

Functioning as both sourcebook and critical edition of Perkins Gilman's widely debated text, this book offers:

- the complete original text as published in the *New England Magazine* in 1892, including illustrations and full commentary
- extensive introductory comment on the contexts and many interpretations of the text, from publication to the present
- annotated extracts from key contextual documents, reviews, and critical works
- cross-references between documents and sections of the guide, in order to suggest links between contexts and criticism
- suggestions for further reading.

Part of the Routledge Guides to Literature series, this volume is essential reading for all those beginning detailed study of *The Yellow Wall-Paper* and seeking a way through Perkins Gilman's text and the wealth of contextual and critical material that surrounds it.

Catherine J. Golden is Professor of English at Skidmore College, USA.

Routledge Guides to Literature*

Editorial Advisory Board: Richard Bradford (University of Ulster at Coleraine), Jan Jedrzejewski (University of Ulster at Coleraine), Duncan Wu (St Catherine's College, University of Oxford)

Routledge Guides to Literature offer clear introductions to the most widely studied authors and literary texts.

Each book engages with texts, contexts, and criticism, highlighting the range of critical views and contextual factors that need to be taken into consideration in advanced studies of literary works. The series encourages informed but independent readings of texts by ranging as widely as possible across the contextual and critical issues relevant to the works examined and highlighting areas of debate as well those of critical consensus. Alongside general guides to texts and authors, the series includes "sourcebooks," which allow access to reprinted contextual and critical materials as well as annotated extracts of primary text.

Available in this series:

* Some books in this series were originally published in the Routledge Literary Sourcebooks series, edited by Duncan Wu, or the Complete Critical Guide to English Literature series, edited by Richard Bradford and Jan Jedrzejewski.

Charlotte Perkins Gilman's
The Yellow Wall-Paper
A Sourcebook and Critical Edition

Edited by Catherine J. Golden

Routledge
Taylor & Francis Group

NEW YORK AND LONDON

First published 2004
by Routledge
711 Third Avenue, New York, NY 10017

Simultaneously published in the UK
by Routledge
2 Park Square, Milton Park, Abingdon, Oxon, OX14 4RN

Routledge is an imprint of the Taylor & Francis Group

Selection and editorial matter © 2004 Catherine J. Golden

Typeset in Sabon and Gill Sans by RefineCatch Ltd, Bungay, Suffolk

Library of Congress Cataloging in Publication Data
Gilman, Charlotte Perkins, 1860–1935.
The yellow wall-paper: a sourcebook and critical edition/edited by Catherine J. Golden.
    p.cm.
Includes bibliographical references and index.
    1. Gilman, Charlotte Perkins, 1860–1935. Yellow wallpaper. 2. Feminism and
literature–United States. 3. Mentally ill women in literature. 4. Married women
in literature. 5. Sex role in literature. 6. Mentally ill women–Fiction. 7. Married
women–Fiction. 8. Sex role–Fiction. I. Golden, Catherine. II. Title.
    PS1744.G57Y45 2004
    813'.4–dc22   2004002077

British Library Cataloguing in Publication Data
A catalogue record for this book is available from the British Library.

ISBN 0–415–26357–3 (hbk)
ISBN 0–415–26358–1 (pbk)

For my husband, Michael Steven Marx,
And my sons, Jesse and Emmet Golden-Marx

Contents

2: Interpretations

3: Text

4: Further Reading

Illustrations

Annotation and Footnotes

Annotation is a key feature of the sourcebooks within this series. Both the original notes from reprinted texts and new annotations by the volume editor appear at the bottom of the relevant page. The reprinted notes are prefaced by the author's name in square brackets, e.g. "[Robinson's note.]"

Parenthetical page number references in Contexts and Interpretations refer to the editions the authors used.

Acknowledgments

A book is a production of many hands. I am particularly grateful to Duncan Wu, series editor, for encouraging me to undertake this project. I am also thankful for the expert and prompt editorial assistance I received from Fiona Cairns, Duncan Wu, Liz Thompson, Ruth Whittington, and the entire staff at Routledge. Their enthusiasm, thoughtful responses to queries, and commitment to the sourcebook series have been invaluable.

I am fortunate to have a community of Gilman scholars with whom to discuss ideas for research and teaching. Like all those who work on Gilman, I am indebted to the pioneering scholarship on the story by the late Elaine R. Hedges, the bibliographical and biographical work of Gary Scharnhorst, and the scholarship of Denise D. Knight. While working on this project, I benefited from the scholarly insights of Denise D. Knight, Gary Scharnhorst, Charlotte Rich, Jennifer Tuttle, Cynthia J. Davis, Shelley Fisher Fishkin, Ann J. Lane, and Joanna Zangrando—generous Gilman colleagues and friends.

I am grateful to Linda Simon and Mason Stokes, Skidmore colleagues and friends, who offered help in clarifying annotations on Alice James and queer theory, their respective areas of expertise. Several staff members of the Lucy Scribner Library at Skidmore College skillfully answered my queries and helped me to find sources for inclusion in this book. I thank, in particular, John Cosgrove, Melinda Taormina, Amy Syrell, and Marilyn Sheffer. This volume also reflects the insights of the many Skidmore students to whom I have taught "The Yellow Wall-Paper" in an English and Women's Studies course entitled "Women and Literature" (EN 223). I am particularly grateful to four students—Jeanne O'Farrell Eddy '03, Nicole Zuckerman '04, Jamie Glover '04, and Camila Lertora '04—for reading text and annotations. Nicole Zuckerman, who served as my student assistant for two years, also offered excellent help in finding sources, Xeroxing, and proofreading. I owe special thanks to Skidmore College for providing a Faculty Major Project Completion Grant to fund my research in the summer of 2003, enabling me to bring the sourcebook to prompt completion.

Foremost, my husband, Michael Marx, was an excellent sounding board, offering expert editorial advice and encouragement. My sons, Jesse Benjamin and Emmet Gabriel Golden-Marx, are avid readers of books and pictures. Our family cats, Lee and Rose, purred contentedly beside me as I researched, drafted, and revised this sourcebook.

I am also grateful for my mother, Nancy Golden, my sister, Pam Golden, and my close women friends—Lollie Abramson, Daria Schewe, Peggy Trounstine, Jeanne Eddy, Marilyn Sandberg, Mary Carr, and Ellen Sheets—who supported me throughout this project.

The following publishers, institutions, and individuals have kindly given permission to reprint materials:

Associated University Presses for Ann Heilmann, "Overwriting Decadence: Charlotte Perkins Gilman, Oscar Wilde, and the Feminization of Art in 'The Yellow Wall-Paper' " from *The Mixed Legacy of Charlotte Perkins Gilman* eds. Catherine J. Golden and Joanna Schneider Zangrando, University of Delaware Press, 2000.

The author for Annette Kolodny, "A Map for Rereading: or Gender and the Interpretation of Literary Texts" from *New Literary History* 11:3, 1980. © 1980 by Annette Kolodny, all rights reserved.

Cornell University Press for Tom Lutz, *American Nervousness, 1903: An Anecdotal History*, 1991.

The Feminist Press at the City University of New York and the Time Warner Book Group UK for "Afterword" to *The Yellow Wall-Paper*, © 1973 by Elaine R. Hedges, www.feministpress.org.

Feminist Studies Inc. and the author for Susan S. Lanser, "Feminist Criticism, 'The Yellow Wallpaper,' and the Politics of Color in America," *Feminist Studies* 15:3, 1989.

The Modern Language Association of America for Guiyou Huang, "The Use of Audiovisual Material as an Aid in Teaching 'The Yellow Wall-Paper' " in *Approaches to Teaching Gilman's "The Yellow Wall-Paper" and "Herland"* eds. Denise D. Knight and Cynthia J. Davis, 2003.

Mosaic: a journal for the interdisciplinary study of literature for Marty Roth, "Gilman's Arabesque Wallpaper," 34: 4, 2001.

The Mütter Museum, The College of Physicians of Philadelphia, for the portrait of S. Weir Mitchell MC by Dvorak, 1890.

Special Collections, Schaeffer Library, Union College, for the opening page of "The Yellow Wall-Paper," and for Jo. H. Hatfield's illustrations "She didn't know I was in the Room," and the tailpiece for "The Yellow Wall-Paper," *New England Magazine*, 1892.

The Schlesinger Library, Radcliffe Institute, Harvard University, for the portrait of Charlotte Perkins Gilman, 1903, the portrait of Charlotte and George Houghton (Ho) Gilman, 1909, the portrait of Charles Walter Stetson, n.d., 1905, the cover of "The Yellow Wall Paper" for the Small, Maynard and Company edition, 1899.

Studies in American Fiction for Catherine J. Golden, "The Writing of 'The Yellow Wallpaper': A Double Palimpsest," vol. 17, 1989.

University of California Press for Walter Benn Michaels, "Introduction" to *The Gold Standard and the Logic of Naturalism: American Literature at the Turn of the Century*, copyright © 1987 The Regents of the University of California.

William Morris Agency, Inc. on behalf of the author for Joseph Leon Edel, *The Diary of Alice James*. Copyright © 1934 by Leon Edel.

Women's Studies for Janice Haney-Peritz, "Monumental Feminism and Literature's Ancestral House; Another Look at 'The Yellow Wallpaper' " in *Women's Studies* (1983) 12:2. http:///www.tandf.co.uk/journals/titles/00497878.html.

Yale University Press for Sandra M. Gilbert and Susan Gubar, *The Madwoman in the Attic: The Woman Writer and the Nineteenth-Century Literary Imagination*, 1979.

Every effort has been made to trace and contact copyright holders. The publishers would be pleased to hear from any copyright holders not acknowledged here so that these acknowledgment pages can be amended at the earliest opportunity.

Figure 1 Charlotte Perkins Gilman, *ca.*1903. Reprinted by permission of Schlesinger Library, Radcliffe Institute, Harvard University.

Introduction

It is hard to picture a text more readily associated with Charlotte Perkins Gilman than "The Yellow Wall-Paper" (1892). Although Gilman's extensive oeuvre includes poetry, short fiction, novels, lectures, theoretical works, and an auto-biography, her literary reputation mainly rests on this striking example of psychological realism, which, ironically, she dismisses in her autobiography as "no more 'literature' than my other stuff, being definitely written 'with a purpose' " (*Living* 121, see **p. 52**). Gilman (1860–1935) (Fig. 1) began her professional career as a poet. She earned the praise of luminaries including Upton Sinclair, Lester Frank Ward, George Bernard Shaw, Woodrow Wilson, and William Dean Howells, who compared "Similar Cases" (1890) and her other "civic satire" to James Russell Lowell's *The Biglow Papers* (1848). At the turn of the twentieth century, she lectured widely across America and in England and earned an international reputation for her theoretical treatise on women's subjugation, *Women and Economics* (1898), which Carl N. Degler reissued in 1966. During an era when the home and family were sacrosanct and the angel in the house was the Victorian ideal, Gilman argued persuasively for equal gender relations, women's autonomy, meaningful work outside the home, payment for housework, kitchen-less homes, and community child care—the most radical part of her agenda for social change.

Gilman's reputation waned along with the women's movement following the passage of the nineteenth amendment in 1920, granting women's suffrage. "The Yellow Wall-Paper" was never "lost" or forgotten, as a quick glance at its publication history reveals. However, with the revival of the women's movement in the 1960s and 1970s, feminist critics embraced the story, a first-person narrative of a young wife and mother undergoing a three-month rest cure for a depression seemingly brought on by the birth of her child, in clinical terms a postpartum depression. The 1973 Feminist Press republication of "The Yellow Wall-Paper" with an "Afterword" by Elaine R. Hedges directed unprecedented international attention to the story. Hailed in feminist circles, "The Yellow Wall-Paper" is now among the most studied texts in the English-speaking world. It is part of the contemporary canon, widely anthologized, and reprinted in European countries including England, Spain, France, Sweden, and Germany. The story has found its way into courses in literature, history, Women's Studies, and American Studies and interdisciplinary courses, such as the history of medicine. It is the subject of books and doctorial dissertations as well as major articles in respected scholarly journals.

If critics of the 1970s and early 1980s elevated "The Yellow Wall-Paper" to majestic proportions in feminist criticism, scholars beginning in the mid-1980s have chastized its privileged status, equating it to Coleridge's albatross or Melville's white whale. This sourcebook appears at an important crossroads in Gilman studies. Beginning in the 1990s, scholars working to recover much of Gilman's prodigious output of theoretical and literary work have urged for examination of her full oeuvre, blemishes and all. Today, we embrace the author, lecturer, and socialist who wanted to create a truly "human world" as a woman ahead of her time, but uncomfortably rooted in her time. Her oeuvre has decided strengths and weaknesses, prejudices and promise. In an age of political correctness, Gilman's ethnic and racial biases and ethnocentrism show her to be insensitive to the struggles of working-class and immigrant women, some of whom she labeled as "undesirables." Her classism and biases against Italians, Asians, Blacks, and Jews reflect the nativist tendencies embedded in the psychic geography of turn-of-the-twentieth-century Anglo-America evident in the work of other leading contemporaries, such as Virginia Woolf. Scholars have identified but not sufficiently confronted Gilman's persistent presentation of class, racial, and ethnic stereotypes, palpable in her posthumously published work of fiction, *Unpunished* (*ca.*1929) (see Further Reading, p. 162): for example, detective Bess Hunt arranges for "our little black Jenny to come as laundress" (63) to aid the Vaughns; characters refer to two immigrants of Italian descent, brothers Emilio and Carlo respectively, as "that little dago in the alley" (199) and a "Wop" (29, published by The Feminist Press, 1997). These beliefs and Gilman's xenophobia and faith in eugenics jar with her progressive evolutionist beliefs in a truly human world as well as her foresighted reforms concerning professionalized housekeeping, child care, women's autonomy, gender relations, and the opening of professions to release women from the restricting confines of the home. In essence, Gilman was an astute social critic who—like many visionaries—embodied her society's prejudices. Her optimist reforms make her a visionary for her own time and, to an extent, our time. Gilman wrote with a "purpose" in the service of social reform, and her incisive dream of women's full participation in society—not yet realized today—remains relevant in the twenty-first century. Perhaps some of the changes Gilman predicted for women will become a reality in this millennium. Moreover, in the twenty-first century, the interest in Gilman and her best-known tale remains at an all-time high and shows no signs of waning.

Critics from disciplines including American Studies, Women's Studies, sociology, psychology, and literary studies have used a range of theoretical perspectives variously to interpret a story that always prompts spirited debate. Artistically superior to Gilman's other, often hurriedly written, fiction, "The Yellow Wall-Paper" skillfully employs two devices she calls upon in her larger oeuvre (e.g. "Through This," *Unpunished*)—first-person narration (in this case in the form of a journal or diary the narrator is writing) and writing as therapy. To borrow the terms of classical rhetoric, the story demonstrates that form or *verba* conveys meaning or *res*. Critics have examined the diary format; first-person narration; discourse of diagnosis; themes of madness and regression versus emancipation and empowerment; word choice; symbolism; and the ambiguous ending, which simultaneously invites interpretations of liberation, defeat, and dubious victory. For example, the short paragraphs, many composed of a single sentence, arguably express the narrator's shift from neurosis to full-blown psychosis. The breaks between diary entries and the namelessness of the narrator augment this sense of fragmentation.

The psychic evolution of the enigmatic narrator continues to captivate, puzzle, and perplex students and scholars of Gilman alike, who may be as engaged in reading the wide-ranging criticism about the tale as the story itself. Scholars present their arguments about "The Yellow Wall-Paper" in conversation with other critics, fostering lively debate on complex questions not easily resolved. Does the narrator's creeping at the end of the story signal regression or rebirth? Is the narrator simply trapped in a wallpapered room whose bars connote patriarchal repression? Alternatively, in locking John out of her room, has the narrator achieved what Virginia Woolf deemed necessary for all literary women—a room of her own? The narrator's release of the woman trapped behind the wallpaper also invites contrasting interpretations: has the narrator gained a degree of personal liberation? Rather, from a Lacanian perspective, has she firmly installed herself in the realm of the imaginary? Since the narrative unfolds as a diary, has the narrator who is presumably writing the very story we are reading sufficiently recovered to finish the tale? (Such an interpretation denies any disjunction between the narrator and the narrated.) Then again, do the journal entries, beginning with the third one, function as interior monologue, as John Sutherland suggests (see Further Reading, p. 159)? Most critics are quick to remark on the power of the narrator who exclaims, " 'I've got out at last' . . . 'in spite of you and Jane!' " (see p. 144). But who is Jane?

Further questions invite pondering. Do the various spellings of the ubiquitous wallpaper (wall paper, wall-paper, wallpaper, and paper) profoundly indicate the changing nature of the narrator's reading of the wallpaper or merely reflect Gilman's notoriously inconsistent spelling? Is the narrator, denied any other form of paper, successfully reading the pattern of the wallpaper as she vows she alone will do? Does the transformation of a figure into a woman trapped behind the bars of the patterned wallpaper document her increasingly hallucinatory state or a larger awareness of the limitations of her patriarchal world? What kind of character is John: is he a well-intentioned husband advocating current medical practices, or is he a suffocating patriarch or a villain? At the end of the tale, is John dead or alive? If he is alive, how will he respond to the creeping narrator when he awakes from his dead faint? What of the narrator's fate? Will she be hidden away like other characters filled with rage, madness, or excess, such as Charlotte Brontë's madwoman in the attic of Thornfield Hall in *Jane Eyre* (1847) or Louisa May Alcott's incarcerated Sybil in "A Whisper in the Dark" (1863)? And how might John tell his side of the story?

The goal of this sourcebook is to provide resources to debate such provocative questions and to generate more. It aims to stimulate critical inquiry and independent thinking and thus to encourage students to make their own arguments and connections. To facilitate these processes, annotations include cross-references between the story and various materials included in the sourcebook. Each of the sections—Contexts, Interpretations, and Text—includes a general introduction and an editorial headnote to each item in that section.

Contexts provides contemporary documents, many not readily available or easily acquired. It consists of extracts from Gilman's autobiography, short fiction, and poems; selections from Edgar Allan Poe, as well as from Gilman's contemporaries, Alice James and Kate Chopin; period conduct literature; medical discourse on neurasthenia and hysteria; and Charles Eastlake on period wallpapers. These materials give insight into notions with which Gilman was familiar, many of which she challenges in "The Yellow Wall-Paper." They also offer a window into the literary, political, and cultural milieu of turn-of-the-twentieth-century America to help readers place the story in its historical moment. For example, background material on nervous diseases and invalid women show the seriousness of the narrator's condition to period readers. The wallpaper design on the Small, Maynard edition helps readers envision the dominant symbol of the story. Photographs of individuals close to the creation of the story and autobiographical excerpts communicate the context in which Gilman conceived "The Yellow Wall-Paper." The Chronology highlights key incidents in Gilman's life, useful to those studying Gilman's larger oeuvre as well as her landmark story.

Interpretations brings together viewpoints of period and modern critics to enable students to witness and engage in an ongoing spirited discussion about the story. Nineteenth-Century and Early Twentieth-Century Interpretations presents the several significant lines of response to the story when it first appeared. Modern Criticism reflects a judicious choice of articles from among the extensive critical discourse—feminist, psychoanalytical, queer theory, Marxist, Derridean, Lacanian, new historicist, and sociological approaches as well as a combination of these. The headnotes introduce challenging criticism and help readers to navigate the critical discourse about Gilman's landmark tale and make connections among materials in this sourcebook.

Text, the third section, provides annotations and footnotes to open up Gilman's provocative and richly ambiguous text. Annotations accompany each of the twelve entries in Gilman's first-person narrative. Not presented as exhaustive, annotations steer a course through a puzzling yet richly rewarding work. They call attention to theme, characterization, plot, and style or form (e.g. sentence and paragraph structure, word choice, and pronoun usage), make reference to works by Gilman and her contemporaries, and set the story in its cultural moment. Different from other Routledge sourcebooks, this edition includes the story in its entirety. Due to its brevity, I advise readers to approach the story in one uninterrupted reading session, as Edgar Allan Poe recommended short stories be read. Numbered annotations correlated with each entry appear at the end of the text (see **p. 144**). Thus, this sourcebook can be used independently of any additional text. Contrary to the trend of anthologizing "The Yellow Wall-Paper," this sourcebook reprints the January 1892 version in *New England Magazine*, preserving many of what critic Jerome McGann calls its original "bibliographical codes"[1]—a pictorial capital, asterisks between entries, and illustrations by staff illustrator Jo. H. Hatfield. Page and column breaks in square brackets indicate the form in which period readers first encountered the story. Biographical information, historical documents, and critical interpretations included in this

---

1   See McGann's *The Textual Condition*, Princeton, NJ: Princeton University Press, 1991, 13.

sourcebook inform the annotations on the text. The annotated bibliography offers further reading for those interested in the extra challenge of augmenting the varied materials provided.

While readers may turn to one section of this sourcebook, I encourage them to read it in its entirety and give ample attention both to historical documents and criticism. Readers will find oft-reprinted excerpts from Gilman's autobiography and journal *Forerunner* as well as from works by groundbreaking feminist scholars who often dipped into her autobiography, an approach which dominated Gilman scholarship in the 1970s and 1980s. Alongside these celebratory voices are excerpts from those who, beginning in the 1980s, call attention to the darker side of the author and her landmark story. Gilman's imperialist tendencies and racial and ethnic prejudices are more visible in subsequent works within her larger oeuvre—e.g. in her fiction, such as *Herland* (1915) and *Unpunished* (*ca*.1929); theoretical works, such as *Concerning Children* (1900); and essays including "A Suggestion on the Negro Problem" (1908); these repugnant aspects, nonetheless, infect this story written early in her career, as Susan Lanser and Marty Roth argue in their respective readings of the color and arabesque design of the dominant symbol of the story (see **pp. 105–8** and **pp. 117–21**).

It is my hope that students will feel compelled to reread, discuss, and debate "The Yellow Wall-Paper" as they confront seminal issues—patriarchal repression, madness, liberation, infantilization, feminism, consumerism, ethnocentrism, and imperialism. I urge readers to analyze the wealth of visual and textual evidence—and even to draw their own evolving representations of the wallpaper in response to the descriptions in the text—as they craft an interpretation of their own and consider alternative viewpoints. If readers become as engrossed in interpretations of the story as the narrator does in attempting to decipher the pattern of her yellow wallpaper, I will have accomplished my goal for this sourcebook.

1

Contexts

Contextual Overview

"The Yellow Wall-Paper" (1892) appeared during the era of the "New Woman," a transitional time in American history and literary history. Progressives increasingly challenged the inequalities between the sexes. Along with a widening of woman's sphere and changes in gender roles lively debate arose over what came to be called "the woman question." During this period of growing industry, opportunity, and advancement, advocates for social change grew angered that progress came too slowly for women or excluded them from equal citizenship. At the same time, conservatives fought to maintain the status quo, supported by the doctrine of separate spheres rising out of the Industrial Revolution.

In the nineteenth century, traditionalists on both sides of the Atlantic regarded the home as a refuge from the bustle of the workplace. Woman, heralded for her purity and morality, was installed as "chief minister" of the home, to quote Gilman's great-aunts, Catharine Beecher and Harriet Beecher Stowe, (in their popular domestic manual *The American Woman's Home* [1869] [see **pp. 52–5**]). Although fiercely proud of her Beecher heritage, Charlotte Perkins Stetson Gilman did not heed much of her great-aunts' advice regarding women's education, marriage, and motherhood. Gilman was one among a number of prominent progressives (including Elizabeth Cady Stanton, Olive Schreiner, and Ellen Key) who rejected stereotypical notions of women as fragile, passive, sickly, dependent beings. Gilman advocated equal education, suffrage, payment for house service, careers for women, and dress reform. She promoted gender equality, so women might—to cite Gilman's frequently used terms—be "world servants," not "house servants," and benefit a more "human world."

Deemed a leading feminist in her own time, Gilman was a social reformer, lecturer, and author who considered herself a "humanist" and repudiated the term "feminist," coined in 1891. Fired with a revolutionary spirit for social change, she laments in her autobiography, *The Living of Charlotte Perkins Gilman* (1935), that she was born on the eve of America's Independence Day (July 3, 1860 in Hartford, Connecticut). Her parents, Frederick Beecher Perkins and Mary Fitch Westcott, came from prominent families; they married in 1857 and divorced in 1873. One of four children (two died in infancy), Gilman never experienced the love or security of home: her father deserted the family when she was a child, stigmatizing his wife and children; her mother was emotionally undemonstrative and moved her family habitually (nineteen times in eighteen years) due to chronic poverty.

A precocious learner, Charlotte Anna Perkins taught herself to read before age five, wrote imaginative tales by age eight, and became an avid reader of essays by Ralph Waldo Emerson and fiction by Charles Dickens, George Eliot, and Edgar Allan Poe. Although she had limited formal education, in 1880 she successfully completed a two-year course at the Rhode Island School of Design. She made a modest income as a freelance commercial artist and a private teacher, but longed for a more independent literary and artistic life. She achieved her goal only the decade following her second marriage to her first cousin George Houghton Gilman (nicknamed Ho) on June 11, 1900. "The Yellow Wall-Paper" dates to the period of her first marriage when she launched her career.

"The Yellow Wall-Paper" does not exude the fiery spirit of her internationally acclaimed theoretical treatise, *Women and Economics* (1898), which argues against women's "sexuoeconomic condition." Gilman invented this term to illustrate that the female sex has an economic function which leaves woman financially and socially dependent on her mate, bound to the home for her very survival. "The Yellow Wall-Paper" graphically presents the consequences of women's subordination in marriage. Written early in her career, it has invited biographical criticism for two reasons: in the story, Gilman names and indicts her eminent physician, Dr. S. Weir Mitchell, who treated her for a nervous depression following the birth of her only child, and creates a fictional Dr. John, who administers a Mitchell-like rest cure; Gilman based the story on the difficulties of her first marriage to Charles Walter Stetson, a Providence, Rhode Island artist (Fig. 2). Stetson and Perkins wed on May 2, 1884. Marrying reluctantly, she feared that matrimony would preclude her ability to do meaningful work. Stetson consoled her with the promise that he would not object to her writing when they married, giving her pens and blank writing tablets to affirm a pledge that the conventional Walter failed to keep. Problems in her marriage intensified after the birth of daughter Katharine Beecher Stetson on March 23, 1885. She temporarily recovered on a trip west, visiting her brother (Thomas, b. 1858) and her father, then staying in Pasadena, California with her close friend Grace Ellery Channing (who became Walter's second wife in 1894). However, she grew despondent a month after her return: "for now I saw the stark fact—that I was well while away and sick while at home" (*Living* 95, see p. 49). At age 26, Charlotte Stetson traveled to Philadelphia to undergo a one-month rest cure in the sanatorium of the leading neurologist, who diagnosed her condition as a breakdown of the nervous system then called neurasthenia or nervous prostration. Adhering to the predominant medical model, Mitchell's well-respected rest cure, of which Sigmund Freud later approved, aimed to heal the mind by treating the body. Inactivity and seclusion were essential to his prescription for health, explicated in *Fat and Blood* (see pp. 61–8).

Separated from but still married to Stetson when she wrote "The Yellow Wall-Paper," Gilman may have consciously redirected her criticism of Stetson—who adhered to the gender-based division of separate spheres—and projected her anger onto Weir Mitchell, who became the decided "villain" of the story. In her autobiography, she says she objected to the conventions of marriage, not to Walter *per se*, whom she describes as tender and caring. She narrates how she

Figure 2 Charles Walter Stetson, n.d., *ca.* 1905. Reprinted by permission of Schlesinger Library, Radcliffe Institute, Harvard University.

attempted to follow Mitchell's often quoted parting advice: to devote herself to her child, limit her intellectual activity, and "never touch pen, brush or pencil as long as you live" (*Living* 96, see **p. 50**). She could not follow this regimen—her condition worsened (she cried uncontrollably and crawled into closets)—nor could she forfeit her sense of purpose to perform meaningful work required in marriage to the traditional Stetson. She did not believe that her "highest duty is so often to suffer and be still," to recall the advice of Sarah Stickney Ellis from *The Daughters of England* (published by D. Appleton, 1843, 73). Rather, Gilman wrote poetry, fiction, and non-fiction to make a case for social change, and her prodigious output stands as a major contribution to modern feminist thought.

Gilman publicly maintains that she created this story for didactic purposes: "to reach Dr. S. Weir Mitchell, and convince him of the error of his ways" (*Living* 121, see **p. 52**). Scholars and biographers often comment on a palpable biographical dimension underpinning her characterizations of powerful husband and intelligent wife forbidden to write as well as the suffocating walls of a nursery/prison (a symbol of patriarchal marriage) and the bars of a wallpaper pattern, restricting the figure of a woman, a symbol of the narrator herself. Scholars who have pursued biographical criticism may have over-zealously read into its autobiographical basis—socially minded Charlotte, committed to devoting her life to her work and improving the world; handsome young artist, Walter Stetson, whose conventionality limited his understanding of his wife's plight; and commanding Dr. S. Weir Mitchell, respected for designing a popular cure that had merits despite its punitive edge. If Gilman's most powerful short story grew out of her anger toward Mitchell and Stetson, as critics have argued, it allowed her to expose the Mitchell rest cure, which came as a result of an entrapping marriage. Gilman's heroine undergoing a three-month rest cure succumbs to a form of madness, a state Gilman avoided by rejecting her doctor's "sage" advice and separating from her husband in 1888; the two divorced officially in 1894.

Nervous diseases from which Gilman suffered and to which her heroine succumbs were widespread among women in Victorian Britain and America. The cult of female frailty and the female predilection for invalidism and nervousness grew out of the dominant theory of male and female energy promoted by Scottish biologist Patrick Geddes along with his pupil J. Arthur Thomson. In *The Evolution of Sex* (1889), they argue that men's superior and women's inferior social positions result from habits of body associated with males and females throughout the animal kingdom: "on an average the females incline to passivity, the males to activity" (New York: Scribner & Welford, 1890, 18). The male, with a "katabolic" constitution, has a more lively physiological habit of body than his mate and exhibits greater physical stamina, intelligence, independence, and courage. In contrast, the female is innately more passive given her "anabolic" constitution, marked by a need to conserve energy for survival and reproduction (26).

Trained as a neurologist (as was Sigmund Freud), Dr. S. Weir Mitchell designed his rest cure for female versus male neurasthenics on the supposition of innate differences between the sexes: he prescribed for males a course of vigorous physical exercise (e.g. work in the west on a cattle ranch) whereas he literally put women to bed (see Jennifer Tuttle's essay in *The Mixed Legacy of Charlotte Perkins Gilman*, Further Reading, **p. 161**). In *Wear and Tear* (1873), a popular treatise on physical and medical health, Mitchell expresses his fear that even the hardiest girls and young women attempting the same education as their brothers could expect their health to break down. During an era which witnessed a marked increase in women's education and in which female invalidism became fashionable among the upper reaches, medical authorities linked women's reading—particularly of novels and sensation fiction—to a host of ailments: infertility, painful menstruation, early menstruation, neurasthenia, insanity, and even premature death. As Catherine J. Golden explains in *Images of the Woman Reader in Victorian British and American Fiction* (published by University Press of Florida, 2003), a woman needed to conserve her energy, and reading and studying were thought to drain her vigor away from her vital organs. In *Sex in Education* (1873, reprinted by Ayer in 1972), Dr. Edward H. Clarke of the Harvard Medical School provides damning testimonials of women who pursued a rigorous education and "graduated from school or college excellent scholars, but with undeveloped ovaries. Later they married, and were sterile" (39). Moreover, due to her greater sensitivity, woman was considered prone to shock from reading exciting love stories or sensational novels. In creating a heroine longing to but forbidden to write, Gilman responds to this nineteenth-century transatlantic debate over women's reading.

Gilman's characterization of John's sister Jennie—who "thinks it is the writing which made [the narrator] sick!" (see **p. 135**)—also lends insight into the rigid ideal of femininity for the middle and upper classes in Victorian America. In her theoretical works *Women and Economics* (1898) and *The Home* (1903), Gilman lambastes the bourgeois home as the source of women's infantilization and oppression; her ideas complement Henrik Ibsen's depiction of the petted Nora Helmer in *A Doll's House* (1879) and Kate Chopin's characterizations of the rebellious Edna Pontellier of *The Awakening* (1899) and the briefly liberated Louise Mallard of "The Story of an Hour" (1894) (see **pp. 37–9**). If the ideal woman was to be fragile, emotional, and dependent, how could she easily become the ideal strong, protective, moral guide for husband and children? Many middle-class American girls could not easily assume the trials of motherhood or bear the challenges of marriage, and their health broke down. Nonetheless, Chopin's Madame Ratignolle of *The Awakening* is an ideal wife and mother, and John's sister is a "perfect and enthusiastic housekeeper, and hopes for no better profession" (**p. 135**). Conduct literature on motherhood, such as by Sylvanus Stall (see **p. 57**), similarly projects the sanctity of motherhood and establishes the quintessential ideal of woman as angel in the house or mother-woman, the Victorian American equivalent of this model. In *The American Woman's Home* (see **pp. 52–5**), Catharine Beecher and Harriet Beecher Stowe endorse woman's role as moral guide of the family, a rhetoric that—to Gilman—was a mandate to maintain the status quo, against which she rebelled.

Separated from her husband and living in California in the 1890s, Gilman published widely. Her poetry collection entitled *In This Our World* first appeared in 1893; subsequent expanded editions came out in 1895 and 1898. The collection contains three sections: "The World," mainly nature poems, prayers, and hymns; "Woman," principally feminist verses (many poems are reprinted from *Woman's Journal*); and "Our Human Kind," featuring political anthems on the themes of labor and Nationalism. To support herself and Katharine, she also wrote articles and short stories. Along with her adoptive "mother" Helen

Campbell, she began to edit the short-lived magazine *Impress*, sponsored by the Pacific Coast Women's Press Association. She eventually sent her daughter east in May of 1894 to live with her father and "co-mother," Grace Channing, whom Stetson married in June 1894. Although Gilman faced heavy criticism for being a divorcée and an "unnatural mother," as she was often called, she continued to lecture widely in England and America and earned an international reputation with the publication of *Women and Economics*, translated into seven languages and used as a college textbook in the 1920s.

Intending not to remarry, she changed her mind after renewing an acquaintance with her first cousin Houghton Gilman (Fig. 3). Like other activists including Carrie Chapman Cat and Elizabeth Cady Stanton, Gilman found a way to balance marriage with an active career of writing and public speaking. In fact, the two decades following her second marriage were ones of extreme productivity, witnessing the publication of numerous theoretical works, regular magazine contributions to *Woman's Home Companion*, *Harper's Bazaar* [sic], and *Scribner's*, and the launching of *Forerunner* in which she brought out her major novels including *What Diantha Did* (1910), *The Crux* (1911), and her best-known utopian novel, *Herland* (1915). Houghton supported her efforts by attending her lectures, reading her work, and assisting with her research.

A prolific writer, Gilman founded *Forerunner* (1909–16)—a magazine she wrote entirely and published single-handedly for seven years. *Forerunner* showcases Gilman's range as a writer of editorials, book reviews, sermons, verse, novels (published serially), short stories, and current events pieces on dress reform, women's suffrage, and child labor laws. In fact, in *Forerunner* she published her well-known essay "Why I Wrote 'The Yellow Wallpaper'?" (1913). Gilman, who vowed there was no point in writing without a purpose, used any and every literary vehicle to present her agenda for equal gender relations, socialized housekeeping, and social motherhood. In her large oeuvre of fiction and nonfiction written at a time when motherhood and the home were sacrosanct, she viewed the private home as a source of women's oppression. The verse and short fiction included in this section demonstrate themes central to "The Yellow Wall-Paper" and her agenda for reform. "To the Young Wife" and "The Mother's Charge" critique the institutions of marriage and motherhood that subordinate and overwhelm the nameless narrator of "The Yellow Wall-Paper" as well as her nameless narrator in "Through This"; in fact, Gilman's 1893 short story of an overwhelmed wife and mother who struggles to be an angel in the house can profitably be read as a companion or prequel to her landmark tale. "She Walketh Veiled and Sleeping" speaks to a woman's unfulfilled potential and evokes the imagery of creeping women who come out of the barred wallpaper in "The Yellow Wall-Paper." "In Duty Bound" chillingly points to the restrictions on a woman that leave her "hemmed" in the private sphere. "An Obstacle" illustrates the force of patriarchal oppression confronting the nameless narrator, who, in the dramatic denouement of the tale, creeps over her own "obstacle," her husband, Doctor John.

Anticipating needs of our modern age, Gilman understood that not all women are equally endowed with the gift of rearing children or wholly committed to the domestic sphere. In her fiction and theoretical treatises, she offered women solutions: apartment houses equipped with "baby gardens"—equivalent to modern

Figure 3 Photograph of Charlotte and George Houghton (Ho) Gilman, 1909, inscribed with a poem. Reprinted by permission of Schlesinger Library, Radcliffe Institute, Harvard University.

day care centers—and communal meals to enable women to work outside the home and contribute to the betterment of their society. She critiqued the personal, private, and domestic arena. Although she may not always have credited those who inspired her, she had a gift in being able to recognize, appropriate as her own, and synthesize ideas for a general public audience. Her work is informed by, for example, Lester Ward, the country's leader of Reform Darwinism—a movement that believed in the necessity of intellectual intervention in the process of natural selection to improve the world. Like Thorstein Veblen—whose book *The Theory of the Leisure Class* (1899) became a classic economics and sociology text—Gilman alleged that women's subjugation dated from prehistoric times. In her theoretical works following "The Yellow Wall-Paper"—*Women and Economics* as well as *Concerning Children* (1900) and *The Home: Its Work and Influence* (1903)—she refined her visionary arguments for economic emancipation of women and socialized housekeeping as well as her social analyses of men and women contributing equally to the work of the world. She stopped *Forerunner* in 1916 when her readership was waning. In fact, once American women received the vote in 1920, the question of women's rights lost its urgency, and Gilman found herself less and less in demand. She even turned to the popular genre of detective fiction in the late 1920s to present a message about domestic abuse, but she could not place *Unpunished* (*ca.*1929, published posthumously in 1997).

Diagnosed with inoperable breast cancer in 1932, Gilman lived her final years with conviction and spirit and finished her autobiography, *The Living of Charlotte Perkins Gilman*, published posthumously in 1935. After her beloved Houghton died unexpectedly of a cerebral hemorrhage on May 4, 1934, Gilman returned to her former home in Pasadena, California to be near her daughter, Katharine, and her grandchildren; Grace Channing Stetson (now widowed) joined her there. Planning her suicide as her disease progressed, Gilman also arranged for her cremation, leaving instructions for her ashes to be scattered. Gilman inhaled chloroform and took her life on August 17, 1935. Daughter Katharine scattered Charlotte's ashes in the Sierra Madre mountains. The ending of her life was filled with dignity, much like her living.

Chronology

Biographical and contextual information appear in this chronology of Gilman's life and times. For the sake of consistency, the author of "The Yellow Wall-Paper" typically appears as "Gilman" throughout the sourcebook although she does not take that name until her marriage to Houghton Gilman in 1900. First names appear at points to avoid confusion between Gilman and her first and second husbands. The partial list of reprintings of "The Yellow Wall-Paper" indicates publication trends. Bullet points denote events in Gilman's life; asterisks denote significant historical and literary events.

1860
* Charlotte Anna Perkins born on July 3 in Hartford, Connecticut to Mary Fitch Westcott Perkins (1828–93) and Frederick Beecher Perkins (1826–99), distant cousins; Frederick Perkins is nephew to Harriet Beecher Stowe and Catharine Beecher
* Abraham Lincoln elected President of the United States

1861
* American Civil War begins

1864
* Abraham Lincoln elected to second term as President

1865
* American Civil War ends
* Founding of Ku Klux Klan in Pulaski, Tennessee. The Klan dies out by 1900, is reorganized in 1915, and flourishes in the 1920s

1868
* Volume One of Louisa May Alcott's *Little Women* is published; Volume Two comes out in 1869
* Passing of the Fourteenth Amendment grants African-Americans citizenship

1869
* Gilman's mother and father permanently separate; mother retains custody of Charlotte and her older brother, Thomas Perkins (b. 1858)

* Passing of the Fifteenth Amendment grants African-American males the right to vote
* Founding of National Woman Suffrage Association (NWSA) by Elizabeth Cady Stanton and Susan B. Anthony

1873
* Frederick and Mary Perkins divorce
* Publication of Dr. Edward H. Clarke's *Sex in Education*
* Publication of Dr. S. Weir Mitchell's popular treatise on mental and physical health entitled *Wear and Tear*

1877
* Gilman begins close friendship with Martha Luther Lane (1862–1948)
* Publication of S. Weir Mitchell's medical treatise *Fat and Blood*

1878–79
* Gilman follows a course of study at Rhode Island School of Design

1879
* Publication of Henrik Ibsen's *A Doll's House*

1880
* Publication of Gilman's first poem, "To D[andelion]. G[reens].," in May 20 issue of *New England Journal of Education*

1881
* Gilman founds "Perkins & Co. Designers" with her cousin Robert Brown and designs advertisement cards for a household cleansing agent, Soapine, produced by Kendall Manufacturing Co.
* Martha Luther becomes engaged, marries, and moves away; Gilman mourns the loss of her closest friend

1882
* January. Gilman meets Charles Walter Stetson, a Providence, RI artist. Seventeen days later, Stetson proposes marriage; she does not accept the proposal

1883
* May. Stetson experiences "a keen personal disappointment," and she agrees to marry him in a year's time. Gilman's bouts of depression continue

1884
* Publication of "In Duty Bound," in *Woman's Journal*
* May 2. Marries Charles Walter Stetson in Providence, RI despite reservations of balancing her "life's work" with marriage
* Discovers she is pregnant in August; periods of depression augment
* S. Weir Mitchell publishes his first novel, *In War Time*

1885
* March 23. Birth of Katharine Beecher Stetson, her only child

1885–86
* Gilman experiences a severe postpartum depression; she takes a solo trip west, visiting father and brother and staying with Grace Ellery Channing in Pasadena, CA. She recovers from "hysteria" but worsens upon her return to Providence, RI

1886
* S. Weir Mitchell publishes his second novel, *Roland Blake*

1887
* April. Undergoes treatment for nervous prostration by leading nerve specialist, Dr. S. Weir Mitchell of Philadelphia, who administers the rest cure
* Health declines further; suffers from a nervous breakdown
* Publication of S. Weir Mitchell's medical treatise *Doctor and Patient*

1888
* Charlotte and Walter Stetson separate. Gilman spends summer with close friend, Grace Ellery Channing, in Bristol, RI; her health improves
* Publication of *Art Gems for the Home and Fireside*
* October. Gilman moves to Pasadena, California with daughter Katharine to recuperate with Grace Channing
* December. Walter Stetson joins them in hope of a reconciliation
* Publication of Edward Bellamy's *Looking Backward, 2000–1887*

1889
* Spending a year in Pasadena, Walter becomes engaged to Grace Channing
* Jane Addams establishes Hull House in Chicago along with Ellen Gates Starr

1890–94
* Gilman becomes active in California Nationalist movement

1890
* Gilman begins her lecturing career; she also begins publishing short stories as well as poems
* January. Walter Stetson travels to Providence, RI to attend his dying mother; Gilman and Walter Stetson permanently separate
* April. Satirical poem "Similar Cases" published in *Nationalist*; Charlotte Stetson starts writing plays with Grace Channing
* June. Receives William Dean Howells's letter of praise about "Similar Cases"
* Summer. Writes her most famous short story, "The Yellow Wall-Paper," based on her own experiences with postpartum depression
* Grace Channing leaves Pasadena to join Walter Stetson, who is living on the east coast

*   Publication of William James's *Principles of Psychology*

1891
- Gilman moves to Oakland, California
- She joins the Pacific Coast Women's Press Association, where she meets Adeline Knapp (also called "Delle" or "Dora")
- In September, she shares boarding-house rooms with Knapp, daughter Katharine, and her ailing mother, Mary Fitch Perkins; she starts divorce proceedings against Walter Stetson
*   The *Athenaeum* book review coins the term "feminist"
*   Publication of S. Weir Mitchell's novel *Characteristics*

1892
- January. Publication of "The Yellow Wall-Paper" in *New England Magazine* under the name of Charlotte Perkins Stetson
*   Ellis Island becomes a station for immigration

1893
- Death of Mary Perkins, Charlotte's mother, on March 6
- Publication of a collection of verse entitled *In This Our World*; composed of three books, it contains satirical and Nationalist verse as well as poems critiquing domesticity and the social construction of domestic femininity
- Publication of "Through This" in *Kate Field's Washington*, September 13, 1893

1894
- April. Divorce from Walter Stetson becomes final
- May. Charlotte Stetson sends Katharine east to live with her father and Channing
- June. Walter Stetson marries Grace Channing
- Gilman relocates to San Francisco and becomes editor of *Impress*
*   Publication of "The Story of an Hour" by Kate Chopin in *Vogue*

1895
- *Impress* stops publication; Gilman goes into debt
- Publication of the second edition of *In This Our World*
- Gilman meets Jane Addams when visiting Hull House in Chicago
- She launches an extensive lecturing circuit throughout the United States, speaking on women's rights in terms of social evolution, economics, marriage, and the home

1896
- January. Gilman meets sociologist Lester Frank Ward at the Women's Suffrage Convention in Washington, D.C.
- July. Travels to London to attend the International Socialist and Labour Congress; she meets eminent playwright George Bernard Shaw, who invites her to join the Fabian Society
*   Publication of S. Weir Mitchell's novel *Hugh Wynne*, his most popular book

1897
- Gilman remeets a younger first cousin, George Houghton (Ho) Gilman, a patent attorney; a courtship ensues between 1897 and 1900
* Publication of *Studies in the Psychology of Sex* by Havelock Ellis

1898
- Publication of *Women and Economics*, a treatise exploring the "sexuo-economic condition" or women's economic dependence on man; the book secures her international reputation
- The third expanded edition of *In This Our World* is published

1899
- Gilman travels to London to attend the International Women's Congress and resides in England for five months
- Publication of "The Yellow Wall-Paper" as a single chapbook edition by Small, Maynard & Co.
* Publication of *The Awakening* by Kate Chopin
* Publication of *The Theory of the Leisure Class* by Thorstein Veblen

1900
- Charlotte Perkins Stetson marries Houghton Gilman on June 11 in Detroit, Michigan. Charlotte and Houghton Gilman move to New York City on the upper west side of Manhattan. Daughter Katharine comes to live with them
- Publishes *Concerning Children*, a study of children in relation to social progress; it reveals her racism and nativism
* Publication of S. Weir Mitchell's novel *Dr. North and His Friends*

1903
- Publication of *The Home: Its Work and Influence*, a critique of the private single-family home, which Gilman considered an oppressive and inefficient institution

1904
- Publication of *Human Work*, a less successful sequel to *Women and Economics*
- Gilman travels to Berlin, Germany to attend the International Congress of Women

1905
- Gilman embarks on a lecture tour through England, Germany, Holland, Austria, and Hungary
* Publication of *The House of Mirth* by Edith Wharton
* Publication of *Constance Trescott*, a novel by S. Weir Mitchell

1907
- Publication of *Women and Social Service*, a tract arguing for social motherhood

1909

- Gilman issues *Forerunner* (1909–16), a monthly periodical with an international subscription; she single-handedly writes, edits, and publishes it for seven years; her goal is to bring out "important truths" that otherwise might not be heard

1910

- Publication of first novel, *What Diantha Did*, serialized in *Forerunner* in 1909–10; in the arena of fiction, she outlines her plans for socialized housekeeping and domestic reform

1911

- Publication in *Forerunner* of *The Man-Made World; Or, Our Androcentric Culture*, a theoretical treatise arguing against male domination, and two novels, *The Crux*—a romance that lambastes the spread of venereal diseases and promotes the West—and *Moving the Mountain*, a utopian novel revolutionizing the home and workplace
- First husband, Charles Walter Stetson, dies on July 20
- * The Triangle Shirtwaist Company disaster; 146 (mainly women) die in fire; outrage over safety hazards and horrific working conditions

1912
- * Sinking of the *Titanic* on its maiden voyage

1913

- Gilman travels to Budapest, Hungary to attend the International Women's Suffrage Congress, her last European conference

1914–18
- * World War I

1914
- * May. Mother's Day made an official holiday
- * January 4. Death of S. Weir Mitchell

1915

- Serial publication of her feminist utopian novel *Herland* in *Forerunner*

1916

- Gilman ends *Forerunner*
- Gilman shows anti-German sentiments and voices support for World War I
- Publication of *With Her in Ourland*, sequel to *Herland*
- * Margaret Sanger opens birth control clinic in New York City, the first in the United States

1919

- Gilman contributes articles to the syndicate of the *New York Tribune*
- * Eighteenth Amendment establishes Prohibition

1920
- Ratification of the Nineteenth Amendment, guaranteeing women the right to vote
- "The Yellow Wall-Paper" appears in *The Great Modern American Stories*, edited by William Dean Howells

1922
- Charlotte and Houghton move to Norwich Town, Connecticut
- "The Yellow Wall-Paper" reprinted in *New York Evening Post*
* Fascist leader Benito Mussolini comes to power in Italy

1923
- Publication of *His Religion and Hers*, Gilman's final social treatise arguing that mainstream religions are patriarchal; created by hunters and fighters, traditional religions center on a fear of death and a belief in the afterlife

1925
- Gilman begins her appropriately titled autobiography *The Living of Charlotte Perkins Gilman*
* Scopes Monkey Trial: John T. Scopes is convicted of teaching evolution in the public schools (as opposed to the creationist doctrine)

1927
- "The Yellow Wall-Paper" appears in *American Mystery Stories*, edited by Carolyn Wells
* Highly charged trial and execution of Nicóla Sacco and Bartolomeo Vanzetti, admitted anarchists

1929
- Gilman completes *Unpunished*, her final work of fiction and first detective novel; with her popularity waning, she is unable to find a publisher

1932
- Gilman receives a terminal diagnosis, inoperable breast cancer
* Amelia Earhart makes history as first woman to fly solo across the Atlantic
* Notorious crime: kidnapping of the Lindbergh baby

1933
- "The Yellow Wall-Paper" reprinted in *The Golden Book Magazine*
* Repeal of Prohibition

1934
- May 4. Husband Houghton Gilman dies unexpectedly from a cerebral hemorrhage
- August. Gilman moves to Pasadena to be near her daughter, Katharine; she revises her autobiography and chooses pictures for it
* Publication of Alice James's diary, forty-two years after her death in 1892

*   Adolf Hitler assumes presidency and chancellorship of Germany and adopts title of *Der Führer*

1935
- The widowed Grace Channing Stetson joins Charlotte in Pasadena
- Charlotte elects to end her life with dignity; on 17 August, she inhales chloroform; her body is cremated, her ashes scattered
- October. Posthumous publication of her autobiography, *The Living of Charlotte Perkins Gilman*, with a foreword by Zona Gale, an eminent novelist

1937
- "The Yellow Wall-Paper" reprinted in *The Haunted Omnibus*, edited by Alexander Laing

1942
- "The Yellow Wall-Paper" reprinted in *The Midnight Reader: Great Stories of Haunting and Horror*, edited by Philip Van Doren Stern; abridged paperback edition published in 1948

1943
- "The Yellow Wall-Paper" reprinted in *About Women: A Collection of Short Stories*, edited by Helene Reed

1950
- "The Yellow Wall-Paper" reprinted in *Ghostly Tales to be Told*, edited by Basil Davenport

1960
- "The Yellow Wall-Paper" reprinted in *More Macabre*, edited by Donald Wollheim

1965
- "The Yellow Wall-Paper" reprinted in *A Chamber of Horrors: An Anthology of the Macabre in Words and Pictures*, edited by John Hadfield

1966
- "The Yellow Wall-Paper" reprinted in *Psychopathology and Literature*, edited by Leslie Y. Rabkin

1972
- Reprinting of "The Yellow Wall-Paper" in *Eight Strange Tales*, edited by Vic Ghidalia
- Reprinting of "The Yellow Wall-Paper" in *The Oven Birds: American Women on Womanhood, 1820–1920*, edited by Gail Parker

1973
- The Feminist Press republication of "The Yellow Wall-Paper" as a single-volume edition with an afterword by Elaine R. Hedges, revised edition published in 1996

1979
- "The Yellow Wall-Paper" reprinted in *Wolf's Complete Book of Terror*, edited by Leonard Wolf

1980
- Publication of *The Charlotte Perkins Gilman Reader*, edited and with an introduction by Gilman biographer Ann J. Lane, revised in 1999; "The Yellow Wall-Paper" is included alongside stories and excerpts from novels

1985
- "The Yellow Wall-Paper" reprinted in *Haunted Women: The Best Supernatural Tales by American Women Writers*, edited by Alfred Bendixen
- "The Yellow Wall-Paper" included in *The Norton Anthology of Literature by Women*, eds. Sandra Gilbert and Susan Gubar, 2nd edition 1996

1989
- Reprinting of "The Yellow Wall-Paper" in *The Yellow Wallpaper and Other Writings by Charlotte Perkins Gilman*, ed. Lynne Sharon Schwartz

1990
- Founding of the Charlotte Perkins Gilman Society by Elaine R. Hedges and Shelley Fisher Fishkin

1992
- Publication of *The Captive Imagination: A Casebook on "The Yellow Wallpaper,"* edited by Catherine J. Golden, to mark the centenary of the story's first publication

1993
- Publication of *The Yellow Wallpaper*, edited by Thomas L. Erskine and Connie Richards

1994
- Induction of Charlotte Perkins Gilman into the National Woman's Hall of Fame in Seneca Falls, New York
- Publication of *"The Yellow Wall-Paper" and Selected Stories of Charlotte Perkins Gilman*, edited by Denise D. Knight; this collection prints the manuscript version of "The Yellow Wall-Paper"

1995
- Publication of *The Yellow Wall-Paper and Other Stories*, edited by Robert Shulman

1997
- Posthumous publication of *Unpunished*, edited and with an afterword by Catherine J. Golden and Denise D. Knight

1998
- Publication of *The Yellow Wallpaper*, edited by Dale Bauer

Contemporary Documents

Selected Letters

These three letters illuminate the publication history of "The Yellow Wall-Paper" and its initial reception. Gilman's relationship with Martha Luther was the most important female friendship she had in her adolescence, although the intimacy changed in 1881 when Martha married Charles A. Lane. In this 1890 letter, Gilman reveals to Martha how Charles Walter Stetson reacted to her story. The stress on ghastliness in the "husband's opinion" is indicative of one of the original lines of response to "The Yellow Wall-Paper" as a horror story akin to Poe's tales of madness. Gilman herself calls "The Yellow Wall-Paper" "a simple tale, but highly unpleasant."

The second letter is by the well-known nineteenth-century author, critic, poet, and editor, William Dean Howells (1837–1920), who admired Gilman's satiric poetry and supported her early literary efforts. He writes to his friend Horace Scudder, then editor of *Atlantic Monthly*, recommending that he read her "blood curdling, but strong" story. Howells refers to Gilman as poet and cites her as a relation of Edward Everett Hale; a noted author and Unitarian clergyman, Hale was Gilman's uncle.

Horace Scudder's dramatic rejection of "The Yellow Wall-Paper" is often quoted in Gilman criticism, particularly the line: "I could not forgive myself if I made others as miserable as I have made myself!" Using Scudder's response to her advantage, Gilman created a persona of an aspiring woman author struggling to place her story in a male-dominated late nineteenth-century literary marketplace.

From **Charlotte Perkins Stetson, Letter to Martha Luther Lane**, July 27, 1890, Charlotte Perkins Gilman Letters, Rhode Island Historical Society

When my awful story "The Yellow Wallpaper" comes out, you must try & read it. Walter says he has read it <u>four</u> times, and thinks it the most ghastly tale he ever read. Says it beats Poe and Doré! But that's only a husband's opinion.

I read the thing to three women here however, and I never saw such squirms! Daylight too. It's a simple tale, but highly unpleasant.

I don't know yet where it will be. If none of the big things will take it I mean to try the New York Ledger. Have you seen that in its new form? Kipling and Stevenson etc. etc. write for that now, so I guess I can.

William Dean Howells, Letter to Horace E. Scudder,
October 5, 1890, Houghton Library, bMs Am 1784.1 (92)

Lynn, Oct. 5, 1890.

My dear Scudder:

The author wished me to send you this. It's pretty blood curdling, but strong, and is certainly worth reading—by you, I mean.

Mrs. Stetson is a relation of E. E. Hale's, I think, and she wrote that clever poem, Parallel Cases.[1]

Yours ever
W. D. Howells

184 Com'th Ave.

Horace E. Scudder, Letter to Charlotte Perkins Stetson,
October 18, 1890, Schlesinger Library, Gilman Papers, folder 126

[printed heading]

EDITORIAL OFFICE OF   18 October 1890
The Atlantic Monthly
  BOSTON
Dear Madam
  Mr. Howells has handed me this story. I could not forgive myself if I made others as miserable as I have made myself!

Sincerely yours
H. E. Scudder.

---

1   Howells is likely referring to "Similar Cases," a poem that brought Gilman international attention.

Literary Context

Edgar Allan Poe, "The Tell-Tale Heart," *The Pioneer* (January 1843): 29–31

American poet, critic, and short-story writer Edgar Allan Poe had a great influence in America and abroad. An avid reader of Poe's tales, Gilman imitated Poe's style in her "Studies in Style" series in *Impress*, which includes her imitations of George Eliot, Charles Dickens, Olive Schreiner, Nathaniel Hawthorne, Louisa May Alcott, and Mark Twain (see Kenneth Baldwin, "Critics," in Knight's 1997 *Charlotte Perkins Gilman: A Study of the Short Fiction*, Further Reading, p. 161). "The Tell-Tale Heart," one of Poe's best-known tales of horror, offers an interesting comparison to "The Yellow Wall-Paper": both stories employ first-person narration and have a mad narrator. While issues of guilt and paranoia dominate this Poe tale about a man haunted by the sound of the still beating heart of his murder victim, madness and the power of imagination loom large in both tales.

Period readers often associated "The Yellow Wall-Paper" with the horror genre made popular by Poe (see Selected Reviews of *The Yellow Wall-Paper*). This includes Gilman's first husband, Charles Walter Stetson. Gilman notes in her autobiography that Walter Stetson "says it beats Poe, and Doré! But that's only a husband's opinion." Denise D. Knight corroborates this point in " 'Only a husband's opinion': Walter Stetson's view of Gilman's 'The Yellow Wall-Paper'—An Inscription" (*American Literary Realism* 36: 1 [Fall 2003]: 86–7). In an inscription on an early off-print of the story, Walter calls it a "masterpiece" and admits "it fairly makes me shudder," a response not unlike that of William Dean Howells, who included the story in his 1920 collection of American masterpieces (see **pp. 86–7**).

Between its 1920 publication in Howells's *The Great Modern American Stories* and today, "The Yellow Wall-Paper" has appeared in numerous collections of mysteries, horror tales, Gothic tales, and strange tales (see Chronology, **pp. 23–5**). In addition to early critics who align the story with Poe (see Interpretations, **pp. 85–6**), scholars today continue this association. Judith Fetterley compares "The Yellow Wall-Paper" to Poe's "The Murders in the Rue Morgue" and Susan Glaspell's "A Jury of Her Peers" (see Further Reading, **pp. 158–9**). Beverly Hume examines Gilman's landmark tale in relation to Poe's "The Black Cat" in "Managing Madness in Gilman's 'The Yellow Wall-Paper' " (*Studies in American Fiction* 30: 1 [Spring 2002]: 3–20). Marty Roth explores the Gilman–Poe connection in "Gilman's Arabesque Wallpaper" (see **pp. 117–21**). To what extent does "The Yellow Wall-Paper," complete with Gothic elements, continue the horror genre made popular by Poe?

THE TELL-TALE HEART.
BY EDGAR A. POE

Art is long and Time is fleeting,
    And our hearts, though stout and brave,
Still, like muffled drums, are beating
    Funeral marches to the grave.
                        Longfellow.

[column 1:]

TRUE!—nervous—very, very dreadfully nervous I had been, and am; but why *will* you say that I am mad? The disease had sharpened my senses—not destroyed—not dulled them. Above all was the sense of hearing acute. I heard all things in the heaven and in the earth. I heard many things in hell. How, then, am I mad? Harken! and observe how healthily—how calmly I can tell you the whole story.

It is impossible to say how first the idea entered my brain; but, once conceived, it haunted me day and night. Object there was none. Passion there was none. I loved the old man. He had never wronged me. He had never given me insult. For his gold I had no desire. I think it was his eye!—yes, it was this! He had the eye of a vulture—a pale blue eye, with a film over it. Whenever it fell upon me, my blood ran cold; and so, by degrees—very gradually—I made up my mind to take the life of the old man, and thus rid myself of the eye forever.

Now this is the point. You fancy me mad. Madmen know nothing. But you should have [column 2:] seen *me*. You should have seen how wisely I proceeded—with what caution—with what foresight—with what dissimulation I went to work! I was never kinder to the old man than during the whole week before I killed him. And every night, about midnight, I turned the latch of his door and opened it—oh so gently! And then, when I had made an opening sufficient for my head, I first put in a dark lantern, all closed, closed, so that no light shone out, and then I thrust in my head. Oh, you would have laughed to see how cunningly I thrust it in! I moved it slowly—very, very slowly, so that I might not disturb the old man's sleep. It took me an hour to place my whole head within the opening so far that I could see the old man as he lay upon his bed. Ha!—would a madman have been so wise as this? And then, when my head was well in the room, I undid the lantern cautiously—oh, so cautiously (for the hinges creaked)—I undid it just so much that a single thin ray fell upon the vulture eye. And this I did for seven long nights—every night just at midnight—but I found the eye always closed; and so it [page 30, column 1:] was impossible to do the work; for it was not the old man who vexed me, but his Evil Eye. And every morning, when the day broke, I went boldly into his chamber, and spoke courageously to him, calling him by name in a hearty tone, and inquiring how he has passed the night. So you see he would have been a very profound old man, indeed, to suspect that every night, just at twelve, I looked in upon him while he slept.

Upon the eighth night I was more than usually cautious in opening the door. A watch's minute-hand moves more quickly than did mine. Never, before that night, had I *felt* the extent of my own powers—of my sagacity. I could scarcely contain my feelings of triumph. To think that there I was, opening the door, little by little, and the old man not even to dream of my secret deeds or thoughts. I fairly chuckled at the idea. And perhaps the old man heard me; for he moved in the bed suddenly, as if startled. Now you may think that I drew back—but no. His room was as black as pitch with the thick darkness, (for the shutters were close fastened, through fear of robbers,) and so I knew that he could not see the opening of the door, and I kept on pushing it steadily, steadily.

I had got my head in, und [and] was about to open the lantern, when my thumb slipped upon the tin fastening, and the old man sprang up in bed, crying out—"Who's there?"

I kept quite still and said nothing. For another hour I did not move a muscle, and in the meantime I did not hear the old man lie down. He was still sitting up in the bed, listening;—just as I have done, night after night, hearkening to the death-watches in the wall.

Presently I heard a slight groan, and I knew that it was the groan of mortal terror. It was not a groan of pain, or of grief—oh, no!—it was the low, stifled sound that arises from the bottom of the soul when overcharged with *awe*. I knew the sound well. Many a night, just at midnight, when all the world slept, it has welled up from my own bosom, deepening, with its dreadful echo, the terrors that distracted me. I say I knew it well. I knew what the old man felt, and pitied him, although I chuckled at heart. I knew that he had been lying awake ever since the first slight noise, when he had turned in the bed. His fears had been, ever since, growing upon him. He had been trying to fancy them causeless, but could not. He had been saying to himself—"It is nothing but the wind in the chimney—it is only a mouse crossing the floor," or "it is merely a cricket which has made a single chirp." Yes, he had been trying to comfort himself with these suppositions; but he had found all in vain. *All in vain:* because death, in approaching the old man had stalked with his black shadow before him, and the shadow had now reached and enveloped the victim. And it was the mournful influence of the unperceived shadow that caused him to feel—although he [column 2:] neither saw nor heard me—to *feel* the presence of my head within the room.

When I had waited a long time, very patiently, without hearing the old man lie down, I resolved to open a little—a very, very little crevice in the lantern. So I opened it—you cannot imagine how stealthily, stealthily—until, at length, a simple dim ray, like the thread of the spider, shot from out the crevice and fell full upon the vulture eye.

It was open—wide, wide open—and I grew furious as I gazed upon it. I saw it with perfect distinctness—all a dull blue, with a hideous veil over it that chilled the very marrow in my bones; but I could see nothing else of the old man's face or person; for I had directed the ray, as if by instinct, precisely upon the damned spot.

And now—have I not told you that what you mistake for madness is but over acuteness of the senses?—now, I say, there came to my ears a *low, dull, quick sound—much such a sound as a watch makes when enveloped in cotton.* I knew *that* sound well, too. It was the beating of the old man's heart. It increased my fury, as the beating of a drum stimulates the soldier into courage.

But even yet I refrained and kept still. I scarcely breathed. I held the lantern motionless. I tried how steadily I could maintain the ray upon the eye. Meantime the hellish tattoo of the heart increased. It grew quicker, and louder and louder every instant. The old man's terror *must* have been extreme! It grew louder, I say, louder every moment:—do you mark me well? I have told you that I am nervous:—so I am. And now, at the dead hour of the night, and amid the dreadful silence of that old house, so strange a noise as this excited me to uncontrollable wrath. Yet, for some minutes longer, I refrained and kept still. But the beating grew louder, *louder!* I thought the heart must burst! And now a new anxiety seized me—the sound would be heard by a neighbor! The old man's hour had come! With a loud yell, I threw open the lantern and leaped into the room. He shrieked once—once only. In an instant I dragged him to the floor, and pulled the heavy bed over him. I then sat upon the bed and smiled gaily, to find the deed so far done. But, for many minutes, the heart beat on, with a muffled sound. This, however, did not vex me; it would not be heard through the walls. At length it ceased. The old man was dead. I removed the bed and examined the corpse. Yes, he was stone, stone dead. I placed my hand upon the heart and held it there many minutes. There was no pulsation. The old man was stone dead. His eye would trouble *me* no more.

If, still, you think me mad, you will think so no longer when I describe the wise precautions I took for the concealment of the body. The night waned, and I worked hastily, but in silence. First of all I dismembered the corpse. I cut off the head and the arms and the legs. **[page 31, column 1:]** I then took up three planks from the flooring of the chamber, and deposited all between the scantlings. I then replaced the boards so cleverly, so cunningly, that no human eye—not even *his*— could have detected anything wrong. There was nothing to wash out—no stain of any kind—no blood-spot whatever. I had been too wary for that. A tub had caught all—ha! ha!

When I had made an end of these labors, it was four o'clock—still dark as midnight. As the bell sounded the hour, there came a knocking at the street door. I went down to open it with a light heart,—for what had I *now* to fear? There entered three men, who introduced themselves, with perfect suavity, as officers of the police. A shriek had been heard by a neighbor during the night; suspicion of foul play had been aroused; information had been lodged at the police-office, and they (the officers) had been deputed to search the premises.

I smiled,—for *what* had I to fear? I bade the gentlemen welcome. The shriek, I said, was my own in a dream. The old man, I mentioned, was absent in the country. I took my visiters all over the house. I bade them search—search *well*. I led them, at length, to *his* chamber. I showed them his treasures, secure, undisturbed. In the enthusiasm of my confidence, I brought chairs into the room, and desired them *here* to rest from their fatigues; while I myself, in the wild audacity of my perfect triumph, placed my own seat upon the very spot beneath which reposed the corpse of the victim.

The officers were satisfied. My *manner* had convinced them. I was singularly at ease. They sat, and, while I answered cheerily, they chatted of familiar things. But, ere long, I felt myself getting pale and wished them gone. **[column 2:]** My head ached, and I fancied a ringing in my ears: but still they sat and still chatted. The ringing became more distinct: I talked more freely, to get rid of the feeling; but it continued and gained definiteness—until, at length, I found that the noise was *not* within my ears.

No doubt I now grew *very* pale;—but I talked more fluently, and with a height- ened voice. Yet the sound increased—and what could I do? It was *a low, dull, quick sound—much such a sound as a watch makes when enveloped in cotton*. I gasped for breath—and yet the officers heard it not. I talked more quickly—more vehemently;—but the noise steadily increased. I arose, and argued about trifles, in a high key and with violent gesticulations;—but the noise steadily increased. Why *would* they not be gone? I paced the floor to and fro, with heavy strides, as if excited to fury by the observations of the men;—but the noise steadily increased. Oh God! what *could* I do? I foamed—I raved—I swore! I swung the chair upon which I had sat, and grated it upon the boards;—but the noise arose over all and continually increased. It grew louder—louder—*louder!* And still the men chatted pleasantly, and smiled. Was it possible they heard not? Almighty God!—no, no! They heard!—they suspected!—they *knew!*—they were making a mockery of my horror!—this I thought, and this I think. But anything was better than this agony! Anything was more tolerable than this derision! I could bear those hypocritical smiles no longer! I felt that I must scream or die!—and now—again!—hark! louder! louder! louder! *louder!*—

"Villains!" I shrieked, "dissemble no more! I admit the deed!—tear up the planks!—here, here!—it is the beating of his hideous heart!"

Excerpts from **The Diary of Alice James** (1889) (posthumously published in 1934), ed. Leon Edel, with an introduction by Linda Simon (Boston: Northeastern University Press, 1999), 25, 148–50

Alice James (1848–92) was the only daughter in the illustrious James family. Long overshadowed by her famous brothers—novelist Henry James, Jr. and philosopher/psychologist William James—Alice wrote diaries, beginning about age forty, that reveal she was a gifted and curious intellectual in her own right. Alice James lived at a time when society circumscribed even the lives of intelligent women and was born into a family that treated women as inferior. She spent her brief lifetime at home (both in England and America) with only erratic formal education and little opportunity for social recognition. With an inherited propensity toward severe depression, Alice gained attention in her family circle as *invalid*, and was subjected, as patient, to scrutiny and misinterpretation. Alice James underwent galvanic cures (electrical stimulation), exercise therapy, and rest cures (introduced in England in the 1880s), a treatment about which she—like Gilman—complained bitterly.

Like the narrator of "The Yellow Wall-Paper" who keeps a diary as she suffers from hysteria, Alice James made a "habit" of writing in her diary for the last four years of her life to "lose a little of the sense of loneliness and desolation which abides with me." Just as Gilman's narrator hides her diary when Doctor John approaches, Alice James kept her diary a secret from her brothers so that she could write freely and independently. While the first of these two diary excerpts gives Alice James's reasons for writing, the second describes with chilling precision Alice's battle with hysteria, which she suggests is "Owing to some physical weakness, excess of nervous susceptibility." Moreover, in the second excerpt, she helps us understand further why she needs the outlet of a diary. Except through this private writing, she cannot give vent to her pain but instead must constrain the "horrors and suffering" that she feels by taking on "the duties of doctor, nurse, and strait-jacket." Likewise, the narrator sees writing as therapy and recognizes that she, too, needs a diary to relieve her mind and vent her frustrations: "John is a physician, and *perhaps*—(I would not say it to a living soul, of course, but this is dead paper and a great relief to my mind—) *perhaps* that is one reason I do not get well faster" (p. 131). James's diary, which was a necessary outlet throughout her treatments, offers an interesting comparison to the fictional diary of Gilman's narrator and authenticates Gilman's decision to compose her story as a diary.

May 31st, 1889

I THINK that if I get into the habit of writing a bit about what happens, or rather doesn't happen, I may lose a little of the sense of loneliness and desolation which abides with me. My circumstances allowing of nothing but the ejaculation of one-syllabled reflections, a written monologue by that most interesting being, *myself*, may have its yet to be discovered consolations. I shall at least have it all my own way and it may bring relief as an outlet to that geyser of emotions, sensations, speculations and reflections which ferments perpetually within my poor old carcass for its sins; so here goes, my first Journal!

[. . .]

October 26th

William uses an excellent expression when he says in his paper on the "Hidden Self"[1] that the nervous victim "abandons" certain portions of his consciousness. It may be the word commonly used by his kind. It is just the right one at any rate, altho' I have never unfortunately been able to abandon my consciousness and get five minutes' rest. I have passed thro' an infinite succession of conscious abandonments and in looking back now I see how it began in my childhood, altho' I wasn't conscious of the necessity until '67 or '68 when I broke down first, acutely, and had violent turns of hysteria. As I lay prostrate after the storm with my mind luminous and active and susceptible of the clearest, strongest impressions, I saw so distinctly that it was a fight simply between my body and my will, a battle in which the former was to be triumphant to the end. Owing to some physical weakness, excess of nervous susceptibility, the moral power *pauses*, as it were for a moment, and refuses to maintain muscular sanity, worn out with the strain of its constabulary functions. As I used to sit immovable reading in the library with waves of violent inclination suddenly invading my muscles taking some one of their myriad forms such as throwing myself out of the window, or knocking off the head of the benignant pater as he sat with his silver locks, writing at his table, it used to seem to me that the only difference between me and the insane was that I had not only all the horrors and suffering of insanity but the duties of doctor, nurse, and strait-jacket imposed upon me, too. Conceive of never being without the sense that if you let yourself go for a moment your mechanism will fall into pie and that at some given moment you must abandon it all, let the dykes break and

1 [Edel's note.] William James's paper "The Hidden Self" had appeared in *Scribner's* in March 1920. Alice is referring to her brother's discussion of Binet's "contractions of the field of consciousness" in hysterical persons.

the flood sweep in, acknowledging yourself abjectly impotent before the immutable laws. When all one's moral and natural stock in trade is a temperament forbidding the abandonment of an inch or the relaxation of a muscle, 'tis a never-ending fight. When the fancy took me of a morning at school to *study* my lessons by way of variety instead of shirking or wiggling thro' the most impossible sensations of upheaval, violent revolt in my head overtook me so that I had to "abandon" my brain, as it were. So it has always been, anything that sticks of itself is free to do so, but conscious and continuous cerebration is an impossible exercise and from just behind the eyes my head feels like a dense jungle into which no ray of light has ever penetrated. So, with the rest, you abandon the pit of your stomach, the palms of your hands, the soles of your feet, and refuse to keep them sane when you find in turn one moral impression after another producing despair in the one, terror in the other, anxiety in the third and so on until life becomes one long flight from remote suggestion and complicated eluding of the multi-fold traps set for your undoing.

[. . .]

Charlotte Perkins Gilman, "Through This," *Kate Field's Washington*, September 13, 1893, 166

"Through This" appeared one year after publication of "The Yellow Wall-Paper." Also drawing upon Gilman's trials as a young wife and mother, it similarly exhibits Gilman's anger toward patriarchy and a gender-based division of work. Denise D. Knight, the first critic to call attention to the story, dubs it a "companion" to "The Yellow Wall-Paper" in a 1992 article in *Women's Studies*; she also anthologized it in her 1994 collection. The story yet deserves wider recognition for its vivid depiction of the demands of marriage and motherhood in Victorian America that overwhelm a young wife and mother who simply cannot get "through this."

Gilman recalls nearly the entire cast of characters from her landmark story: John, the nameless narrator—who Knight posits is Jane—Jennie, Mary, Jane's brother, and a first-born male child. Gilman varies their personalities and changes some points. John assumes a different position of authority as a politician. The narrator and Jennie reverse roles: Jennie has intellectual ambitions while the narrator aims to be "a perfect and enthusiastic housekeeper, and hopes for no better profession" (see **p. 135**). The narrator moves at a frenzied pace as she cleans, cooks delicious meals, runs errands, and lovingly tends to her children. As in "The Yellow Wall-Paper," form conveys meaning. The story reads like a stream of consciousness narrative, riddled by one-sided conversations and fragmented speech (the narrator even interrupts herself mid-sentence). Overwhelmed by the mother-woman ideal, the narrator contemplates the colors of dawn and darkness that creep down her bedroom wall, eerily evoking the narrator's fate in "The Yellow Wall-Paper."

"Through This" exists as a story in its own right. It can be read independent of "The Yellow Wall-Paper," as a companion to it, or—I would argue—as a "prequel" to Gilman's landmark tale, much as Jean Rhys's *Wide Sargasso Sea* (1966), written well after Charlotte Brontë's *Jane Eyre* (1847), informs a reading of another pair of "mad" heroines. From the vantage point of a "prequel," "Through This" illuminates the rigid expectations of nineteenth-century marriage and motherhood against which the narrator of "The Yellow Wall-Paper" rebels.

The dawn colors creep up my bedroom wall, softly, slowly. Darkness, dim gray, dull blue, soft lavender, clear pink, pale yellow, warm gold—sunlight.

A new day.

With the great sunrise great thoughts come.

I rise with the world. I live, I can help. Here close at hand lie the sweet home duties through which my life shall touch the others! Through this man made happier and stronger by my living; through these rosy babies sleeping here in the growing light; through this small, sweet, well-ordered home, whose restful influence shall touch all comers; through me too, perhaps—there's the baker, I must get up, or this bright purpose fades.

How well the fire burns! Its swift kindling and gathering roar speak of accomplishment. The rich odor of coffee steals through the house.

John likes morning-glories on the breakfast table—scented flowers are better with lighter meals. All is ready—healthful, dainty, delicious.

The clean-aproned little ones smile milky-mouthed over their bowls of mush. John kisses me good-bye so happily.

Through this dear work, well done, I shall reach, I shall help—but I must get the dishes done and not dream.

"Good morning! Soap, please, the same kind. Coffee, rice, two boxes of gelatine. That's all, I think. Oh—crackers! Good morning."

There, I forgot the eggs! I can make these go, I guess. Now to soak the tapioca.[1] Now the beets[2] on, they take so long. I'll bake the potatoes—they don't go in yet. Now babykins must have her bath and nap.

A clean hour and a half before dinner. I can get those little nightgowns cut and basted. How bright the sun is! Amaranth lies on the grass under the rosebush, stretching her paws among the warm, green blades. The kittens tumble over her. She's brought them three mice this week. Baby and Jack are on the warm grass too—happy, safe, well. Careful, dear! Don't go away from little sister!

By and by when they are grown, I can—O there! the bell!

Ah, well!—yes—I'd like to have joined. I believe in it, but I can't now. Home duties forbid. This is my work. Through this, in time—there's the bell again, and it waked the baby!

As if I could buy a sewing machine every week! I'll put out a bulletin, stating my needs for the benefit of agents. I don't believe in buying at the door anyway, yet I suppose they must live. Yes, dear! Mamma's coming!

---

1 Tapioca is a starch from the root of the cassava plant, used in puddings and as a thickening agent.
2 The root of a beet is eaten as a vegetable; the bulbous root is dark red and fleshy.

I wonder if torchon would look better, or Hamburg?[3] Its [sic] softer but it looks older. Oh, here's that knit edging grandma sent me. Bless her dear heart!

There! I meant to have swept the bed-room this morning so as to have more time to-morrow. Perhaps I can before dinner. It does look dreadfully. I'll just put the potatoes in. Baked potatoes are so good! I love to see Jack dig into them with his little spoon.

John says I cook steak better than anyone he ever saw.

Yes, dear?

Is that so? Why, I should think they'd *know* better. Can't the people do anything about it?

Why no—not *personally*—but I should think you might. What are men for if they can't keep the city in order.

Cream on the pudding, dear?

That was a good dinner. I like to cook. I think housework is noble if you do it in a right spirit.

That pipe must be seen to before long. I'll speak to John about it. Coal's pretty low, too.

Guess I'll put on my best boots, I want to run down town for a few moments— in case mother comes and can stay with baby. I wonder if mother wouldn't like to join that—she has time enough. But she doesn't seem to be a bit interested in outside things. I ought to take baby out in her carriage, but it's so heavy with Jack, and yet Jack can't walk a great way. Besides, if mother comes I needn't. Maybe we'll all go in the car—but that's such an undertaking! Three o'clock!

Jack! Jack! Don't do that—here—wait a moment.

I ought to answer Jennie's letter. She writes such splendid things, but I don't go with her in half she says. A woman cannot do that way and keep a family going. I'll write to her this evening.

Of course if one *could*, I'd like as well as anyone to be in those great live currents of thought and action. Jennie and I were full of it in school. How long ago that seems. But I never thought then of being so happy. Jennie isn't happy, I know—she can't be, poor thing, till she's a wife and mother.

O, there comes mother! Jack, deary, open the gate for Grandma! So glad you could come, mother dear! Can you stay awhile and let me go down town on a few errands?

Mother looks real tired. I wish she would go out more and have some outside interests. Mary and the children are too much for her, I think. Harry ought not to have brought them home. Mother needs rest. She's brought up one family.

There, I've forgotten my list, I hurried so. Thread, elastic, buttons; what was that other thing? Maybe I'll think of it.

How awfully cheap! How can they make them at that price! Three, please. I guess with these I can make the others last through the year. They're so pretty, too. How much are these? Jack's got to have a new coat before long—not to-day.

O dear! I've missed that car, and mother can't stay after five! I'll cut across and hurry.

---

3 Torchon is a type of lace made from coarse linen or cotton thread and twisted into geometric patterns; Hamburg refers to a type of lace imported from Hamburg, Germany.

Why the milk hasn't come, and John's got to go out early to-night. I wish election was over.

I'm sorry, dear, but the milk was so late I couldn't make it. Yes, I'll speak to him. O, no, I guess not; he's a very reliable man, usually, and the milk's good. Hush, hush, baby! Papa's talking!

Good night, dear, don't be too late.

> Sleep, baby, sleep!
> The large stars are the sheep,
> The little stars are the lambs, I guess,
> And the fair moon is the shepherdess.
> Sleep, baby, sleep!

How pretty they look! Thank God, they keep so well.

It's no use, I can't write a letter to-night—especially to Jennie. I'm too tired. I'll go to bed early. John hates to have me wait up for him late. I'll go now, if it is before dark—then get up early to-morrow and get the sweeping done. How loud the crickets are! The evening shades creep down my bedroom wall—softly—slowly.

Warm gold—pale yellow—clear pink—soft lavender—dull blue—dim gray—darkness.

Kate Chopin, "The Story of an Hour," (under the title "The Dream of an Hour") *Vogue* 4: 360, December 6, 1894

The turn-of-the-century American author most associated with Gilman is Kate Chopin (1851–1904). Her controversial novel *The Awakening* (1899) attacks the restrictions of patriarchy and the bourgeois home while also radically embracing a married woman's sexual desire outside of marriage. Chopin wrote her brief but memorable "The Story of an Hour" (1894) about a woman's reaction to news of her husband's death in the same decade Gilman composed "The Yellow Wall-Paper." Both stories feature a female patient whom the nineteenth-century medical establishment misunderstands and misdiagnoses.

Like Doctor John in "The Yellow Wall-Paper," Louise Mallard's unnamed doctors and family poorly read her condition. In projecting accepted theories onto Louise as female "patient," they create a final diagnosis noted for its irony and shock value—qualities it shares with "The Yellow Wall-Paper" and Poe's horror tales. Moreover, in Louise Mallard's hour of freedom, Chopin delivers a convincing critique of the marital and social mores of her time. Important to the denouement is the moment when Louise Mallard utters the words " 'free, free, free!' " in the privacy of her upstairs bedroom while contemplating an independent life; here we find a woman gaining her liberty, however brief. In this respect, Chopin—much like Gilman—anticipates Virginia Woolf in calling attention to the importance of a woman having a "room of her own," both literally and metaphorically.

"The Story of an Hour," when paired with "The Yellow Wall-Paper," foregrounds the foibles of the male medical model and the social construction of
domestic femininity in Victorian America. Louise's movement between the
upper and lower stories of her home, her rejection of traditional domesticity
during her hour of freedom, and her fate invite interesting comparisons to the
actions and destiny of the narrator of "The Yellow Wall-Paper."

Knowing that Mrs Mallard was afflicted with a heart trouble, great care was
taken to break to her as gently as possible the news of her husband's death.

It was her sister Josephine who told her, in broken sentences; veiled hints that
revealed in half concealing. Her husband's friend Richards was there, too, near
her. It was he who had been in the newspaper office when intelligence of the
railroad disaster was received, with Brently Mallard's name leading the list of
'killed.' He had only taken the time to assure himself of its truth by a second
telegram, and had hastened to forestall any less careful, less tender friend in
bearing the sad message.

She did not hear the story as many women have heard the same, with a para-
lyzed inability to accept its significance. She wept at once, with sudden, wild
abandonment, in her sister's arms. When the storm of grief had spent itself she
went away to her room alone. She would have no one follow her.

There stood, facing the open window, a comfortable, roomy armchair. Into this
she sank, pressed down by a physical exhaustion that haunted her body and
seemed to reach into her soul.

She could see in the open square before her house the tops of trees that were all
aquiver with the new spring life. The delicious breath of rain was in the air. In the
street below a peddler was crying his wares. The notes of a distant song which
some one was singing reached her faintly, and countless sparrows were twittering
in the eaves.

There were patches of blue sky showing here and there through the clouds that
had met and piled one above the other in the west facing her window.

She sat with her head thrown back upon the cushion of the chair, quite motionless, except when a sob came up into her throat and shook her, as a child who has
cried itself to sleep continues to sob in its dreams.

She was young, with a fair, calm face, whose lines bespoke repression and even
a certain strength. But now there was a dull stare in her eyes, whose gaze was
fixed away off yonder on one of those patches of blue sky. It was not a glance of
reflection, but rather indicated a suspension of intelligent thought.

There was something coming to her and she was waiting for it, fearfully. What
was it? She did not know; it was too subtle and elusive to name. But she felt it,
creeping out of the sky, reaching toward her through the sounds, the scents, the
color that filled the air.

Now her bosom rose and fell tumultuously. She was beginning to recognize this
thing that was approaching to possess her, and she was striving to beat it back
with her will – as powerless as her two white slender hands would have been.

When she abandoned herself a little whispered word escaped her slightly parted
lips. She said it over and over under her breath: 'free, free, free!' The vacant stare

and the look of terror that had followed it went from her eyes. They stayed keen and bright. Her pulses beat fast, and the coursing blood warmed and relaxed every inch of her body.

She did not stop to ask if it were or were not a monstrous joy that held her. A clear and exalted perception enabled her to dismiss the suggestion as trivial.

She knew that she would weep again when she saw the kind, tender hands folded in death; the face that had never looked save with love upon her, fixed and gray and dead. But she saw beyond that bitter moment a long procession of years to come that would belong to her absolutely. And she opened and spread her arms out to them in welcome.

There would be no one to live for her during those coming years; she would live for herself. There would be no powerful will bending hers in that blind persistence with which men and women believe they have a right to impose a private will upon a fellow-creature. A kind intention or a cruel intention made the act seem no less a crime as she looked upon it in that brief moment of illumination.

And yet she had loved him – sometimes. Often she had not. What did it matter! What could love, the unsolved mystery, count for in face of this possession of self-assertion which she suddenly recognized as the strongest impulse of her being!

'Free! Body and soul free!' she kept whispering.

Josephine was kneeling before the closed door with her lips to the keyhole, imploring for admission. 'Louise, open the door! I beg; open the door – you will make yourself ill. What are you doing, Louise? For heaven's sake open the door.'

'Go away. I am not making myself ill.' No; she was drinking in a very elixir of life through that open window.

Her fancy was running riot along those days ahead of her. Spring days, and summer days, and all sorts of days that would be her own. She breathed a quick prayer that life might be long. It was only yesterday she had thought with a shudder that life might be long.

She arose at length and opened the door to her sister's importunities. There was a feverish triumph in her eyes, and she carried herself unwittingly like a goddess of Victory. She clasped her sister's waist, and together they descended the stairs. Richards stood waiting for them at the bottom.

Someone was opening the front door with a latchkey. It was Brently Mallard who entered, a little travel-stained, composedly carrying his gripsack and umbrella. He had been far from the scene of accident, and did not even know there had been one. He stood amazed at Josephine's piercing cry; at Richards' quick motion to screen him from the view of his wife.

But Richards was too late.

When the doctors came they said she had died of heart disease – of joy that kills.

Selected poems from **Charlotte Perkins Gilman, In This Our World** (1898) (New York: Arno Press, 1974; reprint of the 1898 Small, Maynard edition) pp. 102–3, 125, 129–31, 160.

Gilman wrote poems with a purpose throughout her lifetime. Her first book of verse, In This Our World (1893), enjoyed a near cult following among socialists in

England and America, resulting in multiple editions (1895 and 1898). Con-temporary luminaries including sociologist Lester Frank Ward and authors Upton Sinclair, George Bernard Shaw, and William Dean Howells praised her satirical verse. As a poet, she did not adhere to any prevailing literary school, making it hard to place her verse in the context of turn-of-the-twentieth-century American women's poetry. In some respects, Gilman's poetry suggests the influence of Walt Whitman, whom she considered America's greatest poet; her work is more didactic than Whitman's, however, sacrificing imagery to promote her agenda, as critics such as Denise D. Knight and Gary Scharnhorst have noted.

Gilman's feminist theories from *Women and Economics* (1898), the treatise that established her international reputation as a social critic, emerge in her nearly five hundred poems. Her verse exposes problems with the patriarchal construction of domestic femininity and argues for a reorganization of house service, including child care. Emphasizing the didactic intent of *In This Our World*, Gilman told an interviewer for the *Topeka State Journal* (15 June 1896, vol. 7), "I don't call it a book of poems. I call it a tool box. It was written to drive nails with." Poetry, like fiction, became a vehicle to critique the dynamics of gender, which, she contended, denied white upper- and middle-class women participation in the new industrial world. "The Obstacle" and "In Duty Bound" appear in the first section of *In This Our World* entitled "The World" while the other three poems come from "Woman," the short but forceful middle section of her three-part volume of poetry. Poems in "Woman" challenge female subjugation, subvert patriarchal ideologies, and argue for women's rights.

In "She Walketh Veiled and Sleeping," Gilman skilfully employs repetition to recall the "creeping" narrator in "The Yellow Wall-Paper," who only comes to "knoweth . . . her power" at the end of "The Yellow Wall-Paper" when she crawls over John. "The Obstacle" also illuminates the denouement of the story when the narrator shows total disregard for her husband; John is reduced to a mere impediment along a woman's path: "And I walked directly through him/ As if he wasn't there." The aptly titled poem "In Duty Bound" forcefully expresses a woman's obligations determined by her sex in the piercing lines: "An obliga-tion pre-imposed, unsought,/ Yet binding with the force of natural law." "To the Young Wife" confronts the emotional and economic dependence of married women in the nineteenth century. Debunking the rhetoric placating women as "queens" of the hearth, she makes the young wife "Queen of a cook-stove throne." In this poem, as in much of her verse, the regular meter and end rhyme could be seen as a strategic means to offset her bitter message. "The Mother's Charge," a dark poem, grimly portrays a mother passing down the limitations of her gendered world through endless housekeeping tips. Preserving the trad-ition of a powerful concluding couplet, Gilman fixes a pattern of unfulfilled mothers and daughters who repeat their mother's lives and mistakes. (See essays on Gilman's poetry by Knight and Golden in *Charlotte Perkins Gilman: Optimist Reformer*, edited by Jill Rudd and Val Gough, published by University of Iowa Press in 1999, Further Reading, p. 161.)

SHE WALKETH VEILED AND SLEEPING.

SHE walketh veiled and sleeping,
For she knoweth not her power;
She obeyeth but the pleading
Of her heart, and the high leading
Of her soul, unto this hour.
Slow advancing, halting, creeping,
Comes the Woman to the hour! —
She walketh veiled and sleeping,
For she knoweth not her power.

AN OBSTACLE

I WAS climbing up a mountain-path
   With many things to do,
Important business of my own,
   And other people's too,
When I ran against a Prejudice
   That quite cut off the view.

My work was such as could not wait,
   My path quite clearly showed,
My strength and time were limited,
   I carried quite a load;
And there that hulking Prejudice
   Sat all across the road.

So I spoke to him politely,
   For he was huge and high,
And begged that he would move a bit
   And let me travel by.
He smiled, but as for moving! —
   He did n't even try.

And then I reasoned quietly
   With that colossal mule:
My time was short — no other path —
   The mountain winds were cool.
I argued like a Solomon;[1]
   He sat there like a fool.

Then I flew into a passion,
   I danced and howled and swore.
I pelted and belabored him
   Till I was stiff and sore;
He got as mad as I did —
   But he sat there as before.

---

1   Solomon, son of King David and Bathsheba, was king of the ancient Hebrews and noted for his
   wisdom and sage proverbs.

And then I begged him on my knees;
　　I might be kneeling still
If so I hoped to move that mass
　　Of obdurate ill-will —
As well invite the monument
To vacate Bunker Hill![2]

So I sat before him helpless,
　　In an ecstasy of woe —
The mountain mists were rising fast,
　　The sun was sinking slow —
When a sudden inspiration came,
　　As sudden winds do blow.

I took my hat, I took my stick,
　　My load I settled fair,
I approached that awful incubus
　　With an absent-minded air —
And I walked directly through him,
　　As if he was n't there!

IN DUTY BOUND

IN duty bound, a life hemmed in
　　Whichever way the spirit turns to look;
No chance of breaking out, except by sin;
　　　　Not even room to shirk —
　　　　Simply to live, and work.

An obligation pre-imposed, unsought,
　　Yet binding with the force of natural law;
The pressure of antagonistic thought;
　　　　Aching within, each hour,
　　　　A sense of wasting power.

A house with roof so darkly low
　　The heavy rafters shut the sunlight out;
One cannot stand erect without a blow;
　　　　Until the soul inside
　　　　Cries for a grave — more wide.

2　Bunker Hill was a pivotal battle in the American Revolution on June 17, 1775 (though it actually
　took place in nearby Breed's Hill). The British won but suffered heavy losses, and the strong
　American defense heightened the Patriots' morale.

A consciousness that if this thing endure,
  The common joys of life will dull the pain;
The high ideals of the grand and pure
    Die, as of course they must,
    Of long disuse and rust.

That is the worst. It takes supernatural strength
  To hold the attitude that brings the pain;
And they are few indeed but stoop at length
    To find something less than best,
    To find, in stooping, rest.

TO THE YOUNG WIFE

ARE you content, you pretty three-years' wife?
  Are you content and satisfied to live
  On what your loving husband loves to give,
    And give to him your life?

Are you content with work, — to toil alone,
  To clean things dirty and to soil things clean;
  To be a kitchen-maid, be called a queen, —
    Queen of a cook-stove throne?

Are you content to reign in that small space —
  A wooden palace and a yard-fenced land —
  With other queens abundant on each hand,
    Each fastened in her place?

Are you content to rear your children so?
  Untaught yourself, untrained, perplexed, distressed,
  Are you so sure your way is always best?
    That you can always know?

Have you forgotten how you used to long
  In days of ardent girlhood, to be great,
  To help the groaning world, to serve the state,
    To be so wise — so strong?

And are you quite convinced this is the way,
  The only way a woman's duty lies —
Knowing all women so have shut their eyes?
    Seeing the world to-day?

Have you no dream of life in fuller store?
  Of growing to be more than that you are?
  Doing the things you now do better far,
    Yet doing others — more?

Losing no love, but finding as you grew
   That as you entered upon nobler life
   You so became a richer, sweeter wife,
     A wiser mother too?

What holds you? Ah, my dear, it is your throne,
   Your paltry queenship in that narrow place,
   Your antique labors, your restricted space,
     Your working all alone!

Be not deceived! 'T is not your wifely bond
   That holds you, nor the mother's royal power,
   But selfish, slavish service hour by hour —
     A life with no beyond!

THE MOTHER'S CHARGE.

SHE raised her head. With hot and glittering eye,
"I know," she said, "that I am going to die.
Come here, my daughter, while my mind is clear.
Let me make plain to you your duty here;
My duty once — I never failed to try —
But for some reason I am going to die."
She raised her head, and, while her eyes rolled wild,
Poured these instructions on the gasping child:

"Begin at once — don't iron sitting down —
Wash your potatoes when the fat is brown —
Monday, unless it rains — it always pays
To get fall sewing done on the right days —
A carpet-sweeper and a little broom —
Save dishes — wash the summer dining-room
With soda — keep the children out of doors —
The starch is out — beeswax on all the floors —
If girls are treated like your friends they stay —
They stay, and treat you like their friends — the way
To make home happy is to keep a jar —
And save the prettiest pieces for the star
In the middle — blue's too dark — all silk is best —
And don't forget the corners — when they're dressed
Put them on ice — and always wash the chest
Three times a day, the windows every week —
We need more flour — the bedroom ceilings leak —
It's better than onion — keep the boys at home —
Gardening is good — a load, three loads of loam —
They bloom in spring — and smile, smile always, dear —
Be brave, keep on — I hope I've made it clear."

She died, as all her mothers died before.
Her daughter died in turn, and made one more.

Charlotte Perkins Gilman, "Why I Wrote 'The Yellow Wallpaper'?," *Forerunner* 4 (October 1913): 271

Gilman founded *Forerunner* in 1909 because of a fervent desire "to express important truths, needed yet unpopular"; in fact, she proclaims in her 1935 autobiography, *The Living of Charlotte Perkins Gilman*: " 'If the editors and publishers will not bring out my work, I will!' "(304). She single-handedly wrote and edited the thirty-two-page monthly to promote the rights of women. It includes articles, book reviews, editorials, advertisements, poems, short stories, and two serials each year (one fiction and one non-fiction). Its circulation was small but far-reaching. In its seven-year run (1909–16), *Forerunner* attracted subscribers from Europe, India, and Australia as well as across the United States.

In this *Forerunner* article, Gilman explains the autobiographical roots of "The Yellow Wall-Paper" and her alleged motivation for writing it—to educate her doctor, S. Weir Mitchell, about his mistaken treatment for nervous depression. Many readers today are familiar with Mitchell's name because Gilman implicates him in her fiction; in the third of twelve entries that comprise her story, Gilman's narrator observes, "John says if I don't pick up faster he shall send me to Weir Mitchell in the fall" (**p. 135**). Gilman's breakdown also forms the subject of Chapter 8 of her autobiography ("The Breakdown," **pp. 48–50**).

Best known as Weir Mitchell, this leading late nineteenth-century specialist in women's nervous diseases treated Gilman in 1887. He prescribed a rest cure for a depression that followed the birth of her daughter, Katharine. Gilman admits differences between fiction and reality—she never objected to her wallpaper decorations or gave way to hallucinations. Nonetheless, she proudly states that she sent her story to "the physician who so nearly drove me mad" and makes a claim that Mitchell confessed to his friends that he changed his treatment for neurasthenia (nervous depression) after reading Gilman's story; in her words, "Many years later I was told that the great specialist had admitted to friends of his that he had altered his treatment of neurasthenia since reading *The Yellow Wallpaper*."

In the first wave of criticism following The Feminist Press's 1973 republication of the story, scholars echoed Gilman's account of Mitchell's change of heart. By the 1990s, critics began to acknowledge how Gilman often remembered imprecisely or altered a point to her advantage. For example, "The Yellow Wall-Paper" came out in January 1892, although in this article she dates it "about 1891." Using the passive voice in her claim, Gilman leaves her source of information unstated. She does not name Mitchell's friends. "Many years" have passed between the time she sends the story to him and learns of a positive outcome. Moreover, twenty-one years separate the publication of "The Yellow Wall-Paper" and this *Forerunner* article. In that period, Gilman may have altered or exaggerated her conviction about Mitchell's conversion in an attempt to mythologize her life.

Gilman here refers to M. D., the anonymous author of a review published in *Boston Transcript* entitled "Perilous Stuff" (1892), as a Boston male physician (see

Many and many a reader has asked that. When the story first came out, in the *New England Magazine* about 1891, a Boston physician made protest in *The Transcript*. Such a story ought not to be written, he said; it was enough to drive anyone mad to read it.

Another physician, in Kansas I think, wrote to say that it was the best description of incipient insanity he had ever seen, and – begging my pardon – had I been there?

Now the story of the story is this:

For many years I suffered from a severe and continuous nervous breakdown tending to melancholia – and beyond. During about the third year of this trouble I went, in devout faith and some faint stir of hope, to a noted specialist in nervous diseases, the best known in the country. This wise man put me to bed and applied the rest cure, to which a still good physique responded so promptly that he concluded there was nothing much the matter with me, and sent me home with solemn advice to "live as domestic a life as far as possible," to "have but two hours' intellectual life a day," and "never to touch pen, brush or pencil again as long as I lived." This was in 1887.

I went home and obeyed those directions for some three months, and came so near the border line of utter mental ruin that I could see over.

Then, using the remnants of intelligence that remained, and helped by a wise friend, I cast the noted specialist's advice to the winds and went to work again – work, the normal life of every human being; work, in which is joy and growth and service, without which one is a pauper and a parasite; ultimately recovering some measure of power.

Being naturally moved to rejoicing by this narrow escape, I wrote *The Yellow Wallpaper*, with its embellishments and additions to carry out the ideal (I never had hallucinations or objections to my mural decorations) and sent a copy to the physician who so nearly drove me mad. He never acknowledged it.

The little book is valued by alienists and as a good specimen of one kind of literature. It has to my knowledge saved one woman from a similar fate – so terrifying her family that they let her out into normal activity and she recovered.

But the best result is this. Many years later I was told that the great specialist had admitted to friends of his that he had altered his treatment of neurasthenia since reading *The Yellow Wallpaper.*

It was not intended to drive people crazy, but to save people from being driven crazy, and it worked.

From **Charlotte Perkins Gilman,** *The Living of Charlotte Perkins Gilman:* **"The Breakdown"** and **"Pasadena"** (1935) (Madison, Wis.: The University of Wisconsin Press, 1991). Chapters VIII and IX, 90–7, 118–21

Gilman wrote her autobiography at a time when few women writers chose to work in a genre now growing in popularity among women writers. She began it in 1925 when she felt the loss of her audience in a climate of increasing conservatism. She finished *The Living of Charlotte Perkins Gilman* just before her death from cancer at age seventy-five. While dying, she completed her text, revised it, proofread it, and chose the cover and photographic illustrations before taking chloroform to end her long suffering. Published posthumously on October 4, 1935, it forms an essential part of her literary legacy.

Autobiography offered Gilman a vehicle to call attention to her achievements at the twilight of a brilliant career, but also to grant herself authority. Looking backwards, Gilman describes her oft-noted difficult and impoverished childhood, her marriage to artist Charles Walter Stetson, her pregnancy and subsequent breakdown, her journey to California, personal struggles (e.g. allowing Katharine to live with her first husband following his remarriage to her lifelong friend), and literary accomplishments (e.g. her international acclaim for *Women and Economics* [1898]), as well as her second marriage to Houghton Gilman in 1900. Time seems to have softened her memories. For example, she paints a glowing picture of her first husband. Even if Stetson failed her merely by being a perfectly conventional husband, her depression so vital to the creation of "The Yellow Wall-Paper" is rooted in her first marriage, resulting in separation in 1888 and ending in divorce in 1894. Despite her whitewashing of Stetson, whom her biographer Ann J. Lane calls a prototype for John, the chapters entitled "The Breakdown" and "Pasadena" shed insight into the creation of her landmark story.

In "The Breakdown," Gilman describes her nervous depression following the birth of Katharine, leading to a melancholy that debilitated her. Weaning her daughter, she took a solo trip west—a prescription for rehabilitation that she grants Vivian Lane of *The Crux* (1911) and Jacqueline "Jack" Warner of *Unpunished* (ca. 1929). In California, staying with the Channings, Gilman restored her health yet discovered home was the source of her sickness. She recounts her visit to the Philadelphia sanatorium of Dr. S. Weir Mitchell and graphically recounts the disastrous consequences of following Mitchell's treatment; she played with a baby rag doll and crawled on the floor.

In "Pasadena," she repeats many of the same points that appear in her 1913 *Forerunner* article; however, the autobiography is more comprehensive. She begins by stating that "The Yellow Wall-Paper" is a case of a nervous break-down that begins as hers did but progresses to full-blown insanity because of a Mitchell-type rest cure treatment. She reprints *Atlantic Monthly* editor Horace E. Scudder's rejection of her story and the anonymous protest published in the *Boston Evening Transcript*, closing up the gap between the initials M. D. and follow-ing the letter with one from Brummel Jones, whom Gilman identifies as "another doctor." She also repeats her claim that she wrote the story to convince Mitchell of the "error of his ways." She alters a few other facts from her *Forerunner* article: Mitchell's friends to whom he admits changing his treat-ment after reading her story are now "close friends"; in fact, Gilman actually meets someone who knew them. Gilman also presents her oft-quoted convic-tion that "The Yellow Wall-Paper" "was no more 'literature' than my other stuff, being definitely written 'with a purpose.' In my judgment it is a pretty poor thing to write, to talk, without a purpose."

Significant is the title of the autobiography. Gilman recounts not her "life," but her "living." Her use of the present progressive participle in the title involves us actively as readers in the *living* of an author who once again holds a prominent place in the history of literature and feminism.

[. . .]

THE BREAKDOWN

In those days a new disease had dawned on the medical horizon. It was called "nervous prostration." No one knew much about it, and there were many who openly scoffed, saying it was only a new name for laziness. To be recognizably ill one must be confined to one's bed, and preferably in pain.

That a heretofore markedly vigorous young woman, with every comfort about her, should collapse in this lamentable manner was inexplicable. "You should use your will," said earnest friends. I had used it, hard and long, perhaps too hard and too long; at any rate it wouldn't work now.

"Force some happiness into your life," said one sympathizer. "Take an agree-able book to bed with you, occupy your mind with pleasant things." She did not realize that I was unable to read, and that my mind was exclusively occupied with unpleasant things. This disorder involved a growing melancholia, and that, as those know who have tasted it, consists of every painful mental sensation, shame, fear, remorse, a blind oppressive confusion, utter weakness, a steady brainache that fills the conscious mind with crowding images of distress.

The misery is doubtless as physical as a toothache, but a brain, of its own nature, gropes for reasons for its misery. Feeling the sensation fear, the mind suggests every possible calamity; the sensation shame – remorse – and one remembers every mistake and misdeeds of a lifetime, and grovels to the earth in abasement.

"If you would get up and do something you would feel better," said my mother. I rose drearily, and essayed to brush up the floor a little, with a dustpan and small whiskbroom, but soon dropped those implements exhausted, and wept again in helpless shame.

I, the ceaselessly industrious, could do no work of any kind. I was so weak that the knife and fork sank from my hands – too tired to eat. I could not read nor write nor paint nor sew nor talk nor listen to talking, nor anything. I lay on that lounge and wept all day. The tears ran down into my ears on either side. I went to bed crying, woke in the night crying, sat on the edge of the bed in the morning and cried – from sheer continuous pain. Not physical, the doctors examined me and found nothing the matter.

The only physical pain I ever knew, besides dentistry and one sore finger, was having the baby, and I would rather have had a baby every week than suffer as I suffered in my mind. A constant dragging weariness miles below zero. Absolute incapacity. Absolute misery. To the spirit it was as if one were an armless, legless, eyeless voiceless cripple. Prominent among the tumbling suggestions of a suffering brain was the thought, "You did it yourself! You did it yourself! You had health and strength and hope and glorious work before you – and you threw it all away. You were called to serve humanity, and you cannot serve yourself. No good as a wife, no good as a mother, no good at anything. And you did it yourself!" . . .

The baby? I nursed her for five months. I would hold her close – that lovely child! – and instead of love and happiness, feel only pain. The tears ran down on my breast. . . . Nothing was more utterly bitter than this, that even motherhood brought no joy.

The doctor said I must wean her, and go away, for a change. So she was duly weaned and throve finely on Mellins' Food, drinking eagerly from the cup – no bottle needed. With mother there and the excellent maid I was free to go.

Those always kind friends, the Channings, had gone to Pasadena to live, and invited me to spend the winter with them. Feeble and hopeless I set forth, armed with tonics and sedatives, to cross the continent. From the moment the wheels began to turn, the train to move, I felt better.

[. . .]

Leaving California in March, in the warm rush of its rich spring, I found snow in Denver, and from then on hardly saw the sun for a fortnight. I reached home with a heavy bronchial cold, which hung on long, the dark fog rose again in my mind, the miserable weakness – within a month I was as low as before leaving. . . .

This was a worse horror than before, for now I saw the stark fact – that I was well while away and sick while at home – a heartening prospect! Soon ensued the same utter prostration, the unbearable inner misery, the ceaseless tears. A new tonic had been invented, Essence of Oats, which was given me, and did some good for a time. I pulled up enough to do a little painting that fall, but soon slipped down again and stayed down. An old friend of my mother's, dear Mrs. Diman, was so grieved at this condition that she gave me a hundred dollars and urged me to go away somewhere and get cured.

At that time the greatest nerve specialist in the country was Dr. S. W. Mitchell of Philadelphia. Through the kindness of a friend of Mr. Stetson's living in that city, I went to him and took "the rest cure"; went with the utmost confidence, prefacing the visit with a long letter giving "the history of the case" in a way a modern psychologist would have appreciated. Dr. Mitchell only thought it proved self-conceit. He had a prejudice against the Beechers. "I've had two women of your blood here already," he told me scornfully.[1] This eminent physician was well versed in two kinds of nervous prostration; that of the business man exhausted from too much work, and the society woman exhausted from too much play. The kind I had was evidently beyond him. But he did reassure me on one point – there was no dementia, he said, only hysteria.

I was put to bed and kept there. I was fed, bathed, rubbed, and responded with the vigorous body of twenty-six. As far as he could see there was nothing the matter with me, so after a month of this agreeable treatment he sent me home, with this prescription:

"Live as domestic a life as possible. Have your child with you all the time." (Be it remarked that if I did but dress the baby it left me shaking and crying – certainly far from a healthy companionship for her, to say nothing of the effect on me.) "Lie down an hour after each meal. Have but two hours' intellectual life a day. And never touch pen, brush or pencil as long as you live."

I went home, followed those directions rigidly for months, and came perilously near to losing my mind. The mental agony grew so unbearable that I would sit blankly moving my head from side to side – to get out from under the pain. Not physical pain, not the least "headache" even, just mental torment, and so heavy in its nightmare gloom that it seemed real enough to dodge.

I made a rag baby, hung it on a doorknob and played with it. I would crawl into remote closets and under beds – to hide from the grinding pressure of that profound distress. . . .

Finally, in the fall of '87, in a moment of clear vision, we agreed to separate, to get a divorce. There was no quarrel, no blame for either one, never an unkind word between us, unbroken mutual affection – but it seemed plain that if I went crazy it would do my husband no good, and be a deadly injury to my child.

What this meant to the young artist, the devoted husband, the loving father, was so bitter a grief and loss that nothing would have justified breaking the marriage save this worse loss which threatened. It was not a choice between going and staying, but between going, sane, and staying, insane. If I had been of the slightest use to him or to the child, I would have "stuck it," as the English say. But this progressive weakening of the mind made a horror unnecessary to face; better for that dear child to have separated parents than a lunatic mother.

PASADENA

Besides "Similar Cases" the most outstanding piece of work of 1890 was "The Yellow Wallpaper." It is a description of a case of nervous breakdown beginning something as mine did, and treated as Dr. S. Weir Mitchell treated me with what I considered the inevitable result, progressive insanity.

This I sent to Mr. Howells, and he tried to have the *Atlantic Monthly*[2] print it, but Mr. Scudder, then the editor, sent it back with this brief card:

---

1 Harriet Beecher Stowe's daughter Georgiana Stowe did undergo Mitchell's rest cure; if there was a second Beecher, the identity remains unknown, or this could be another of Gilman's unsupported claims.
2 Founded in Boston in 1857, *Atlantic Monthly* was a prestigious magazine guided by distinguished editors including James Russell Lowell, William Dean Howells, James T. Fields, and Horace Scudder, who rejected Gilman's landmark tale.

DEAR MADAM,

Mr. Howells has handed me this story.

I could not forgive myself if I made others as miserable as I have made myself!

Sincerely yours,

H. E. SCUDDER.

This was funny. The story was meant to be dreadful, and succeeded. I suppose he would have sent back one of Poe's on the same ground. Later I put it in the hands of an agent who had written me, one Henry Austin, and he placed it with the *New England Magazine*.[3] Time passed, much time, and at length I wrote to the editor of that periodical to this effect:

DEAR SIR,

A story of mine, "The Yellow Wallpaper," was printed in your issue of May, 1891. Since you do not pay on receipt of ms. nor on publication, nor within six months of publication, may I ask if you pay at all, and if so at what rates?

They replied with some heat that they had paid the agent, Mr. Austin. He, being taxed with it, denied having got the money. It was only forty dollars anyway! As a matter of fact I never got a cent for it till later publishers brought it out in book form, and very little then. But it made a tremendous impression. A protest was sent to the Boston *Transcript*, headed "Perilous Stuff" –

TO THE EDITOR OF THE TRANSCRIPT:

In a well-known magazine has recently appeared a story entitled "The Yellow Wallpaper." It is a sad story of a young wife passing the gradations from slight mental derangement to raving lunacy. It is graphically told, in a somewhat sensational style, which makes it difficult to lay aside, after the first glance, til it is finished, holding the reader in morbid fascination to the end. It certainly seems open to serious question if such literature should be permitted in print.

The story can hardly, it would seem, give pleasure to any reader, and to many whose lives have been touched through the dearest ties by this dread disease, it must bring the keenest pain. To others, whose lives have become a struggle against an heredity of mental derangement, such literature contains deadly peril. Should such stories be allowed to pass without severest censure?

M.D.

Another doctor, one Brummel Jones, of Kansas City, Missouri, wrote me in 1892 concerning this story, saying: "When I read 'The Yellow Wallpaper' I was very much pleased with it; when I read it again I was delighted with it, and now that I have read it again I am overwhelmed with the delicacy of your touch and the

---

3 A relatively conservative periodical, *New England Magazine* featured stories, poems, travel, history, and biographical sketches.

correctness of portrayal. From a doctor's standpoint, and I am a doctor, you have made a success. So far as I know, and I am fairly well up in literature, there has been no detailed account of incipient insanity." Then he tells of an opium addict who refused to be treated on the ground that physicians had no real knowledge of the disease, but who returned to Dr. Jones, bringing a paper of his on the opium habit, shook it in his face and said, "Doctor, you've been there!" To which my correspondent added, "Have you ever been – er –; but of course you haven't." I replied that I had been as far as one could go and get back.

One of the *New England Magazine*'s editors wrote to me asking if the story was founded on fact, and I gave him all I decently could of my case as a foundation for the tale. Later he explained that he had a friend who was in similar trouble, even to hallucinations about her wallpaper, and whose family were treating her as in the tale, that he had not dared show them my story till he knew that it was true, in part at least, and that when he did they were so frightened by it, so impressed by the clear implication of what ought to have been done, that they changed her wallpaper and the treatment of the case – and she recovered! This was triumph indeed.

But the real purpose of the story was to reach Dr. S. Weir Mitchell, and convince him of the error of his ways. I sent him a copy as soon as it came out, but got no response. However, many years later, I met some one who knew close friends of Dr. Mitchell's who said he had told them that he had changed his treatment of nervous prostration since reading "The Yellow Wallpaper." If that is a fact, I have not lived in vain.

A few years ago Mr. Howells asked leave to include this story in a collection he was arranging – *Masterpieces of American Fiction*. I was more than willing, but assured him that it was no more "literature" than my other stuff, being definitely written "with a purpose." In my judgment it is a pretty poor thing to write, to talk, without a purpose.

All these literary efforts providing but little, it was well indeed that another avenue of work opened to me at this time.

[. . .]

Cultural Context

From **Catharine E. Beecher and Harriet Beecher Stowe's** *The American Woman's Home* (New York: J. B. Ford & Co., 1869; reprinted 1870), 19, 255–9

Harriet Beecher Stowe and Catharine Beecher were daughters of Lyman Beecher, a well-known American Calvinist preacher. They were also Gilman's great-aunts, a legacy of which she was proud. Harriet Beecher Stowe (1811–96) is best known as author of the most widely read, controversial novel of the nineteenth century, *Uncle Tom's Cabin* (1852). In fiction, she set out to raise America's consciousness that slavery subjugated human rights, undermining, in her opinion, the Christianity of the nation. Juggling a prolific writing career with the demands of child raising and housekeeping, Beecher Stowe grew keenly aware of the difficulties of proper home management. Whereas Gilman pressed for a reorganization of traditional domesticity, Harriet Beecher Stowe wrote, with her older sister, an advice manual on how women could manage effectively and efficiently in the private home. Co-author Catharine Beecher (1800–78) earned a reputation for championing young women's education. She was among the first to organize girls' schools in numerous American cities including Hartford, Cincinnati and Milwaukee. She wrote about social and political problems, women's suffrage, and slavery as well as women's moral education and home management.

The subtitle of their domestic manual—*Principles of Domestic Science; Being A Guide to the Formation and Maintenance of Economical, Healthful, Beautiful, and Christian Homes*—reveals its scope (covering all aspects of women's sphere) as well as its conservative nature. The Beecher sisters give advice on how to raise a Christian family; the value of exercise, nutritious diet, and mental health; sewing, proper ventilation, and home decoration; and care for the aged and homeless, household servants, and domestic animals. Interestingly, in the chapter on "Home Decoration," they describe pale "buff" paper with a maroon border as ideal wallpaper and recommend indoor plants in a glass case for an invalid's chamber: "it will refresh many a weary hour to watch it."

In the excerpt from Chapter 1 entitled "The Christian Family," the Beechers urge women to practice "self-denial," serving their families and communities as "chief minister" of the domestic hearth. This rhetoric no doubt reconciled some women to remaining contented in their domestic sphere. Their advice in Chapter XX, "Health of Mind," supports Mitchell's rest cure and Clarke's fears surrounding intellectual activity for women (see **pp. 61–8** and **57–9**). Endorsing the pervasive medical model, the Beechers caution that "many of the most promising minds sink to an early grave, or drag out a miserable existence"; novel reading, for which the narrator of "The Yellow Wall-Paper" admits a penchant, "wastes time and energies" and "undermines the vigor of the nervous system" (259) unless balanced by sufficient physical exercise.

Gilman broke from the Beecher mold in creating a protagonist who longs to write and secretly defies her physician husband. Doctor John prescribes many of the principles set forth in the Beechers' well-respected domestic manual, with one noticeable exception: he does not heed their advice on home decoration.

[. . .]

The family state then, is the aptest earthly illustration of the heavenly kingdom, and in it woman is its chief minister. Her great mission is self-denial, in training its members to self-sacrificing labors for the ignorant and weak: if not her own children, then the neglected children of her Father in heaven. She is to rear all under her care to lay up treasures, not on earth, but in heaven. All the pleasures of this life end here; but those who train immortal minds are to reap the fruit of their labor through eternal ages.

[. . .]

XX.
HEALTH OF MIND.

THERE is such an intimate connection between the body and mind that the health of one can not be preserved without a proper care of the other. And it is from a neglect of this principle, that some of the most exemplary and conscientious persons in the world suffer a thousand mental agonies from a diseased state of body, while others ruin the health of the body by neglecting the proper care of the mind.

[. . .]

Another cause of mental disease is the excessive exercise of the intellect or feelings. If the eye is taxed beyond its strength by protracted use, its blood-vessels become gorged, and the bloodshot appearance warns of the excess and the need of rest. The brain is affected in a similar manner by excessive use, though the suffering and inflamed organ can not make its appeal to the eye. But there are some indications which ought never to be misunderstood or disregarded. In cases of pupils at school or at college, a diseased state, from over-action, is often manifested by increased clearness of mind, and temporary ease and vigor of mental action. In one instance, known to the writer, a most exemplary and industrious pupil, anxious to improve every hour and ignorant or unmindful of the laws of health, first manifested the diseased state of her brain and mind by demands for more studies, and a sudden and earnest activity in planning modes of improvement for herself and others. When warned of her danger, she protested that she never was better in her life; that she took regular exercise in the open air, went to bed in season, slept soundly, and felt perfectly well; that her mind was never before so bright and clear, and study never so easy and delightful. And at this time, she was on the verge of derangement, from which she was saved only by an entire cessation of all intellectual efforts.

[. . .]

In our colleges, too, many of the most promising minds sink to an early grave, or drag out a miserable existence, from this same cause. And it is an evil as yet little alleviated by the increase of physiological knowledge. Every college and professional school, and every seminary for young ladies, needs a medical man or woman, not only to lecture on physiology and the laws of health, but empowered by official capacity to investigate the case of every pupil, and, by authority, to enforce such a course of study, exercise and repose, as the physical system requires. The writer has found by experience that in a large institution there is one class of pupils who need to be restrained by penalties from late hours and excessive study, as much as another class need stimulus to industry.

Under the head of excessive mental action, must be placed the indulgence of the imagination in novel-reading and "castle-building."[1] This kind of stimulus, unless

---

1   This expression commonly used in the nineteenth century refers to the creation of elaborate day-dreams engendered in response to reading romantic fiction and imaginative literature. The reader enters into the fictional world, journeys with the characters, and elaborates upon what he or she finds, thus building castles in the air.

counterbalanced by physical exercise, not only wastes time and energies, but undermines the vigor of the nervous system. The imagination was designed by our wise Creator as a charm and stimulus to animate to benevolent activity; and its perverted exercise seldom fails to bring a penalty.

[. . .]

From **Charles Eastlake, *Hints on Household Taste: The Classic Handbook of Victorian Interior Decoration*** (1878). (New York: Dover Books, 1969; reprint of the 1878 revised edition), 119–23

This book by Charles Eastlake enticed Victorians with a passion for self-improvement. The title word "hints" implies that the interested reader can confidently improve taste in household furnishings—including wallpaper—without exerting too much effort.

Trained in the British Royal Academy schools, Eastlake developed an interest in architecture and apprenticed himself to the noted architect Philip Hardwick the elder. He supplemented his training with a trip to Europe where he developed a passion for interior design including furniture, metalwork, jewellery, and wallpaper patterns, which he created. Eastlake's comprehensive book, first printed in 1868, gives advice about household furniture (for all types of rooms), carpets, wallpaper, ornaments, doors, mirrors, and glassware. The book spurred interest in the Arts and Crafts Movement, initiated by William Morris. Unlike Morris, Eastlake did not allow his own passion for things medieval to influence his insights about nineteenth-century industry and domestic life. His work attracted readers because of its lucid writing and practical approach, as exemplified in this excerpt on wallpapers from Chapter IV, "The Floor and the Wall." A steady seller in England, *Hints on Household Taste* received excellent reviews and gained great popularity in America. By 1881, six American editions had appeared.

The wallpaper that at first repulses and then captivates the narrator in "The Yellow Wall-Paper" boldly violates the aesthetics of Charles Eastlake. The author advises "quiet colours" that "relieve" the surrounding furnishings; in contrast, the wallpaper that comes to preoccupy the narrator entirely looks a "smouldering unclean yellow" with a "sickly sulphur tint" and a "dull yet lurid orange in some places" (**p. 133**). The intensity of the colors seems all the more significant in light of Lois and William Katzenbach's argument in *The Practical Book of American Wallpaper* (published by J. B. Lippincott, 1951): "there is little doubt that the average eye is more sensitive to color than to form and line" (101). Eastlake also favors simplicity in papers for all rooms though he allows for greater variety in design if no pictures cover the wallpaper—seemingly the case in "The Yellow Wall-Paper" (Gilman makes no mention of wall hangings). But would he agree to "flamboyant patterns committing every artistic sin" and "great slanting waves of optic horror" that sprout toadstools and slap a viewer in the face (**pp. 132, 136**)? Eastlake cautions that a sitting room should not have "an unrelieved pattern of monotonous design," precisely the type of wallpaper pattern covering the room Doctor John chooses for the narrator (she prefers a different room or at least another wallpaper design).

Gilman, who studied art at the Rhode Island School of Design, endows her narrator with knowledge about the principles of design, including geometrical arrangements, repetition, alternation, and symmetry. The narrator precisely pinpoints a lack of order in the pattern as "torturing"; she labels the lack of sequence as a "defiance of law" but, nonetheless, vows to figure out the pattern. The Eastlake diapered design—a popular pattern either enclosed by boundary lines or divided into geometric compartments, typically of a uniform size— suggests the complexities of Victorian wallpapers, giving support to the narrator's conviction that a back pattern exists in the wallpaper. The busily patterned wallpaper design on the cover of the 1899 Small, Maynard chapbook edition (which Gilman presumably approved prior to publication) illustrates the fluid movements of period wallpaper that Gilman intensifies in her tale (see Fig. 5, **p. 73**). Critics Tom Lutz and Ann Heilmann, respectively, explore the monotony of design and poisonous dyes of Victorian wallpapers and read the wallpaper as an expression of male aestheticism associated with William Morris and Oscar Wilde (see **pp. 108–11** and **pp. 114–17**).

. . . the choice of a wall-paper should be guided in every respect by the destination of the room in which it will be used. The most important question will always be whether it is to form a decoration in itself, or whether it is to become a mere background for pictures. In the latter case the paper can hardly be too subdued in tone. Very light stone colour or green (not emerald), and silver-grey will be found suitable for this purpose, and two shades of the *same colour* are generally sufficient for one paper. In drawing-rooms, embossed white or cream colour, with a very small diapered pattern, will not be amiss, where water-colour drawings are hung. As a rule, the simplest patterns are the best for every situation; but where the eye has to rest upon the surface of the wall alone, a greater play of line in the ornament may become advisable. It is obvious that delicate tints admit of more linear complexity than those which are rich or dark. Intricate forms should be accompanied by quiet colour, and variety of hue should be chastened by the plainest possible outlines. In colour, wallpapers should relieve without violently opposing that of the furniture and hangings by which they are surrounded. There should be one dominant hue in the room, to which all others are subordinate. . . . The real secret of success in decorative colour is, however, quite as much dependent on subtle variations and delicate contrast as on similarity of tint; nor can real artistic effect be expected without the employment of both.

[. . .]

Paperhangings should in no case be allowed to cover the whole space of a wall from skirting to ceiling. . . . The most dreary method of decorating the wall of a sitting-room is to cover it all over with an unrelieved pattern of monotonous design.

[. . .]

From **Sylvanus Stall,** *What a Young Husband Ought to Know*
(Philadelphia: Vir Publishing, 1897), 293

> This excerpt from a late nineteenth-century advice manual presents the ideal of the mother-woman, also called the angel in the house in Victorian Britain. The perfect mother is nurturing, patient, selfless, self-effacing, uncomplaining— virtually an angel on earth. Gilman's narrator clearly has a "perverted mother sense," according to Stall's definition of mother-woman. Ironic is Stall's comment that "Many otherwise excellent women find the nursery a prison, and the care of their own children irksome": the narrator in "The Yellow Wall-Paper," who finds the company of her baby "irksome," is confined to a room that was formerly a nursery.
>
> Advice books on marriage, motherhood, and child rearing were very common in the nineteenth century. Most authors addressed the young wife, but Stall writes for the young husband. Gilman's traditional Doctor John seemingly shares Stall's expectations of a young wife and mother.

Influence of Mothers

* * * What the child needs pre-eminently above playthings, books, clothes, and every other earthly thing, is *the presence and influence of mother*. No other woman in the world can take her place. Many mothers farm their children out to ⟵ nurses, and then give themselves to household duties, social pleasures, or possibly to duties which may be important in themselves, but which, after all, can only be secondary to the discharge of the all-important duties of motherhood.

Many otherwise excellent women find the nursery a prison, and the care of their own children irksome, simply because they have a perverted mother-sense. The mother should have proper relief from the care of her children, but if she has the true mother-heart the companionship of her children will be the society which she will prefer above that of all others.

[. . .]

Scientific Context

From **Edward H. Clarke, M.D.,** *Sex in Education; Or, A Fair Chance for the Girls* (1873) (Arno Press Inc., 1972; reprint of the 1873 James R. Osgood edition, Boston), 106–17

> Dr. Edward H. Clarke, a retired professor from Harvard Medical School, used scientific reasoning to argue against women's pursuit of intellectual activity and higher education. *Sex in Education* (1873), an influential and widely read book, posits that intellectual activity endangers a woman's health and her ability to bear children. Quoting a like-minded physician named Dr. T. W. Fisher, Clarke

launches his section "Chiefly Clinical" by arguing that excessive study leaves women prone to a host of menstrual irregularities (including amenorrhoea and dysmenorrhoea), robs her of her "chief feminine functions," and may lead to fatal diseases of the nervous system. In other sections of the book, he chides women who graduated from colleges and universities as excellent scholars with "undeveloped ovaries," remaining sterile after marriage. Not all women will succumb to these problems, he admits, but the number of critical cases that could be avoided is too serious for women to risk higher education. With the stamp of science behind him, Clarke offers a convincing argument that supports Mitchell's rest cure for women as well as a gender-specific approach to medicine.

Clarke's popular prescriptions did meet some opposition. In *Sex and Education. A Reply to Dr. E. H. Clarke's "Sex in Education"* (published by Roberts Brothers in 1874), editor Julia Ward Howe calls Clarke's volume "a work of a polemic type" with a marked gender bias. She assembles essays by important men and women, such as Elizabeth Stuart Phelps and Mrs. Horace Mann (one of the three famous Peabody sisters, namely Mary Peabody Mann, Sophia Peabody Hawthorne, and Elizabeth Peabody); they question Clarke's findings while still acknowledging his rank and expertise. A compelling section entitled "Testimony from Colleges" includes statistics of the number of children born to female graduates of Antioch College and a letter from Vassar's female college physician, ensuring that the college's healthy learning environment does not overtax a young woman (Clarke criticizes Vassar in one of his own case studies). Nonetheless, Clarke's *Sex in Education* was an enormously popular and highly influential treatise in its day.

[. . .]

"A certain proportion of girls are predisposed to mental or nervous derangement. The same girls are apt to be quick, brilliant, ambitious, and persistent at study, and need not stimulation, but repression. For the sake of a temporary reputation for scholarship, they risk their health at the *most susceptible period* of their lives, and break down *after the excitement of school-life has passed away.* For *sexual reasons* they cannot compete with boys, whose out-door habits still further increase the difference in their favor. If it was a question of school-teachers instead of school-girls, the list would be long of young women whose health of mind has become bankrupt by a *continuation* of the mental strain commenced at school. Any method of relief in our school-system to these over-susceptible minds should be welcomed, even at the cost of the intellectual supremacy of woman in the next generation."[1]

The fact which Dr. Fisher alludes to, that many girls break down not during but *after* the excitement of school or college life, is an important one, and is apt to be overlooked. The process by which the development of the reproductive system is arrested, or degeneration of brain and nerve-tissue set a going, is an insidious one. At its beginning, and for a long time after it is well on in its progress, it would not

1   [Clarke's note] *Plain Talk about Insanity.* By T. W. Fisher, M.D. Boston. pp. 23, 24.

be recognized by the superficial observer. A class of girls might, and often do, graduate from our schools, higher seminaries, and colleges, that appear to be well and strong at the time of their graduation, but whose development has already been checked, and whose health is on the verge of giving way. Their teachers have known nothing of the amenorrhoea, menorrhagia, dysmenorrhoea, or leucorrhoea which the pupils have sedulously concealed and disregarded; and the cunning devices of dress have covered up all external evidences of defect; and so, on graduation day, they are pointed out by their instructors to admiring committees as rosy specimens of both physical and intellectual education. A closer inspection by competent experts would reveal the secret weakness which the labor of life that they are about to enter upon too late discloses.

[. . .]

It has been reserved for our age and country, by its methods of female education, to demonstrate that it is possible in some cases to divest a woman of her chief feminine functions; in others, to produce grave and even fatal disease of the brain and nervous system; in others, to engender torturing derangements and imperfections of the reproductive apparatus that imbitter a lifetime. Such, we know, is not the object of a liberal female education. Such is not the consummation which the progress of the age demands. Fortunately, it is only necessary to point out and prove the existence of such erroneous methods and evil results to have them avoided. That they can be avoided, and that woman can have a liberal education that shall develop all her powers, without mutilation or disease, up to the loftiest ideal of womanhood, is alike the teaching of physiology and the hope of the race.

In concluding this part of our subject, it is well to remember the statement made at the beginning of our discussion, to the following effect, viz., that it is not asserted here, that improper methods of study and a disregard of the reproductive apparatus and its functions, during the educational life of girls, are the *sole* causes of female diseases; neither is it asserted that *all* the female graduates of our schools and colleges are pathological specimens. But it is asserted that the number of these graduates who have been permanently disabled to a greater or less degree, or fatally injured, by these causes, is such as to excite the *gravest alarm*, and to demand the serious attention of the community.

[. . .]

From **Dr. Fordyce Barker, The Puerperal Diseases: Clinical Lectures Delivered at Bellevue Hospital** (New York: D. Appleton, 1874), 172–84.

According to the nineteenth-century medical model, a woman's ovaries and uterus determined her state of mind and propensity to nervous disorders. In his manual on postpartum illnesses, Fordyce Barker (1819–91) suggests women inherit a predisposition to puerperal mania—akin to a clinical postpartum depression—through the female line, and child bearing triggers it. In The

Puerperal Diseases, Barker describes his "moral treatment" for the disease, which resembles the Mitchell rest cure: constant supervision, warm baths, firm approach, regulated feedings, and induced sleep.

Of interest, Barker notes a high number of intelligent physicians' wives who succumb to this disorder. Similar to *delirium tremens*, symptoms of puerperal mania include delusions, which "The Yellow Wall-Paper" narrator experiences in her hallucinations of a woman trapped in the wallpaper, as well as insomnia, poor appetite, wild behavior, foul language, odd cravings, shyness, a suicidal tendency, and "peculiar" facial expressions. If puerperal mania continues, Barker argues, the result is not death but prolonged insanity.

Barker's clinical account of puerperal mania read alongside "The Yellow Wall-Paper" strengthens the authenticity of Gilman's fictionalized account of mental disorder as well as the contemporary treatment of invalid women. The narrator—who has trouble sleeping and little appetite—contemplates suicide and exhibits a decidedly peculiar look in Hatfield's second illustration accompanying the 1892 version. In making the narrator an intelligent doctor's wife who very much wants to write, Gilman adds a fictional case to Barker's list.

[. . .]

Puerperal mania is the form with which obstetricians have most frequently to deal. In some few rare cases, it is suddenly developed without any forewarning symptoms, but, in by far a larger number, there are very characteristic prodromic symptoms, sometimes continuing for a few days and in other instances only a few hours before the explosion. There is generally an unusual excitement of manner, although, in a few, a morbid melancholy air first attracts attention. A sudden aversion is displayed toward those who have been before best loved; an excessive loquacity, or an obstinate silence, weeping or laughing equally without a motive, a morbid sensibility to light, to noises, to odors, a suspicious watchful expression of the eye, and sleeplessness, are symptoms, which, occurring in a woman who has been confined within ten or fifteen days, indicate an impending attack of puerperal mania. There are often muscular movements of the eyelids, the face, and the hands, very much resembling the appearance of a patient on the brink of delirium tremens. Indeed, the general symptoms are often wonderfully like those which are characteristic of the beginning of delirium tremens, and, in the case of the wife of a medical friend, which I shall presently relate to you, a painful suspicion existed in the mind of her husband at first that the real disease was delirium tremens.

There are certain symptoms which very generally characterize the moment of the attack, but these are usually of short duration. The facial expression is very peculiar, and, having once been seen, will always be remembered. The features are drawn, pallid, the cheeks and forehead are covered with little drops of perspiration, and the whole air of the expression is unsettled, indicative of fright or fury.

When the malady is fully developed, the patient becomes very boisterous and noisy, incoherent in her language and in her gestures. She stares wildly at imaginary objects in the air, seizes any word spoken by those near, and repeats it with "damnable iteration," clutches at every thing and every one near her, throws off all covering, jumps from the bed, and even the most refined and religious women, when possessed with the demon of puerperal mania, will scream out oaths and obscenity with a volubility perfectly astounding. Erotic manifestations occur in a majority of cases. Masturbation is sometimes noticed, but I believe, as Dr. Tuke suggests, that this is more the result of a wish to allay than to excite irritation. Nearly one-half of these cases manifest a suicidal tendency, but rather as a sudden impulse than as a settled determination.

[. . .]

I will mention a curious fact that has occurred in my experience: Since 1855, I have seen thirteen cases of puerperal mania in the wives of physicians, nine in this city, and four in the adjoining cities. All but one were primiparae. It has struck me as very extraordinary, that so large a number should have occurred in one special class, and I think the following is the probable explanation: All of these were ladies of education and more than usual quickness of intellect, and, beginning a new experience in life, and having access to their husband's books, they probably had read just enough on midwifery to fill their minds with apprehensions as to the horrors which might be in store for them, and thus developed the cerebral disturbances, just as any other moral emotions may.

[. . .]

From **Dr. S. Weir Mitchell,** *Fat and Blood: And How to Make Them: "Fat in Its Clinical Relations"* and **"Rest"** (Philadelphia: J. B. Lippincott, 1877) Chapters 2 and 5, 26–33, 40–4

After referring to the internationally acclaimed neurologist and author who went by his middle name, Weir, the narrator of "The Yellow Wall-Paper" confides: "But I don't want to go there at all. I had a friend who was in his hands once, and she says he is just like John and my brother, only more so!" (see **p. 135**) Gilman plants a veiled reference to herself in her narrator's anecdote: Gilman is the narrator's friend who was in Mitchell's hands. In 1887, at age twenty-six, Gilman (then Stetson) traveled to Mitchell's sanatorium in Philadelphia to take his famous rest cure. Although today Mitchell's reputation largely rests on Gilman's indictment of him in her landmark tale, at the turn of the twentieth century, his reputation as an author eclipsed hers.

A third-generation physician, S. Weir Mitchell (1829–1914, Fig. 4) specialized in women's nervous disorders and treated women of prominent families including Jane Addams, Edith Wharton, Winifred Howells (William Dean Howells's daughter), Gilman, and Georgiana Stowe (Harriet Beecher Stowe's daughter). Alice James and Virginia Woolf underwent Mitchell's rest cure treatment, brought to England in 1880; like their Victorian sisters, they complained bitterly about enforced rest and passivity to calm the mind. However, according to George Beard, dubbed the "father" of neurasthenia, the disease was particularly American and infected America in greater proportion than any other nation.

Figure 4 Portrait of S. Weir Mitchell, M.D. *ca.*1890 by Dvorak.
Courtesy of Mütter Museum, College of Physicians of
Philadelphia.

In his book entitled *American Nervousness* (Putnam, 1881), Beard argues: "The
chief and primary cause of this development and very rapid increase of nervousness is *modern civilization*, which is distinguished from the ancient by these
five characteristics: steam power, the periodical press, the telegraph, the sci-
ences, and the mental activity of women" (vi); he concludes, "When civilization,
plus these five factors, invades any nation, it must carry nervousness and nervous diseases along with it" (96). Gilman, from Beard's perspective, succumbed

to a disease that was in itself a product of industrialized modern society and to which certain classes of individuals—men and women of the leisure class, artists, and intellectuals—became most prone given their involvement in modern life. In the late nineteenth century, neurologists posited anxiety and depression as somatic in origin and aimed to heal the mind by healing the body. Psychology did not emerge as a recognized field of study until the end of the nineteenth century. In fact, Mitchell and Sigmund Freud were trained as neurologists.

Akin to Oliver Wendell Holmes, Mitchell was a prolific author and a physician. He maintained an affluent medical practice, but he wrote popular medical treatises and fiction often featuring neurasthenic women (e.g. *Roland Blake* [1886], *Hugh Wynne* [1896]). In fact, his celebrated romance set during the Revolutionary War, *Hugh Wynne*, was the best-selling novel of 1897. Both types of writing fed notions about women's health and assumed frailty, supporting the prevailing nineteenth-century cult of female invalidism. In his first popular medical treatise, *Wear and Tear, or Hints for the Overworked* (1871), Mitchell defines neurasthenia. Excerpts from his subsequent book, *Fat and Blood* (1877), describe his gender-specific rest cures for those who experienced great emotional or physical strain. Male neurasthenics—including Beard and Mitchell himself—frequently suffered from trauma (e.g. nerve wounds incurred during the American Civil War) or strain whereas women were prone to neurasthenia because of their physiology. For men, Mitchell advised vigorous activity, typically on a cattle ranch in the West as he counseled Owen Wister, author of *The Virginian* (1902). In contrast, Mitchell put nervous women to bed. He did not permit women to read, write, cut their food, feed themselves, sit up, or sew; in some cases, they had to pass their bodily fluids without leaving their beds. In *Fat and Blood*, Mitchell devotes a full chapter to each of the components of the rest cure: rest (typically for 6–8 weeks), diet (overfeeding, beginning with milk, to improve the quality of blood, body mass, and energy), seclusion (an unfamiliar setting and nurse), massage, and electricity (to guard against muscular atrophy).

A punitive and authoritarian tone dominates *Doctor and Patient* (1887), such as when Mitchell proclaims: "the man who does not know sick women does not know women." He believed, in line with contemporary medical views, that a woman's physiology made her prone to nervous exhaustion. Mitchell's description of a woman patient crying for no reason and rapidly becoming "a ready victim of hysteria" matches the symptoms of the narrator in "The Yellow Wall-Paper," revealing Gilman's intimate knowledge of a condition from which she herself recovered. As Catherine Golden has argued, Gilman defied Mitchell's attempt to make her more like his ideal patients and tractable fictional characters, such as Serena Vernon in *A Comedy of Conscience* (1900). She "overwrote" Mitchell's prescription for health by writing "The Yellow Wall-Paper" and creating a heroine who also writes (see Golden, " 'Overwriting' the Rest Cure," in *Critical Essays on Charlotte Perkins Gilman*, ed. Joanne Karpinski, Further Reading, **p. 161**). Feminist critics today often characterize the rest cure as an attempt to reform wayward women who rebelled against their traditional submissive domestic role.

Sociologist Carroll Smith-Rosenberg qualifies that not all hysterical women consciously choose their behavior, a concept that the rest cure exploits. Mitchell admittedly put neurasthenic woman to bed in isolation with no stimulation, so they would gladly rise again to resume the duties which they escaped by consciously or unconsciously becoming hysterics. Smith-Rosenberg's ideas suggest, rather, that the narrator's neurasthenic condition be seen as a result of role conflict—the inability of a sensitive, fragile, and highly imaginative individual to adapt to the rigorous social and cultural expectations of her patriarchal society (see Further Reading, p. 159).

Nonetheless, the Mitchell rest cure had merit. It proved preferable to other nineteenth-century cures then in vogue, such as leeches and drugs. It was similar to popular water cures in European spa cities. Preeminently, the rest cure removed a nervous woman from the demands of her home environment and offered her an opportunity to restore her health. Moreover, Mitchell enjoyed popularity among his women patients: many traveled far for consultation and left satisfied.

Fat in Its Clinical Relations

I see every week – almost every day – women who when asked what is the matter reply, "Oh, I have nervous exhaustion." When further questioned, they answer that everything tires them. Now, it is vain to speak of all of these cases as hysterical, or, as Paget has done, as mimetic. It is quite sure that in the graver examples exercise quickens the pulse curiously, the tire shows in the face, or sometimes diarrhoea or nausea follows exertion, and though while under excitement or in the presence of some dominant motive they can do a good deal, the exhaustion which ensues is in proportion to the exercise used.

I have rarely seen such a case which was not more or less lacking in color and which had not lost flesh; the exceptions being those troublesome cases of fat anaemic people which I shall by and by speak of more fully.

Perhaps a full sketch of one of these cases will be better than any list of symptoms: A woman, most often between twenty and thirty, undergoes a season of trial or encounters some prolonged strain. She undertakes the hard task of nursing a relative, and goes through this severe duty with the addition of emotional excitement, swayed by hopes and fears, and forgetful of self and of what every one needs in the way of air and food and change when attempting this most trying task; or possibly it is mere physical strain, such as teaching. In another set of cases an illness is the cause, and she never rallies entirely, or else some local uterine trouble starts the mischief, and although this is cured the doctor wonders that his patient does not get fat and ruddy again.

But no matter how it comes about, the woman grows pale and thin, eats little, or if she eats does not profit by it. Everything wearies her, – to sew, to write, to read, to walk, – and by and by the sofa or the bed is her only comfort. Every effort is paid for dearly, and she describes herself as aching and sore, as sleeping ill, and as needing constant stimulus and endless tonics. Then comes the mischievous role of bromides, opium, chloral, and brandy. If the case did not begin with uterine troubles they soon appear, and are usually treated in vain if the general means employed to build up the bodily health fail, as in many of these cases they do fail. The same remark applies to the dyspepsias and constipation which further annoy the patient and embarrass the treatment. If such a person is emotional she does not fail to become more so, and even the firmest women lose self-control at last under incessant feebleness. Nor is this less true of men, and I have many a time seen soldiers who had ridden boldly with Sheridan or fought gallantly with Grant[1] become, under the influence of painful nerve-wounds, as irritable and hysterically emotional as the veriest girl. If no rescue comes, the fate of women thus disordered is at last the bed. . . .

The treatment I am about to describe consists in seclusion, certain forms of diet, rest in bed, massage (or manipulation), and electricity; and I desire to insist anew on the fact that it is the use of these means together that is wanted. The necessities of my subject will of course oblige me to treat of each of them in a separate chapter.

REST

[. . .]

[. . .] As a rule, no harm is done by rest, even in such people as give us doubts about whether it is or is not well for them to exert themselves. There are plenty of these women who are just well enough to make it likely that if they had motive enough for exertion to cause them to forget themselves they would find it useful. In the doubt I am rather given to insisting on rest, but the rest I like for them is not at all their notion of rest. To lie abed half the day, and sew a little and read a little, and be interesting and excite sympathy, is all very well, but when they are bidden to stay in bed a month, and neither to read, write, nor sew, and to have one nurse, –who is not a relative, – then rest becomes for some women a rather bitter medi-cine, and they are glad enough to accept the order to rise and go about when the doctor issues a mandate which has become pleasantly welcome and eagerly looked for. I do not think it easy to make a mistake in this matter unless the woman takes with morbid delight to the system of enforced rest, and unless the doctor is a person of feeble will. I have never met myself with any serious trouble about getting out of bed any woman for whom I thought rest needful, but it has happened to others, and the man who resolves to send any nervous woman to bed must be quite sure that she will obey him when the time comes for her to get up.

I have, of course, made use of every grade of rest for my patients, from insisting upon repose on a lounge for some hours a day up to entire rest in bed. In carrying out my general plan of treatment it is my habit to ask the patient to remain in bed from six weeks to two months. At first, and in some cases for four or five weeks, I do not permit the patient to sit up or to sew or write or read. The only action allowed is that needed to clean the teeth. In some instances I have not permitted the patient to turn over without aid, and this I have done because sometimes I think no motion desirable, and because sometimes the moral influence of absolute repose is of use. In such cases I arrange to have the bowels and water passed while

---

1 Ulysses S. Grant was a major general fighting for the Union in the American Civil War; he became 18th president of the United States. Philip Henry Sheridan also distinguished himself as a Union general and was pivotal in the surrender of Confederate leader, General Robert E. Lee.

lying down, and the patient is lifted on to a lounge at bedtime and sponged, and then lifted back again into the newly-made bed. In all cases of weakness, treated by rest, I insist on the patient being fed by the nurse, and, when well enough to sit up in bed, I insist that the meats shall be cut up, so as to make it easier for the patient to feed herself.

In many cases I allow the patient to sit up in order to obey the calls of nature, but I am always careful to have the bowels kept reasonably free from costiveness, knowing well how such a state and the efforts it gives rise to enfeeble a sick person.

Usually, after a fortnight I permit the patient to be read to,—one to three hours a day,—but I am daily amazed to see how kindly nervous and anaemic women take to this absolute rest, and how little they complain of its monotony. In fact, the use of massage and the battery, with the frequent comings of the nurse with food and the doctor's visits, seem so to fill up the day as to make the treatment less tiresome than might be supposed. And, besides this, the sense of comfort which is apt to come about the fifth or sixth day, – the feeling of ease, and the ready capacity to digest food, and the growing hope of final cure, fed as it is by present relief, – all conspire to make most patients contented and tractable.

The moral uses of enforced rest are readily estimated. From a restless life of irregular hours, and probably endless drugging, from hurtful sympathy and over-zealous care, the patient passes to an atmosphere of quiet, to order and control, to the system and care of a thorough nurse, to an absence of drugs, and to simple diet. The result is always at first, whatever it may be afterwards, a sense of relief, and a remarkable and often a quite abrupt disappearance of many of the nervous symptoms with which we are all of us only too sadly familiar.

All the moral uses of rest and isolation and change of habits are not obtained by merely insisting on the physical conditions needed to effect these ends. If the physician has the force of character required to secure the confidence and respect of his patients he has also much more in his power, and should have the tact to seize the proper occasions to direct the thoughts of his patients to the lapse from duties to others, and to the selfishness which a life of invalidism is apt to bring about. Such moral medication belongs to the higher sphere of the doctor's duties, and if he means to cure his patient permanently, he cannot afford to neglect them. Above all, let him be careful that the masseuse and the nurse do not talk of the patient's ills, and let him by degrees teach the sick person how very essential it is to speak of her aches and pains to no one but himself.

[. . .]

From **Dr. S. Weir Mitchell,** *Doctor and Patient:* **"Introductory"** and **"Nervousness and its Influence on Character"** (Philadelphia: J. B. Lippincott, 1887), 10–11, 116–29

INTRODUCTORY

[. . .] To confess is, for mysterious reasons, most profoundly human, and in weak and nervous women this tendency is sometimes exaggerated to the actual distortion of facts. The priest hears the crime or folly of the hour, but to the physician are oftener told the long, sad tales of a whole life, its far-away mistakes, its failures, and its faults. None may be quite foreign to his purpose or needs. The causes of breakdowns and nervous disaster, and consequent emotional disturbances and their bitter fruit, are often to be sought in the remote past. He may dislike the quest, but he cannot avoid it. If he be a student of character, it will have for him a personal interest as well as the relative value of its applicative side. The moral world of the sick-bed explains in a measure some of the things that are strange in daily life, and the man who does not know sick women does not know women.

I have been often asked by ill women if my contact with the nervous weaknesses, the petty moral deformities of nervous feminine natures, had not lessened my esteem for woman. I say, surely, no! So much of these is due to educational errors, so much to false relationships with husbands, so much is born out of that which healthfully dealt with, or fortunately surrounded, goes to make all that is sincerely charming in the best of women. The largest knowledge finds the largest excuses, and therefore no group of men so truly interprets, comprehends, and sympathizes with woman as do physicians, who know how near to disorder and how close to misfortune she is brought by the very peculiarities of her nature, which evolve in health the flower and fruitage of her perfect life.

With all her weakness, her unstable emotionality, her tendency to morally warp when long nervously ill, she is then far easier to deal with, far more amenable to reason, far more sure to be comfortable as a patient, than the man who is relatively in a like position. [. . .]

[. . .]

NERVOUSNESS AND ITS INFLUENCE ON CHARACTER

[. . .]

The two questions referred to above are these: The woman who consults you says, "I am nervous. I did not use to be. What can I do to overcome it?" Once well again, she asks you, – and the query is common enough from the thoughtful, – "What can I do to keep my girls from being nervous?"

Observe, now, that this woman has other distresses, in the way of aches and feebleness. The prominent thing in her mind, nervousness, is but one of the symptomatic results of her condition . . . If you are wise, you ask what she means by nervousness. You soon learn that she suffers in one of two, or probably in both of two, ways. . . . She has become doubtful and fearful, where formerly she was ready-minded and courageous. Once decisive, she is now indecisive. When well, unemotional, she is now too readily disturbed by a sad tale or a startling newspaper-paragraph. A telegram alarms her; even an unopened letter makes her hesitate and conjure up dreams of disaster. Very likely she is irritable and recognizes the unreasonableness of her temper. Her daily tasks distress her sorely. She can no longer sit still and sew or read. Conversation no longer interests, or it even troubles her. Noises, especially sudden noises, startle her, and the cries and laughter of children have become distresses of which she is ashamed, and of which she complains or not, as her nature is weak or enduring. Perhaps, too, she is so restless as to want to be in constant motion, but that seems to tire her as it once did not. Her sense of moral proportion becomes impaired. Trifles grow large to her; the grasshopper is a burden. With all this, and in a measure out of all this, come certain bodily disabilities. The telegram or any cause of emotion sets her to shaking. She cries for no cause; the least alarm makes her hand shake, and even her writing, if she should chance to become the subject of observation when at the desk, betrays her state of tremor. What caused all this trouble? What made her, as she says, good for nothing? I have, of course, put an extreme case. We may, as a rule, be pretty sure, as to this condition, that the woman has had some sudden shock, some severe domestic trial, some long strain, or that it is the outcome of acute illness or of one of the forms of chronic disturbance of nutrition which result in what we now call general neurasthenia or nervous weakness, – a condition which has a most varied parentage. With the ultimate medical causation of these disorderly states of body I do not mean to concern myself here, except to add also that the great physiological revolutions of a woman's life are often responsible for the physical failures which create nervousness.

If she is at the worst she becomes a ready victim of hysteria. . . .

[. . .]

2

Interpretations

Critical History

Among the best-known rediscovered works by turn-of-the-century American woman writers, "The Yellow Wall-Paper" had difficulty finding its way into print. Conflicting versions exist about the publication history and early critical reception of a story that Gilman penned in two extremely hot days during a heat wave in the summer of 1890 in Pasadena, California shortly after she and Stetson permanently separated.[1] Most scholars agree it took about eighteen months to place "The Yellow Wall-Paper." Gilman elicited help from the eminent novelist, critic, and editor William Dean Howells, who had praised her poems "Similar Cases" and "Women of To-day." She records in her autobiography that, after receiving Howells's "unforgettable letter" of June 9, 1890, she felt "like a 'real' author at last" (*Living* 113). A former editor of the prestigious journal *Atlantic Monthly*, Howells sent the story to the current editor, Horace Elisha Scudder. Often quoted in Gilman criticism is Scudder's curt rejection letter, which he sent directly to Gilman. While the first sentence merely acknowledges receipt of the story from Howells, the second is memorable and bears repeating: "I could not forgive myself if I made others as miserable as I made myself!" Gilman concluded: "This was funny. The story was meant to be dreadful, and succeeded. I suppose he would have sent back one of Poe's on the same ground" (*Living* 119, see **p. 51**).

How then did "The Yellow Wall-Paper" find its way into print? Gilman and Howells suggest different scenarios, leading Julie Bates Dock to call the reception history a "he-says/she-says conundrum" (12) in her 1998 critical edition and documentary casebook published by Penn State University Press (see Further Reading, **p. 160**). Gilman claims in her autobiography that she sent the story to a literary agent, Henry Austin, who placed it in *New England Magazine*, a relatively conservative periodical featuring stories, poems, travel, history, and biographical spotlights (black-and-white illustrations and photographs accompany the selections). She also alleges that Austin pocketed the fee for the story (a claim which he denied). However, in his introduction to *The Great Modern American Stories* (1920), Howells notes that he "corrupted" Edwin Mead, then editor of *New England Magazine*, into publishing the story (see **p. 87**). Howells had

---

1 Gilman records in an undated typescript entitled " 'The Yellow Wall-Paper'—Its History and Reception" (box 17, folder 21 in the Gilman Papers, Schlesinger Library) that the temperature reached 103 degrees.

helped Mead, his wife's cousin, gain entry into the publishing field for which he was forever grateful. If Howells's story is accurate, did Gilman know the role he played, or was it opportune for her to forget it?

Following its 1892 publication in *New England Magazine*, "The Yellow Wall-Paper" "attracted a cult of readers" (18), as biographer Gary Scharnhorst notes in *Charlotte Perkins Gilman* published by Twayne in 1985. In 1899, Small, Maynard & Co. of Boston reprinted "The Yellow Wall-Paper" as a chapbook without its original illustrations; sulphur orange-yellow paper-board covers with a flamboyant wallpaper design make vivid the pattern of the ubiquitous wallpaper (Fig. 5). The 1899 edition and subsequent reprintings of the story gave rise to numerous reviews (see **pp. 82–7**). Period reviewers typically focus on two aspects of the story—its horror, and the wallpaper—but some comment on its feminist undertones and call for its censure.

Nineteenth-century critics who read the story as a Gothic thriller, ghost story, or horror tale liken it to weird tales by Edgar Allan Poe or Nathaniel Hawthorne at their best. In her documentary casebook, Dock aptly notes: "readers in the last quarter of the twentieth century still appreciate the story's chilling qualities, for it has appeared in at least a dozen collections of gothic horror or suspense" (20). Similarly, Beverly Hume compares "The Yellow Wall-Paper" to Poe's "The Black Cat" (*Studies in American Fiction*, 2002), and Marty Roth sets the story in context of Poe's horror tales in "Gilman's Arabesque Wallpaper" (see **pp. 117–21**). Gilman critics today also discuss the deleterious effects of the wallpaper in violating the aesthetic standards of the day, carrying health hazards, and driving the narrator to madness (see Lutz, **pp. 108–11**, and Heilmann, **pp. 114–17**).

Some period reviewers place blame on the narrator's restricted and stifling life in a patriarchal society, although many 1970s and 1980s feminist critics regrettably suggest the feminist thrust needed to wait a century to be noticed or that readers lacked the psychological insight to understand it (see Hedges, **pp. 88–90** and Kolodny, **pp. 92–4**). For example, Henry B. Blackwell, a firm supporter of the women's movement, notes the misguided efforts of the narrator's well-meaning physician-husband and presents the narrator's situation as unbearable in an 1899 review for *Woman's Journal*: "Nothing more graphic and suggestive has ever been written to show why so many women go crazy, especially farmers' wives, who live lonely, monotonous lives." Gilman was close to Blackwell, his wife Lucy Stone, and his daughter Alice Stone Blackwell. Blackwell reviewed much of Gilman's work including *Women and Economics* (1898). Akin to Blackwell, another anonymous 1899 reviewer for *The Literary World* notes, "Perhaps the best or the worst of the sketch is the reasonable suggestion that the end might have been different if the sufferer had been treated more rationally." These late nineteenth-century reviewers recognized the sexual politics of female subjugation even if they did not use the terms that commonly appeared in the explosion of criticism following the story's 1973 republication. Or else they refrained (320), in the words of Elaine R. Hedges, from reading it "for very fear of discovering what it really said" (see " 'Out at Last'? 'The Yellow Wallpaper' after Two Decades of Feminist Criticism" in *The Captive Imagination*, edited by Catherine Golden and published by The Feminist Press in 1992, Further Reading, **p. 158**).

Since the 1970s, the story has experienced near unprecedented attention in literary criticism, giving it a cult status that eventually led to a backlash: critics

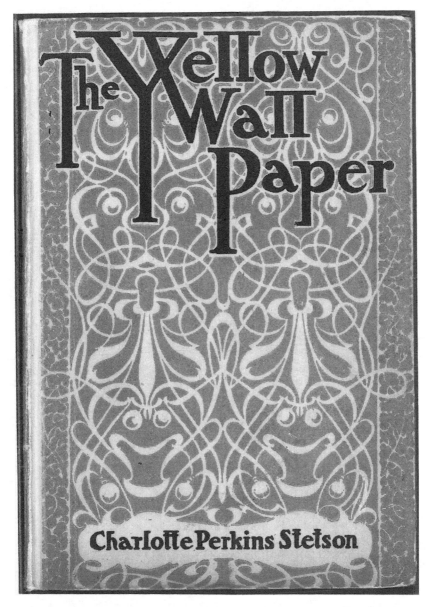

Figure 5 Cover of *The Yellow Wall Paper* for Small, Maynard & Co.,
1899. The 1901 edition reprinted by permission of
Schlesinger Library, Radcliffe Institute, Harvard University.

beginning in the 1980s have questioned the story's canonical status assured by its now frequent appearance in anthologies of women's literature, American literature, and fiction. Just as feminist victories in reproductive rights and equal opportunity in employment and education may have influenced 1970s critics to read the literary text sympathetically, even optimistically, concerns with political correctness and a more conservative feminism in the late 1980s, 1990s, and beyond have turned a more critical eye on the prejudices rooted in the color and odor of the ubiquitous wallpaper and the status of Gilman's text in the canon of American literature and women's literature. Criticism excerpted for this sourcebook represents dominant trends in how scholars have read "The Yellow Wall-Paper" since its 1973 republication and indicates the breadth of critical approaches scholars have used to explore the story—principally reader response theory; new historicism; biographical, feminist, sociological, linguistic, and psychological approaches (e.g. Lacanian, Freudian, Derridean, Adlerian); as well as a combination of theoretical perspectives. The sourcebook also records debates surrounding the ending of the story (defeat versus liberation or a qualified victory), the color of the wallpaper (e.g. evoking sexuality, feces, decadence, the Yellow Peril), the narrator's tearing of the wallpaper (an act of madness versus freedom), her crawling (rebirth or regression), the publication history (did critics lack the conventions to read the story or shun it for fear of the sacrosanct territory it exposed?), the use of the hyphen in the title (the preferred spelling is now "The Yellow Wall-Paper"), and its genre (short story versus novella, likely encouraged by the story's 1899 and 1973 publications as chapbook editions).

There are far more fascinating essays than I can possibly include or even mention in this sourcebook. To provide a sense of the collective terrain and help readers make their way through an evolving criticism as fascinating as the story itself, I offer an overview of important trends and seminal essays included in this sourcebook as well as the larger body of Gilman scholarship. Work by pioneering scholars between 1973 and 1981—and here I include Elaine R. Hedges's "Afterword" (1973), Sandra Gilbert and Susan Gubar's discussion in *The Madwoman in the Attic* (1979), Annette Kolodny's "A Map for Rereading: Or, Gender and the Interpretation of Literary Texts" (1980) (see Modern Criticism, **pp. 88–94**), and Jean Kennard's "Convention Coverage or How to Read Your Own Life" (1981; reproduced in *Captive Imagination*)—tend to read "The Yellow Wall-Paper" sympathetically. All focus on a misunderstood, misdiagnosed woman who attempts to free herself from the restrictions of her gendered world encoded in the wallpaper. Hedges draws attention to the sociological importance of the story, the politics of gender, and its biographical significance while Kennard argues that "The Yellow Wall-Paper" could finally be appreciated as a feminist work because readers of the 1970s, including Elaine Hedges, had access to a set of literary conventions not available when the story was published in the 1890s. Kolodny argues that devotees of Poe-esque fiction could not easily transfer the horror and morbidity of a genre that Poe popularized to the sacrosanct domestic sphere. And Gilbert and Gubar read the tale as a woman's liberation from confinement and woe. While all are sensitive to the narrator's plight, they do not agree on the degree of success the narrator achieves; for example, Hedges ultimately pronounces the narrator defeated while Gilbert and Gubar grant her a higher form of sanity in her madness.

Eagerly bringing "The Yellow Wall-Paper" to the forefront of feminist academic circles and, in turn, helping it achieve a privileged status among literature by women, these and other pioneering scholars seemingly took at face value many of Gilman's claims in her autobiography regarding the story's publication and reception history. In turn, Gilman scholars of the 1980s and early 1990s—and here I include myself—both read and reinforced 1970s interpretations; as a result, some oft-repeated accounts which lack solid backing have admittedly assumed near legendary status in Gilman criticism. For example, the difficulty Gilman had in placing the story has been fodder for an argument that late nineteenth-century American society was not ready to receive Gilman's biting attack on the domestic sphere of home, husband, and children even though some contemporary critics included in this study, notably Henry B. Blackwell, clearly recognized the feminist intent and commented on its value. Equally, critics following the 1973 republication of the story by The Feminist Press also claim "The Yellow Wall-Paper" was virtually out of print and went unnoticed, although bibliographies reveal there were near two dozen printings of the story following its first publication in 1892. The story's inclusion in collections such as *The Midnight Reader* (1942) or *The Chamber of Horrors* (1965) legitimately made it more available to the general public than the academic community that embraced it in the 1970s, but they exist all the same.

I suggest we view studies by pioneering Gilman scholars in their own historical moment. "The Yellow Wall-Paper" achieved acclaim at a time when most authoritative editions were texts written by males and edited by male academicians. Groundbreaking legislative triumphs such as the granting of a woman's right to an abortion in Roe vs. Wade (1973) may have influenced the way feminist scholars optimistically read "The Yellow Wall-Paper" when The Feminist Press reissued it, as Hedges notes in her retrospective essay " 'Out at Last'?". What version of the story pioneering scholars read or brought to the attention of the feminist scholarly community was not an urgent consideration—just that the story be read and given wide visibility. As a result of their efforts, "The Yellow Wall-Paper" is now hailed in the feminist canon and included in the American literary canon. In the early twenty-first century, Gilman scholars maintain a healthy dose of skepticism about Gilman's claims and a respect for pioneering scholarship without a full-fledged acceptance of it. We recognize Gilman offers a mixed legacy—an agenda for widespread reform to liberate women, setting her far ahead of her time, as well as prejudices of class, race, and ethnicity common to early twentieth-century Anglo-America (see p. 2; Lanser, pp. 105–8; and Roth, pp. 117–21). Gilman tended not to credit others for their influence and to allow information to be interpreted to her advantage. In her autobiography published nearly forty years after the publication of "The Yellow Wall-Paper," Gilman may have refashioned the truth about some early responses to her publication (e.g. Mitchell's response to her work). With the passage of time, she may have simply forgotten some of the crucial details of its publication history. While I do not excuse such misinformation and literary transformation, these problems are not unique to Gilman studies: even the most admired classics have become reconstructed over the ages (e.g. Christina Rossetti's *Goblin Market* [1862] offers a prime example). Perhaps the most important lesson we can learn from the legends surrounding the story's reception is that we need to be cautious when reading an author's own account of her work; many of the misconceptions about the story in feminist criticism of the 1970s and 1980s stem from Gilman herself.

The mid-1970s and 1980s also brought forth numerous psychological and feminist readings by, among others, Loralee MacPike (1975), Beate Schöpp-Schilling (1975), and Judith Fetterley (1986). These essays usher in the notion of the narrator achieving a partial victory (they appear in entirety in *Captive Imagination*, along with the work of Jean Kennard [1981]). To MacPike, the narrator's identification with the trapped woman within the wallpaper, even if born of a hallucination, prompts the narrator to free herself from her restrictive world. Schöpp-Schilling applies the psychological principles of Alfred Adler to argue that the narrator, denied other forms of paper, turns to the wall*paper*; her preoccupation with it leads to her psychic degeneration. Fetterley continues this line of argument in suggesting the narrator turns the wallpaper into her text. Expressing herself through the paper (since John forbids her to write on paper), the narrator temporarily achieves control of her script but succumbs to madness, in Fetterley's view, because she validates John's "fiction": creative work leads her to madness.

In the 1980s, critics also directed increasing attention to the narrator's language. In a 1984 essay (reproduced in *Captive Imagination*) entitled "Escaping the Sentence: Diagnosis and Discourse in 'The Yellow Wallpaper,' " Paula Treichler explores the notion of women and language and the narrator as an inventive language user. To Treichler, the narrator authors her own sentences as a rebellion against her doctor-husband's medical "sentencing" of her condition. The result is a partial victory: while the narrator has linguistically freed herself, she remains trapped by a restrictive social reality that she sees more clearly once she is "out at last." In "The Writing of 'The Yellow Wall-Paper': A Double Palimpsest" (1989; see Modern Criticism, p. 101), Catherine Golden reads the story as a palimpsest: a text with a dominant top pattern, comprising her actions, and a muted back pattern, the language of the text itself. She argues that just at the point where the dominant text of the narrator's actions compromises her sanity and condemns her to madness, the narrator exhibits a defiant voice, granting her a dubious victory.

Treichler's essay sparked two responses by critics Carol Neely and Karen Ford printed in *Tulsa Studies* in 1985 alongside a rejoinder by Treichler. This critical exchange offers one striking example of how critics openly debate central aspects of "The Yellow Wall-Paper" in conversation with one another. Summarizing the Neely, Ford, Treichler debate, Richard Feldstein reinvigorates this dialogue in "Reader, Text, and Ambiguous Referentiality in 'The Yellow Wall-Paper' "(1985; reproduced in *Captive Imagination*). Similarly, Schöpp-Schilling sets up her psychological reading by criticizing previous scholars Ann Douglas Wood, Gail Parker, and Elaine Hedges for falling prey to the biographical fallacy in reading Gilman's life into her story. Jean Kennard draws upon the contributions of Hedges, Gilbert and Gubar, and Kolodny in presenting her own argument, while Fetterley, in turn, acknowledges the influence of Kennard and Kolodny. Conrad Shumaker—whose under-utilized essay " 'Too Terribly Good to Be Printed': Charlotte Perkins Gilman's 'The Yellow Wallpaper' " (1985; see Further Reading, p. 159) examines "The Yellow Wall-Paper" in relation to the work of Nathaniel Hawthorne, Henry James, Mark Twain, and Edith Wharton—finds the feminist approaches of Kolodny and Kennard instructive but isolating in separating

Gilman's landmark story from the dominant nineteenth- and early twentieth-century American literary tradition (*Captive Imagination* contains Shumaker's and Feldstein's essays). In reaction to feminist criticism by Hedges, Kennard, Kolodny, and Gilbert and Gubar—who gave "The Yellow Wall-Paper" too hegemonic a reading and too privileged a status in her opinion—Janice Haney-Peritz neither identifies nor sympathizes with the narrator in her 1986 essay, "Monumental Feminism and Literature's Ancestral House: Another Look at 'The Yellow Wall-Paper' " (see Modern Criticism, **pp. 96–9**).

Ushering in a darker phase in Gilman scholarship, Haney-Peritz reads the wallpaper through Lacanian psychoanalytic terms to explore the narrator's struggle with the oppressive structures of male discourse. When the narrator sees the trapped woman as a real woman, not a symbol, she has retreated from the linguistic realm (in which she can construct her speaking and writing identity) into the imaginary. Haney-Peritz's conclusion departs from that of Treichler, Fetterley, and Golden in that she does not allow a partial victory for the narrator, who remains encrypted in the realm of haunted houses. That same year, Mary Jacobus explored the story in her book *Reading Women* (see Modern Criticism, **pp. 94–6**). Offering a more Freudian reading of narrator as "hysteric"—a term derived from the Latin word for "uterus"—Jacobus also perceives the fate of the narrator darkly, arguing that the narrator becomes trapped in a maze from over reading. To Jacobus, the smooch her body makes along the wall represents the repression of female sexuality in Victorian America while the odor of the paper signifies male hysteria.

Of the many essays appearing in the mid-1980s to 1990, I single out Susan Lanser's provocative 1989 essay entitled "Feminist Criticism, 'The Yellow Wallpaper,' and the Politics of Color in America" in which she questions the canonical status of Gilman's story lauded exclusively by white academics (see Modern Criticism, **p. 105**). Offering a different take on the color and smell of the yellow wallpaper, Lanser views the story from the perspective of the late nineteenth-century mass immigration of Asians and southern and eastern Europeans to America and the accompanying prejudices toward "yellow-skinned" peoples—a term which included Chinese, Japanese, and light-skinned African-Americans as well as Poles, Jews, Hungarians, Italians, and Irish. Lanser brings to light racism and privilege in Gilman's mission for changing women's lives. If her attention to the political ideology of the text darkened the story's heretofore privileged status, it urged Gilman scholars to recognize Gilman's prejudices and biases as part of her legacy.

Other critics interpret the color variously—it is fear of sexuality to Jacobus, saturated urine to William Veeder (*Arizona Quarterly*, 1988), and a child's messy feces to Ann J. Lane (see Further Reading, **p. 160**). What builds a case of racism for Lanser becomes, for these critics, a fear of motherhood, which relates to the narrator's postpartum depression and Gilman's own trying experiences with maternity. Moreover, in the 1980s, the story gained the attention of new historicists, such as Walter Benn Michaels who finds the story exemplary as an illustration of American capitalist culture of consumption (see **pp. 99–101**). His Derridean reading in *The Gold Standard and the Logic of Naturalism* (1987) argues the narrator produces herself through writing her body and ultimately consuming herself.

Hedges—the scholar who catapulted the story into the consciousness of feminist academics with her "Afterword" to the 1973 Feminist Press single-volume edition—contextualizes these critics' contributions among others in her retrospective essay on the near unprecedented critical response to Gilman's story entitled " 'Out at Last'? 'The Yellow Wallpaper after Two Decades of Feminist Criticism," commissioned for *Captive Imagination* (1992). Hedges surveys over two dozen essays published on "The Yellow Wall-Paper" between the 1970s and early 1990s. She addresses trends in the criticism and summarizes the accomplishments of far more critics than can possibly be incorporated in this sourcebook. Her essay is informative both on the state of feminist literary criticism from the 1970s to the early 1990s and the various critical readings of the story during this fruitful period. I recommend reading Hedges's important essay in its entirety, after becoming familiar with the territory of scholarship on the story. Golden's introductory essay to *Captive Imagination* entitled "One Hundred Years of Reading 'The Yellow Wall-Paper' " also navigates the rich terrain of critical interpretations.

"The Yellow Wall-Paper" found a niche in gay and lesbian studies and textual studies beginning in the 1990s. Jonathan Crewe's 1995 essay entitled "Queering 'The Yellow Wallpaper'?" draws attention to the queer aspects of the story including the narrator's dawning awareness of her kinship with the woman trapped in the wallpaper to argue that we see elements that John himself sought to squelch in reestablishing heterosexuality as the norm (see **pp. 111–14**). Julie Bates Dock brought forth a critical edition and documentary casebook on "The Yellow Wall-Paper" in 1998, and most recently Shawn St. Jean published "Hanging 'The Yellow Wall-Paper': Feminism and Textual Studies" (2003; see Further Reading, **p. 159**). Recent essays have also focused on the material aspects of "The Yellow Wall-Paper," two of which appear in *The Mixed Legacy of Charlotte Perkins Gilman* (2000), edited by Catherine J. Golden and Joanna Schneider Zangrando. In "Overwriting Decadence: Charlotte Perkins Gilman, Oscar Wilde, and the Feminization of Art," Ann Heilmann associates the dominant motif of the wallpaper with fin-de-siècle decadence; she argues that the narrator must free herself from a wallpaper whose color and design represent a late nineteenth-century male aesthetic movement, symbolic of patriarchy itself, in order to create a new female aesthetic (see **pp. 114–17**). Also focusing on the wallpaper, Heather Kirk Thomas explores how wallpaper not only embodies a male aesthetic promoted by Charles Eastlake and William Morris but also a male monopoly of the decorative arts market and the encoding of gender within domestic places. These critics' attention to the wallpaper continues notions that Tom Lutz raises in *American Nervousness, 1903: An Anecdotal History* (1991) where he discusses Gilman's belief in neurasthenia and her endorsement of concerns regarding the influence of wallpaper on women's mental health (see **pp. 108–11**). Moreover, in appearing together in a section entitled "Re-Envisioning 'The Yellow Wall-Paper' " in *Mixed Legacy*, essays by Heilmann and Kirk Thomas exemplify the trend toward book publication in Gilman scholarship.

While many essays first appeared in periodicals, some subsequently came out in book form, and scholars have reprinted a good number in critical editions and sourcebooks devoted to "The Yellow Wall-Paper." For example, Haney-Peritz's oft-cited 1986 *Women's Studies* essay subsequently appeared in two early 1990s casebooks: *The Captive Imagination* (1992) edited by Golden, and *The Yellow Wallpaper* edited by Thomas L. Erskine and Connie L. Richards (1993); an excerpt of her essay also appears in this sourcebook (see **pp. 96–9**). Another edition entitled *The Yellow Wallpaper* (1998) edited by Dale M. Bauer provides a rich array of background material grounding the story in its historical context.

Sources listed in Further Reading offer additional testimony to the growing field of Gilman studies. This list includes biographies by Mary A. Hill, Gary Scharnhorst, and Ann J. Lane, the Gilman diaries edited by Denise D. Knight, and collections of criticism, such as *Critical Essays on Charlotte Perkins Gilman* (1992) edited by Joanne Karpinski; *Charlotte Perkins Gilman: Optimist Reformer* (1999) edited by Val Gough and Jill Rudd; and *The Mixed Legacy of Charlotte Perkins Gilman* (2000) edited by Golden and Zangrando; the latter two collections are outgrowths of international Charlotte Perkins Gilman conferences, both of which devoted sessions to new readings of "The Yellow Wall-Paper." The University of Liverpool hosted the first Gilman conference in 1995. Skidmore College (1997) and the University of South Carolina (2001) held subsequent conferences sponsored by the Charlotte Perkins Gilman Society (which publishes an annual newsletter and hosts a website). The late Elaine Hedges and Shelley Fisher Fishkin founded the Charlotte Perkins Gilman Society in 1990 to promote interest in her life and oeuvre. The pattern of conference-based collections continues: in 2004, University of Alabama Press published essays from the 2001 conference in a collection edited by Cynthia J. Davis and Denise D. Knight entitled *Charlotte Perkins Gilman and Her Contemporaries: Literary and Intellectual Contexts.* Plans are under way for a fourth conference at the University of New England in 2006.

"The Yellow Wall-Paper" has prompted two books of pedagogy published in 2003, one in the MLA Approaches series on *"The Yellow Wall-Paper" and Herland* edited by Denise D. Knight and Cynthia J. Davis, and another entitled *The Pedagogical Wallpaper*, edited by Jeffrey Weinstock. The explosion of interest in "The Yellow Wall-Paper" has also led to audiovisual materials including a 15-minute international instructional television version directed by John Robbins (1978); a 90-minute film by BBC Education and Training and the WGBH Education Foundation directed by John Clive (1989); a 26-minute film version directed by Tony Romain (1996); and a 14-minute version directed by Marie Ashton and promoted by Women Make Movies (1977). While none of the film versions of the story is considered pre-eminent, Guiyou Huang reports that instructors most commonly show the Clive version, starring Julia Watson and Stephen Dillon. An excerpt of Huang's essay on the use of film, photographs, and other visual materials entitled "The Use of Audiovisual Material as an Aid in Teaching 'The Yellow Wall-Paper' " (2003) appears in this sourcebook (see **pp. 121–4**). In addition to movie adaptations, interested readers might profitably examine period wallpapers, late nineteenth-century women's fashion and coiffure, and photographs of Gilman and members of her personal and professional circles. Visual materials (many included in this sourcebook) help readers situate the story in Gilman's life and its own historical moment.

Critical interest in "The Yellow Wall-Paper" remains ongoing; more than ten essays were published between 2000 and 2003 alone. The next years will witness further editions of criticism, biography, and fiction that can be read as companion pieces to her landmark story—an area which has exploded in recent years (see Further Reading, **pp. 161–2**). Of note, Denise D. Knight and Jennifer Tuttle are editing *Selected Letters of Charlotte Perkins Gilman*, forthcoming from the

University of Alabama Press in 2006. Cynthia J. Davis is writing a biography entitled *Charlotte Perkins Gilman: A Living*, to be published by Stanford University Press in 2006. Charlotte Rich's edition of Gilman's first novella, *What Diantha Did*, is expected to be published by Duke University Press in 2005.

While these volumes give more definition to Gilman's life and oeuvre, she remains best known as author of "The Yellow Wall-Paper," a tale that has been refashioned in response to the way a culture constructs femininity and women's liberation. As the following section on Interpretations reveals, developments in literary studies—feminism, psychoanalytical criticism, new historicism, gay and lesbian studies, and textual studies—in turn have illuminated new dimensions of a story that continues to perplex and fascinate critics and students alike. Scholarship on "The Yellow Wall-Paper" continues to grow in the new millennium as critics puzzle and debate the poignant symbolism of the story. In an era recognizing the needs of women across races, ethnicities, and nations, marked by increasing technological accomplishments, and threatened by violence and global terrorism, we can only imagine what new directions will emerge in the multi-faceted scholarship on "The Yellow Wall-Paper."

Nineteenth-Century and Early Twentieth-Century Interpretations

Selected Reviews of "The Yellow Wall-Paper"

From the initial two reviews in *Boston Evening Transcript*, 1892

These two reviews accompanied the initial publication of "The Yellow Wall-Paper" in January 1892. The first excerpt offers a partial list of the contents of the January 1892 issue. In the single sentence that describes the story, the reviewer calls "The Yellow Wall-Paper" "very paragraphic and very queer generally" (see below). The second "review" is technically a letter to the editor. Gilman believed this was written by a male physician (see Scharnhorst, Further Reading, **p. 159**). Gilman made much of this letter in her January 1913 *Forerunner* article "Why I Wrote 'The Yellow Wall-Paper'?" and reprinted it in her autobiography, closing the gap between the M. and the D. The anonymous reviewer calls her story one of "deadly peril" and ends with a palpably pregnant rhetorical question.

Anon., "January Magazines," *Boston Evening Transcript*, January 1, 1892, p. 6, col. 5 [excerpt]

S. Q. Lapius contributes a fine poem, "The Gray Dawn." Edith Mary Norris has a powerful and pathetic story of the good old days of witchcraft, called "A Salem Witch." Charlotte Perkins Stetson contributes a story called "The Yellow Wallpaper," which is very paragraphic and very queer generally. One of Phillips Brooks's finest sermons on Abraham Lincoln is reproduced, with a commentary upon it by Mr. Mead. A number of other poems and sketches complete a very interesting number.

M. D., "Perilous Stuff," *Boston Evening Transcript*, April 8, 1892, p. 6, col. 2

To the Editor of the Transcript: In a well-known magazine has recently appeared a story entitled "The Yellow Wallpaper." It is a sad story of a young wife passing through the gradations from slight mental derangement to raving lunacy. It is graphically told, in a somewhat sensational style, which makes it difficult to lay aside, after the first glance, til it is finished, holding the reader in morbid fascination to the end. It certainly seems open to serious question if such literature should be permitted in print.

The story can hardly, it would seem, give pleasure to any reader, and to many whose lives have been touched through the nearest ties by this dread disease, it must bring the keenest pain. To others, whose lives have become a struggle against an heredity of mental derangement, such literature contains deadly peril. Should such stories be allowed to pass without protest, without severest censure?

M. D.

A[nne] M[ontgomerie], "The Yellow Wall Paper," *The Conservator* 10 (June 1899): 60–1

This story, which treats of the psychology of mental disorder, appeared some years ago (1892) in The New England Magazine and is now reprinted out of deference to the growing popular interest in the work of its author. Readers who wish further proof of the versatility of Mrs. Stetson need but to examine this monograph to be convinced. It is in style quite different from what may be considered her customary and contemporary, or in a sense even her most serious, mood, although the keen penetration and inevitable touch which characterize that is here also.

The Yellow Wall Paper seems at first to be only a skit—a gentle, mildly amusing joke. But it grows and increases with a perfect crescendo of horror. It is almost uncanny to come upon Mrs. Stetson in the act of making literature of this sort—she is so interested, heart and soul, in such other things as woman's economic status, and so identified with the philosophic assertion of sex independence. Here she is writing about a woman afflicted with nervous prostration. This woman tells her own story. She is taken for quiet and rest to a place in the country that can be described only by using all the adjectives of enjoyment in the language. But in this paradise she meets with one thing she does not like—a certain yellow wall paper. It is a condition, not a wall paper, of course. Anything would have served her fancy; if she had not referred her malady to that yellow wall paper it would have attached itself to some other phenomenon. It is a piteous recital. We reach a fatal but necessary crisis—the victim ceases to be a spectator of the baffling movements of the creeping woman behind the bars of the wall paper and herself becomes the creeper delighted to escape. The story is simple, serious, sly, fascinating, torturing. It is embodied excitement. It is brooding insanity. Imagine Mrs. Stetson tracing out curiously and deftly the lines of such a picture.

And the wall paper in prototype peers at you from the covers of the little book with staring bulbous eyes all over the livid orange and a sulphurous smooch at its base.

A. M.

Anon., "New Books and Those Who Make Them," *Boston Daily Advertiser,* June 10, 1899, p. 8

A second edition of Mrs. Charlotte P. Stetson's "Women and Economics" has been brought out by Small, Maynard & Company. The text, except for a few slight corrections, remains the same, but a full index has been added.

The publishers have just issued Mrs. Stetson's story, published some years ago in one of the magazines. It is called "The Yellow Wall Paper." Those who were fortunate enough to read the tale when it first appeared will welcome it in book form, for there is no doubt that it is one of the most powerful and original short stories published for many years. It appears in a cover of orange and yellow, not beautiful in design, but purposely intended to represent the horrible wall covering that caused the insanity of the poor nervous invalid who was compelled to look at it day after day.

Anon., "A Question of 'Nerves'," */Times (?)/* (Baltimore, Md.), June 10, 1899

A slight but suggestive study in neuroticism is "The Yellow Wall Paper," by Charlotte Perkins Stetson (Boston: Small, Maynard & Company). The writer, who has contributed a good deal of serious matter on the subject of social economics, has in this instance taken up the pen of the fictionist, "The Yellow Wall Paper" being the diary of a nervous woman driven insane by the stupid devotion of a husband and by living in a bedroom decorated with wall paper of "a smouldering, unclean yellow," having "one of those sprawling flamboyant patterns committing every artistic sin." To follow its outrageous writhings was "as good as gymnastics." The book is bound in what one may suppose is a sample of the abhorred paper, and its grotesque design will easily arouse sympathy for the poor lady. The story, far from being ridiculous, has a touch of ghastliness. After reading it the model husband will be inclined seriously to consider the subject of repapering his wife's bed chamber according to the ethics of William Morris.

H[enry] B. B[lackwell], "Literary Notices: The Yellow Wall Paper," *The Woman's Journal,* June 17, 1899, p. 187

This is a most striking and impressive study of morbid psychology, in the shape of a story. A woman goes insane through the effort of her husband, a well-meaning physician, to cure her of "a temporary nervous depression—a slight hysterical tendency" by keeping her confined in a quiet house, where she takes phosphates and tonics and air and exercise, but is absolutely forbidden to work. The poor woman believes that what she needs is congenial work, with excitement and change, less opposition, and more society and stimulus. She keeps a journal, and mopes. With frightful simplicity and naiveté she records from day to day her mind's gradual passage from melancholy to madness, which last takes its hue from a disagreeable yellow wall paper. With pathetic sadness she begins her story thus:

"It is seldom that mere ordinary people like John and myself secure ancestral halls for the summer. A colonial mansion, a hereditary estate, I would say a haunted house and reach the height of romantic felicity,—but that would be asking too much of fate. Still, I will proudly declare that there is something queer about it. John laughs at me, of course. John is practical in the extreme. He has no patience with faith, an intense horror of superstition, and he scoffs openly at any talk of things not to be felt and seen put down in figures. John is a physician, and *perhaps*—(I would not say it to a living soul, of course, but this is dead paper and a great relief to my mind)—*perhaps* that is one reason I do not get well faster. You see, he does not believe I am sick! And what can one do?"

Nothing more graphic and suggestive has ever been written to show why so many women go crazy, especially farmers' wives, who live lonely, monotonous lives. A husband of the kind described in this little sketch once said that he could not account for his wife's having gone insane—"for," said he, "to my certain knowledge she has hardly left her kitchen and bedroom in 30 years."

This story appeared some years ago in the *New England Magazine*, and attracted much attention. A distinguished alienist said to her: "It exactly describes the phenomena of mental disease. By what extraordinary power of imagination and sympathy have you been able to enter into the consciousness of these unfortunates?" Many years ago a story was published, entitled "Miserrimus." It described with frightful intensity the horrors of remorse which preyed upon the unhappy victim until he became the inmate of an insane asylum. Both these books deserve to be perpetuated and widely circulated.

H. B. B.

Anon., "Books: Light and Serious Stories," *Time and the Hour* 10 (June 17, 1899): 9

WITH wonderful word-selection drawing curves and blobs and goggling eyes, with none of the real facts of her story told, but all left to inference, with no plot at all, but the simple "un-narration" of the horrors of the beginnings of puerperal insanity, Charlotte Perkins Stetson has done work in "The Yellow Wall-Paper" (Small, Maynard & Co.), reprinted from the *New England Magazine*, in a startling cover, which should bind and hold her to more as good. It is not good to retail the facts which Mrs. Stetson has hinted at; they are the facts which come to some of us and shake reason, religion, and faith clean out of us. Conan Doyle had no right, say the outraged physicians, to write "Round the Red Lamp." Be it so: this story is calculated to prevent girls from marrying far more surely than Dr. Doyle's "Unto the Third Generation" attacked young men.[1]

The beauty of the work lies in the handling entirely. The wall-paper of hideous color and pattern showed to the new mother, as she became insane, a sub-pattern

---

1   *Round the Red Lamp Being Facts and Fancies of Medical Life* (1893) is a collection of 17 Conan Doyle detective stories conveying his knowledge of medicine, love of the medical profession, and his skill with deductive reasoning evident in his Sherlock Holmes stories. The critic likely refers to "The Third Generation" in that collection. A young baronet, Sir Francis Norton, learns of his constitutional and hereditary taint from the renowned Dr. Horace Selby, who advises him not to marry next week as planned; the baronet dies of an "accident" that very evening.

which grew always clearer. It was the figure of a woman trying to escape through the meshes of the outer pattern, and it makes the reader feel that his own mind is slipping to read behind the mad woman's chatter—which is all the story—the horrible facts. It is a strong book, a little yellow book, a well-done, horrible book,—a book to keep away from the young wife.

Anon., "Minor Fiction," *Literature* (American edition), n.s. 27 (July 14, 1899): 18

Seldom is a strong and original story compressed into so small a number of pages as is "The Yellow Wall-Paper" (Boston: Small, Maynard and Company). Mrs. Stetson's tale of the subtle creeping on of insanity may be read at a sitting, but the haunting effect of the gruesome, realistic diary kept by its helpless victim will cling to the memory for days. The heroine is the wife of a physician, who is singularly blind to the persistent and harrowing distress caused her by confinement in a large, airy room, which is papered with a loathsome fungus sort of yellow paper with innumerable spirals and arabesques and a general motive of toadstools in endless iteration, so that the deadly fascination of the walls finally completes the overthrow of the tottering reason. In many respects the story is worthy of a place beside some of the weird and uncanny masterpieces of Hawthorne and Poe.

Anon., "The Yellow Wall Paper," *The Literary World* (Boston) 22 (July 22, 1899): 236

It may not be exactly wholesome to read about how it feels to go crazy, but *The Yellow Wall Paper* is at least very interesting as well as pathetic. Charlotte Perkins Stetson is its author, and she has drawn an exceedingly vivid and compelling picture of mental sickness and hallucination. Perhaps the best or the worst of the sketch is the reasonable suggestion that the end might have been different if the sufferer had been treated more rationally.

Anon., "Brief Reviews," *The Daily Oklahoman* (Oklahoma City), January 29, 1928

Fourteen stories that are on the way to becoming classics. Not always distinct from ghost and detective stories, mystery stories present riddles which work one into an agony of curiosity and sometimes horror as in the case of What Was It? [by Fitz-James O'Brien] and The Yellow Wall-Paper, by Charlotte Perkins Gilman, a study of madness as powerful as the best of Poe's tales.

Anon., "New Books in Brief Review," *The Independent* 120 (February 11, 1928): 141

. . . The mystery stories are distinctly superior. Besides the tales of Poe, we are given some very real horrors, including those two unequaled stories, "The Yellow Wallpaper" and "The Upper Berth" [by F. Marion Crawford].

From **William Dean Howells, ed., "Introduction,"** *The Great Modern American Stories, An Anthology* (New York: Boni & Liveright, 1920), vii

A dominant figure in the history of American literature, Howells (1837–1920) is often considered the forefather of American realism, a genre that challenged Romantic literary conventions. Best known for *The Rise of Silas Lapham* (1885), he was a prominent author, poet, critic, and editor of the prestigious *Atlantic Monthly*, one of the journals to which Gilman sent her landmark tale. He later contributed "Editor's Study" to *Harper's Monthly*. Ironically Mark Twain and Henry James, whose works Howells promoted, have eclipsed Howells's reputation as a leading late nineteenth-century American author.

Just months before his death in 1920, William Dean Howells wrote to Gilman asking for permission to reprint her story in a collection entitled *The Great Modern American Stories*. Other notable selections include Mary E. Wilkins Freeman's "The Revolt of Mother" (1890) about a woman's rebellion against her husband and Mark Twain's "The Celebrated Jumping Frog of Calaveras County" (1865), a tall tale. Often noted in Gilman criticism is Howells's reaction to "The Yellow Wall-Paper" in his introduction to the collection. He "shivers" over this tale, calling it chilling enough "to freeze our young blood," and "so terribly good that it ought never to be printed." Critics make much of his "shivering." Perhaps more intriguing is why Howells thought it ought "never to be printed." In his 1985 article " 'Too Terribly Good to be Printed': Charlotte Perkins Gilman's 'The Yellow Wall-Paper,' " Conrad Shumaker suggests Howells recognized that Gilman's attack on the home and motherhood was blasphemous at a time when these realms were sacrosanct (see Further Reading, p. 159). And what of Howells's claim that he "could not rest until I had corrupted the editor of *The New England Magazine* into publishing it"? Gilman gives a different account of the publication of the story, which many critics have taken at face value. She explains in her autobiography that she sent the story to a literary agent, Henry Austin, who placed it in *New England Magazine*. She also complains that she never received payment for the story. Howells was known for his honesty and generosity in helping to promote the work of upcoming authors. The editor of *New England Magazine*, Edwin Mead, was a first cousin of Howells's wife and had previously profited from his support.

How do we reconcile the conflicting stories? Did Howells influence Mead? If so, did Gilman know that Howells helped to place the story? Conceivably, Howells might have asked Mead that she not be told, but then why would he disclose this information later, especially since Gilman was still alive? In the years intervening between the story's first publication in 1892 and the publication of her autobiography in 1935, Gilman might have forgotten Howells's role in the story, or he might have forgotten his wish for concealment. Gilman did not always acknowledge Howells for his help, as Joanne Karpinski notes in her essay entitled "When the Marriage of True Minds Admits Impediments: Charlotte Perkins Gilman and William Dean Howells" (228) (printed in Shirley Marchalonis's 1988 collection entitled *Patrons and Protegées*, published by Rutgers University Press).

[. . .]

It wanted at least two generations to freeze our young blood with Mrs. Perkins Gilman's story of *The Yellow Wall Paper*, which Horace Scudder (then of *The Atlantic*) said in refusing it that it was so terribly good that it ought never to be printed. But terrible and too wholly dire as it was, I could not rest until I had corrupted the editor of *The New England Magazine* into publishing it. Now that I have got it into my collection here, I shiver over it as much as I did when I first read it in manuscript, though I agree with the editor of *The Atlantic* of the time that it was too terribly good to be printed.

[. . .]

Modern Criticism

Original endnotes to the articles are converted to footnotes and are selectively reprinted. Those retained (prefaced by the author's name in square brackets) present information essential to a reading of the excerpt or not identifiable from the text itself. Interested readers may return to the original sources to read works in their entirety or pursue further research.

From **Elaine R. Hedges, "Afterword"** to *The Yellow Wall-Paper* (1973) (New York: The Feminist Press, 1996, 8th printing), 37–63

Elaine Hedges reintroduced the scholarly community to "The Yellow Wall-Paper" in 1973 when The Feminist Press reissued it in a single-volume edition followed by her "Afterword." This small paperback with a flamboyant yellow wallpaper design on its cover quickly became a best seller for The Feminist Press and widely known in the feminist academic community.

Hedges calls attention to the sociocultural importance of Gilman's "feminist document" while drawing heavily on the autobiographical roots of a tale "wrenched out of Gilman's own life" and "unique in the canon of her works" for its literary power and directness. In the excerpts presented here, Hedges calls "The Yellow Wall-Paper" "rare" among works by nineteenth-century women writers in confronting "the sexual politics of the male-female, husband-wife relationship." She also connects Gilman's tale to Kate Chopin's *The Awakening* (1899), linking the destruction of both heroines to the patriarchal climate of their times. While critics variously interpret the narrator's fate along a spectrum ranging from entrapment to liberation, Hedges reads the narrator as "destroyed," "defeated," "totally mad." Nonetheless, Hedges recognizes that the narrator, "in her mad-sane way . . . has seen the situation of women for what it is," granting the narrator a clarity of vision that leads other critics, such as Sandra Gilbert and Susan Gubar, to pronounce her liberated (see **pp. 91–2**).

Hedges's criticism is inevitably dated and not without flaws (the 1996 publication essentially updates the text only). For example, in suggesting that the connection between gender, insanity, and patriarchy went unrecognized at the time of its publication, Hedges overlooks early critics who made such a connection (even if they did not couch it in the terms of 1970s feminists). Like many of the pioneering studies, Hedges's essay reads the story in terms of Gilman's life and concludes that even if her heroine "fails," Charlotte Perkins Gilman did not. Nonetheless, this essay by a pioneering feminist critic is still regarded as groundbreaking, paving the way for future criticism.

"The Yellow Wall-Paper" is a small literary masterpiece. For almost fifty years it has been overlooked, as has its author, one of the most commanding feminists of her time. Now, with the new growth of the feminist movement, Charlotte Perkins Gilman is being rediscovered and "The Yellow Wall-Paper" should share in that rediscovery. The story of a woman's mental breakdown, narrated with superb psychological and dramatic precision, it is, as William Dean Howells said of it in 1920, a story to "freeze our . . . blood."

The story was wrenched out of Gilman's own life, and is unique in the canon of her works. Although she wrote other fiction – short stories and novels – and much poetry as well, none of it ever achieved the power and directness, the imaginative authenticity of this piece. Polemical intent often made her fiction dry and clumsily didactic; and the extraordinary pressures of publishing deadlines under which she worked made careful composition almost impossible. (During one seven-year period she edited and published her own magazine, *The Forerunner*, writing almost all of the material for it – a sum total, she estimated, of twenty-one thousand words per month or the equivalent of twenty-eight books.)

Charlotte Perkins Gilman was an active feminist and primarily a nonfiction writer: the author of *Women and Economics*, a witty, bitingly satirical analysis of the situation of women in her society, which was used as a college text in the 1920s and translated into seven languages; and the author of many other non-fiction works dealing with the socio-economic status of women. She was also an indefatigable and inspiring lecturer. Her work during the last decade of the nineteenth century and the first two of the twentieth has led one recent historian to say that she was "the leading intellectual in the women's movement in the United States" in her time.[1]

That interest in her has recently revived is satisfying, and only just. In the past few years several masters theses and doctoral dissertations have been written about her, and *Women and Economics* was reissued in 1966. The recent acquisition of her personal papers by the Schlesinger Library of Radcliffe College is bound to lead to further research and publication. Even "The Yellow Wall-Paper" has resurfaced in several anthologies. However, tucked away among many other selections and frequently with only brief biographical information about its author, the story will not necessarily find in these anthologies the wide audience it deserves.

Yet it does deserve the widest possible audience. For aside from the light it throws on the personal despairs, and the artistic triumph over them, of one of America's foremost feminists, the story is one of the rare pieces of literature we

1 [Hedges's note.] Carl N. Degler, ed., *Women and Economics* (reprinted, New York: Harper and Row, 1966), p. xiii.

have by a nineteenth-century woman which directly confronts the sexual politics of the male-female, husband-wife relationship. In its time (and presumably still today, given its appearance in the anthology *Psychopathology and Literature*), the story was read essentially as a Poe-esque tale of chilling horror – and as a story of mental aberration. It is both of these. But it is more. It is a feminist document, dealing with sexual politics at a time when few writers felt free to do so, at least so candidly. Seven years after Gilman published her story, Kate Chopin published *The Awakening*, a novel so frank in its treatment of the middle-class wife and her prescribed submissive role that it lost its author both reputation and income. It is symptomatic of their times that both Gilman's story and Chopin's novel end with the self-destruction of their heroines.

[. . .]

It is no surprise to find, therefore, that at the end of the story the narrator both does and does not identify with the creeping women who surround her in her hallucinations. The women creep out of the wallpaper, they creep through the arbors and lanes and along the roads outside the house. Women must creep. The narrator knows this. She has fought as best she could against creeping. In her perceptivity and in her resistance lie her heroism (her heroineism). But at the end of the story, on her last day in the house, as she peels off yards and yards of wallpaper and creeps around the floor, she has been defeated. She is totally mad.

But in her mad-sane way she has seen the situation of women for what it is. She has wanted to strangle the woman behind the paper – tie her with a rope. For that woman, the tragic product of her society, is of course the narrator's self. By rejecting that woman she might free the other, imprisoned woman within herself. But the only available rejection is suicidal, and hence she descends into madness. Madness is her only freedom, as, crawling around the room, she screams at her husband that she has finally "got out" – outside the wallpaper – and can't be put back.

[. . .]

The heroine in "The Yellow Wall-Paper" is destroyed. She has fought her best against husband, brother, doctor, and even against women friends (her husband's sister, for example, is "a perfect and enthusiastic housekeeper, and hopes for no better profession"). She has tried, in defiance of all the social and medical codes of her time, to retain her sanity and her individuality. But the odds are against her and she fails.

[. . .]

From **Sandra Gilbert and Susan Gubar, *The Madwoman in the Attic***
(New Haven: Yale University Press, 1979), 89–92

Sandra Gilbert and Susan Gubar include "The Yellow Wall-Paper" in their
groundbreaking *The Madwoman in the Attic*, a book praised for its bold feminist
reinterpretation of works by leading nineteenth-century women novelists (e.g.
Jane Austen, George Eliot, the Brontë sisters) and its persuasive argument for
the existence of a distinctly female literary imagination. Often quoted is their
assertion that Gilman tells "a striking story of female confinement and escape, a
paradigmatic tale which (like *Jane Eyre*) seems to tell the story that all literary
women would tell if they could speak their 'speechless woe.'" Charlotte
Brontë's *Jane Eyre* features the quintessential madwoman in the attic, but
Gilbert and Gubar make a connection based on self-expression: like Jane Eyre,
the narrator escapes her confinement and expresses herself by narrating her
own story.

While acknowledging the narrator's madness, Gilbert and Gubar read the
tale as one of escape and liberation. Even more important than John's feminine
swoon at the end of the story are the narrator's "mirages of health and freedom with which her author endows her like a fairy godmother showering gold
on a sleeping heroine." To these critics, the narrator's active imagination
becomes a source of health and liberation, not of disease and defeat in madness;
in fact, to Gilbert and Gubar, the narrator leaves a state of "dis-ease" as the
story progresses. The narrator watches the woman behind the paper move into
"open country," and the woman behind the paper is "the narrator and the
narrator's double. By the end of the story, moreover, the narrator has enabled
this double to escape from her textual/architectural confinement." Gilbert and
Gubar follow Gilman's view of S. Weir Mitchell and make the same move from
literature to biography as Elaine Hedges does to conclude: "That such an escape
from the numb world behind the patterned walls of the text was a flight from
dis-ease into health was quite clear to Gilman herself."

Gilbert and Gubar brought further attention to Gilman's landmark story in
anthologizing it in their popular and extensively used *Norton Anthology of Literature by Women* (1985). In its second edition (1996), Gilbert and Gubar include
several of Gilman's poems to complement themes of "The Yellow Wall-Paper."

As if to comment on the unity of all these points – on, that is, the anxiety-inducing
connections between what women writers tend to see as their parallel confine-
ments in texts, houses, and maternal female bodies – Charlotte Perkins Gilman
brought them all together in 1890 in a striking story of female confinement and
escape, a paradigmatic tale which (like *Jane Eyre*) seems to tell *the* story that all
literary women would tell if they could speak their "speechless woe." "The
Yellow Wallpaper," which Gilman herself called "a description of a case of nervous breakdown," recounts in the first person the experiences of a woman who is
evidently suffering from a severe postpartum psychosis.

[. . .]

Eventually it becomes obvious to both reader and narrator that the figure creeping through and behind the wallpaper is both the narrator and the narrator's double. By the end of the story, moreover, the narrator has enabled this double to escape from her textual/architectural confinement: "I pulled and she shook, I shook and she pulled, and before morning we had peeled off yards of that paper." Is the message of the tale's conclusion mere madness? Certainly the righteous Doctor John – whose name links him to the anti-hero of Charlotte Brontë's *Villette* – has been temporarily defeated, or at least momentarily stunned. "Now why should that man have fainted?" the narrator ironically asks as she creeps around her attic. But John's unmasculine swoon of surprise is the least of the triumphs Gilman imagines for her madwoman. More significant are the madwoman's own imaginings and creations, mirages of health and freedom with which her author endows her like a fairy godmother showering gold on a sleeping heroine. The woman from behind the wallpaper creeps away, for instance, creeps fast and far on the long road, in broad daylight. "I have watched her sometimes away off in the open country," says the narrator, "creeping as fast as a cloud shadow in a high wind."

Indistinct and yet rapid, barely perceptible but inexorable, the progress of that cloud shadow is not unlike the progress of nineteenth-century literary women out of the texts defined by patriarchal poetics into the open spaces of their own authority. That such an escape from the numb world behind the patterned walls of the text was a flight from dis-ease into health was quite clear to Gilman herself. When "The Yellow Wallpaper" was published she sent it to Weir Mitchell, whose strictures had kept her from attempting the pen during her own breakdown, thereby aggravating her illness, and she was delighted to learn, years later, that "he had changed his treatment of nervous prostration since reading" her story. "If that is a fact," she declared, "I have not lived in vain." Because she was a rebellious feminist besides being a medical iconoclast, we can be sure that Gilman did not think of this triumph of hers in narrowly therapeutic terms. Because she knew, with Emily Dickinson, that "Infection in the sentence breeds,"[1] she knew that the cure for female despair must be spiritual as well as physical, aesthetic as well as social. What "The Yellow Wallpaper" shows she knew, too, is that even when a supposedly "mad" woman has been sentenced to imprisonment in the "infected" house of her own body, she may discover that, as Sylvia Plath was to put it seventy years later, she has "a self to recover, a queen."[2]

From **Annette Kolodny, "A Map for Rereading,"** *New Literary History* 11: 3 (1980): 451–67

To Kolodny, Gilman did not have a ready-made audience for her story even though she worked within a literary tradition made popular by Poe. Kolodny cites similarities between "The Yellow Wall-Paper" and Poe's "The Pit and the

---

1   This line comes from Emily Dickinson's poem 1261, "A Word dropped careless on a page" (1861).
2   This line comes from Sylvia Plath's poem "Stings" (1962) in her volume *Ariel* (1965).

Pendulum"—both of which focus on the effect of insanity-inducing circum-stances on a sane mind—but she argues that Gilman daringly projects mental derangement onto a middle-class wife and mother and makes the home, the sacrosanct sphere for dutiful women, the source of madness. Poe, rather, cre-ates an idiosyncratic character and makes madness a character flaw. Noting this essential distinction, Kolodny argues: "those for whom the woman in the home was a familiar literary character were hard-pressed to comprehend so extreme an anatomy of the psychic price she paid"—or to accept the connection between insanity and the politics of gender. Kolodny concludes that Gilman's readers were not ready to accept these connections, which is why Gilman's story, unlike Poe's tales, took so long in finding its way into print.

Building on Hedges's 1973 "Afterword," Kolodny is one of many 1970s and 1980s critics who perpetuate the notion of dichotomous readings between Gilman's contemporaries, notably Horace Scudder and William Dean Howells, and Kolodny's own feminist contemporaries. A close look at the responses by Scudder and Howells suggests that these reviewers may have comprehended the politics of gender all too well, making it a "literary dead-end" to keep it from influencing impressionable young women.

[. . .]

The appearance of Kate Chopin's novel *The Awakening* in 1899, for example, perplexed readers familiar with her earlier (and intentionally "regional") short stories not so much because it turned away from themes or subject matter implicit in her earlier work, nor even less because it dealt with female sensuality and extramarital sexuality, but because her elaboration of those materials deviated radically from the accepted norms of women's fiction out of which her audience so largely derived its expectations. [. . .]

[. . .]

Charlotte Perkins Gilman's initial difficulty in seeing "The Yellow Wallpaper" into print repeated the problem, albeit in a somewhat different context: for her story located itself not as any deviation from a previous tradition of women's fiction but, instead, as a continuation of a genre popularized by Poe. And insofar as Americans had earlier learned to follow the fictive processes of aberrant per-ception and mental breakdown in *his* work, they should have provided Gilman, one would imagine, with a ready-made audience for *her* protagonist's progres-sively debilitating fantasies of entrapment and liberation. As they had entered popular fiction by the end of the nineteenth century, however, the linguistic mark-ers for those processes were at once heavily male-gendered and highly idio-syncratic, having more to do with individual temperament than with social or cultural situations *per se*. As a result, it would appear that the reading strategies by which cracks in ancestral walls and suggestions of unchecked masculine will-fulness were immediately noted as both symbolically and semantically relevant did not, for some reason, necessarily *carry over* to "the nursery at the top of the house" with its windows barred, nor even less to the forced submission of the woman who must "take great pains to control myself before" her physician husband.

A reader today seeking meaning in the way Harold Bloom outlines that process might note, of course, a fleeting resemblance between the upstairs chamber in Gilman – with its bed nailed to the floor, its windows barred, and metal rings fixed to the walls – and Poe's evocation of the dungeon chambers of Toledo; in fact, a credible argument might be made for reading "The Yellow Wallpaper" as Gilman's willful and purposeful misprision of "The Pit and the Pendulum." Both stories, after all, involve a sane mind entrapped in an insanity-inducing situation. Gilman's "message" might then be that the equivalent revolution by which the speaking voice of the Poe tale is released to both sanity and freedom is unavailable to her heroine. No *deus ex machina*, no General Lasalle triumphantly entering the city, no "outstretched arm" to prevent Gilman's protagonist from falling into her own internal "abyss" is conceivable, given the rules of the social context in which Gilman's narrative is embedded. When gender is taken into account, then, so this interpretation would run, Gilman is saying that the nature of the trap envisioned must be understood as qualitatively different, and so too the possible escape routes.

Contemporary readers of "The Yellow Wallpaper," however, were apparently unprepared to make such connections. Those fond of Poe could not easily transfer their sense of mental derangement to the mind of a comfortable middle-class wife and mother; and those for whom the woman in the home was a familiar literary character were hard-pressed to comprehend so extreme an anatomy of the psychic price she paid. Horace Scudder, the editor of *The Atlantic Monthly* who first rejected the story, wrote only that "I could not forgive myself if I made others as miserable as I have made myself!" (Hedges, p. 40). And even William Dean Howells, who found the story "chilling" and admired it sufficiently to reprint it in 1920, some twenty-eight years after its first publication (in *The New England Magazine* of Jan. 1892), like most readers, either failed to notice or neglected to report "the connection between the insanity and the sex, or sexual role, of the victim" (Hedges, p. 41). For readers at the turn of the century, then, that "meaning" which "is always wandering around between texts" had as yet failed to find connective pathways linking the fanciers of Poe to the devotees of popular women's fiction, or the shortcut between Gilman's short story and the myriad published feminist analyses of the ills of society (some of them written by Gilman herself). Without such connective contexts, Poe continued as a well-traveled road, while Gilman's story, lacking the possibility of further influence, became a literary dead-end.

[. . .]

From **Mary Jacobus, "An Unnecessary Maze of Sign Reading,"** in *Reading Women. Essays in Feminist Criticism* (New York: Columbia University Press), 1986, 229–48

Also building upon Hedges's 1973 "Afterword," Jacobus sets out to examine the smell of the yellow wallpaper and its perturbing color. To Jacobus, the narrator is "an incarnation not only of hysteria but of male fears about women." She sees the yellow dirty "stain" of a "smooch" on the narrator as a literal representation of unmentionable sexuality, repressed in Victorian America, just as women's writing was. The narrator's cultural repression reduces her to overreading the wallpaper and eventually to animalhood.

Jacobus equates the hysterical narrator with Brontë's madwoman in the attic of Thornfield Hall, but her association is far different from Gilbert and Gubar's (see **pp. 91–2**). To Jacobus, "The woman on all fours is like Bertha Mason, an embodiment of the animality of woman unredeemed by (masculine) reason." While some critics read the narrator's act of crawling over her husband as a triumph (e.g. the narrator overcoming John), Jacobus, rather, sees it as a sign of regression, terrifying to her practical and pragmatic doctor/husband who faints at the sight of her. The yellow smell that the narrator exudes is a powerful odor of female genitalia, derived in part from menstruation and associated with sexuality itself. As Jacobus concludes, the foul haunting smell comes not only from the narrator's genitalia but from John's hysteria, a response to the power of "mother" to threaten masculine reason with a return to infancy and castration. Jo. H. Hatfield's third and final illustration for the New England Magazine version of the story supports Jacobus's argument in drawing Doctor John fainted on the floor in a fetal position (see **p. 145**).

[. . .]

"Now why should that man have fainted?" The narrator's question returns us to male hysteria. The body of woman is hystericized as the uncanny—defined by Freud as the sight of something that should remain hidden; typically, the sight of the female genitals. The woman on all fours is like Bertha Mason, an embodiment of the animality of woman unredeemed by (masculine) reason. Her creeping can only be physical—it is the story that assumes her displaced psychic uncanniness to become "creepy"—since by the end she is all body, an incarnation not only of hysteria but of male fears about women. The female hysteric displaces her thoughts onto her body: the male hysteric displaces his fear of castration, his anxiety, onto her genitals. Seemingly absent from "The Yellow Wallpaper," both the female body (female sexuality) and male hysteria leave their traces on the paper in a stain or a whiff—in a yellow "smooch" and a yellow smell that first appear in metonymic proximity to one another in Gilman's text:

[. . .]

At the end of the story, the narrator's own shoulder "just fits in that long smooch around the wall" (p. 35). The mark of repetition, the uncanny trace made by the present stuck in the groove of the past, the "smooch" is also a smudge or smear, a reciprocal dirtying, perhaps (the wallpaper leaves "yellow smooches on all my clothes and John's" p. 27). In the 1890s, "smooch" had not taken on its slangy mid-twentieth-century meaning (as in "I'd rather have hooch/And a bit of

a smooch" [1945]).[1] The "smooch" on the yellow wallpaper cannot yet be a
natural caress, although dirty rubbing might be both Doctor John's medical ver-
dict on sexuality and the story's hysterical literalization of it. As such, the dirty
stain of smooching would constitute not just the unmentionable aspect of the
narrator's genteel marital incapacity, but the unsayable in Gilman's story—the
sexual etiology of hysteria, certainly (repressed in Gilman's as in Breuer's[2] text);
but also the repression imposed by the 1890s on the representation of female
sexuality and, in particular, the repression imposed on women's writing.

And what of the "yellow smell"?—a smell that creeps, like the figure in the text;
presumably the smell of decay, of "old foul, bad yellow things."[. . .]

[. . .]The bad smell that haunts the narrator in "The Yellow Wallpaper" is
both the one she makes and the smell of male hysteria emanating from her
husband—that is, fear of femininity as the body of the mother ("old, foul, bad
yellow things") which simultaneously threatens the boy with a return to the
powerlessness of infancy and with anxiety about the castration she embodies.

[. . .]

From Janice Haney-Peritz, "Monumental Feminism and Literature's Ancestral House: Another Look at 'The Yellow Wallpaper,' " Women's Studies 12:2 (1986): 113–28

Haney-Peritz takes a critical look at the wave of scholarship following the 1973
Feminist Press republication of "The Yellow Wall-Paper." Her essay, which
reads the wallpaper in Lacanian psychoanalytic terms, might best be seen as a
reaction to pioneering critics who, in their sympathetic readings, tried to coun-
ter a "male line of response" to the story—Gilman's first husband, Walter
Stetson; M. D. (the anonymous reviewer for The Boston Evening Transcript); Atlantic Monthly editor Horace Scudder; and noted author William Dean Howells, to
name a few. Haney-Peritz evaluates pioneering feminist interpretations before
positing her own; she models a responsibility facing today's readers in light of
the wealth of criticism on the story that shows no sign of abating. Haney-Peritz
responds specifically to the work of Elaine Hedges, Sandra Gilbert and Susan
Gubar, and Annette Kolodny—reprinted in this sourcebook—as well as Jean
Kennard and then goes on to offer a far darker reading of the story. She looks
not to the oppressive social structures of patriarchy confronting the narrator in
the story, but to the challenges the narrator faces in representing herself
through a language that is itself male-dominated (an approach Paula Treichler
also takes in her essay "Escaping the Sentence: Dialogue and Discourse in 'The
Yellow Wallpaper' " in The Captive Imagination). Haney-Peritz suggests that
the narrator, in bonding with what she perceives as a real woman trapped in

1   [Jacobus's note.] "Once upon a time you 'spooned,' then you 'petted,' after that you 'necked' . . .
     but now you may 'smooch' "(1937); Harold Wentworth and Stuart Berg Flexner, Dictionary of
     American Slang (New York: Thomas Y. Crowell Co., 1975).
2   Jacobus refers to Josef Breuer, the Austrian physician whose theory of hysteria influenced Sigmund
     Freud; Breuer wrote Studies in Hysteria (1895) together with Freud.

the paper, yields to the symbolic realm of male discourse, which constructs her identity as a speaker and writer.

Haney-Peritz categorically disputes Gilbert and Gubar for their metaphorical use of the narrator's phrase "open country" (see **p. 92**). Whereas Gilbert and Gubar perceive the narrator's bonding with and freeing of the trapped woman as liberating—a move into "open country"—Haney-Peritz argues that these same actions embed the narrator firmly in fantasy, "the realm of haunted houses." In Haney-Peritz's view, Gilman's short story has assumed "monumental proportions" as a memorial making vivid the struggles of late nineteenth-century feminists against patriarchal domination and as a boundary marker laying out a viable form of feminist literary criticism. In her provocative conclusion, Haney-Peritz insists that if the story be read as a memorial, it must be considered a "*memento mori*," a Latin term (that signifies the death of (a) woman)—not a model of liberation and identification to inspire a significant body of feminist literary criticism. "The Yellow Wall-Paper" Is but a cautionary tale of what happens as a woman turns to the imaginary when her mode of self-expression in communication—writing in a journal—becomes repressed. However, like many pioneering scholars whom she criticizes (including Hedges and Gilbert and Gubar), Haney-Peritz, at the conclusion of her article, turns from literature to Gilman's life for inspiration.

[. . .]

It is this male line of response that the 1973 edition of "The Yellow Wallpaper" seeks to disrupt and displace, implicitly by affixing to the text the imprint of The Feminist Press and explicitly by appending to the text an afterword in which Elaine Hedges reads the story as a "feminist document," as "one of the rare pieces of literature we have by a nineteenth-century woman which directly confronts the sexual politics of the male-female, husband-wife relationship." So effective has this disruption and displacement been that it is not much of an exaggeration to say that during the last ten years, Gilman's short story has assumed monumental proportions, serving at one and the same time the purposes of a memorial and a boundary marker. As a memorial, "The Yellow Wallpaper" is used to remind contemporary readers of the enduring import of the feminist struggle against patriarchical domination; while as a boundary marker, it is used to demarcate the territory appropriate to a feminist literary criticism.[1] Although I am interested in pointing out some of the more troubling implications of a literary criticism in

---

1   [Haney-Peritz's note.] Although much of this monumentalizing occurs within classes devoted to women's studies or women's literature, at least three influential publications treat the story as both a memorial and a boundary marker: Sandra Gilbert and Susan Gubar, *The Madwoman in the Attic: The Woman Writer and the Nineteenth-Century Literary Imagination* (New Haven: Yale University Press, 1979), pp. 89–92; Annette Kolodny, "A Map for Rereading: Or, Gender and the Interpretation of Literary Texts," *NLH*, 11 (1980), 451–467; and Jean Kennard, "Convention Coverage or How to Read Your Own Life," *NLH* 13 (1981), 69–88.

which Gilman's story functions as a feminist monument, before doing so, it is necessary to take another look at "The Yellow Wallpaper" itself.

[. . .]

In the final words of "The Yellow Wallpaper," the narrator describes how she must crawl over John's astonished body. Like the transitivism[2] of the narrator's "self-realization," this closing image displays a conjunction of erotic and aggressive impulses, a conjunction which once again suggests that by identifying herself with the wallpaper's shadow-woman, the narrator has firmly installed herself in the realm of the imaginary, the realm of haunted houses.

[. . .]

In "The Yellow Wallpaper," the narrator does not move out into open country; instead, she turns an ancestral hall into a haunted house and then encrypts herself therein as a fantasy figure. If we wish to consider the result of this turn to be a feminist monument, then perhaps it would be better to read such a monument as a *memento mori* that signifies the death of (a) woman rather than as a memorial that encloses the body essential to a viable feminist literary criticism. Unlike a memorial, a *memento mori* would provoke sympathy rather than identification and in so doing, would encourage us to apprehend the turn to the imaginary not as a model of liberation but as a sign of what may happen when a possible operation of the feminine in *language* is repressed.

If such an apprehension seems an uninspiring alternative for those of us committed to feminism, then I suggest that we look to Gilman rather than to the narrator of "The Yellow Wallpaper" for the inspiration we seek. By representing the narrator as in some sense mad, Gilman can be said to have preferred sympathy to identification, a preference which becomes all the more significant once we recall that much of "The Yellow Wallpaper" is based on Gilman's personal experience. However, Gilman did more than sympathize, for as Dolores Hayden has documented, she also involved herself in efforts to change the material conditions of social existence through the construction of kitchenless houses and feminist apartment hotels – new architectural spaces in which alternative social and discursive relations might emerge.[3] Although those of us interested in literature may find Gilman's concern for the material conditions of social life a troubling defection, it is also quite possible to consider that concern a thoughtful deferral based on a recognition that the prevailing social structure made it idealistic, if not dangerously presumptuous to lay claim to having identified either the woman's story or female meaning. Indeed, it may just be that what Gilman learned in writing and reading "The Yellow Wallpaper" was that as yet, a woman could only *imagine* that she had found herself, for until the material conditions of social life

---

2 Transitivism describes a transitory state as well as changeableness.
3 [Haney-Peritz's note.] Dolores Hayden, *The Grand Domestic Revolution: A History of Feminist Designs for American Homes, Neighborhoods, and Cities* (Cambridge: MIT Press, 1981), pp. 182–277.

were radically changed, there would be no "real" way out of mankind's ancestral mansion of many apartments.

From **Walter Benn Michaels, "Introduction,"** *The Gold Standard and the Logic of Naturalism: American Literature at the Turn of the Century* (Berkeley, Los Angeles and London: University of California Press, 1987), 4–6, 13–14

Just when some 1980s feminist critics began to deflate "The Yellow Wall-Paper" as an exemplary text, new historicists came to embrace it for its ideological underpinnings. Walter Benn Michaels launches his book on late nineteenth-century American literature and capitalism with an examination of "The Yellow Wall-Paper." Benn Michaels offers a Derridean reading of the story, discussing it in terms of production and consumption, processes essential to capitalism.

To Benn Michaels, the narrator suffers from "overproduction": the story "is about a woman driven crazy (if she is crazy) by a commitment to production so complete that it requires her to begin by producing herself." The production is writing, first in secret on "dead paper" and then with her body when she creeps in the room and rubs against the wallpaper, which gains animation—odor, movement, color—and, in turn, "stains" her clothes with yellow smooches. Benn Michaels equates the narrator's marked body as well as her writing of her own body against the wall as acts that place her in a chain of capitalist production. He reads the narrator's assertion that she "came out of that wall-paper" (see **p. 143**) as a declaration that she has, in essence, written herself into being as she wishes to be or given birth to herself, a process he calls "self-generation." Ultimately, the narrator becomes consumed in this process and succumbs to what some perceive to be madness—Benn Michaels leaves that issue open. From the perspective of consumer capitalism, he concludes firmly that we read the narrator's nursery—a site of patriarchal repression to Hedges and Gilbert and Gubar—as a marketplace; "The Yellow Wall-Paper" itself becomes "the genesis of the marketplace or, more specifically, the birth of what historians have come to call . . . the 'culture of consumption.' "

[. . .]

But while it is perfectly true that the seemingly crazy narrator of "The Yellow Wallpaper" is forbidden by her doctor husband to write, it is by no means the case that she doesn't in fact do a lot of writing. For one thing, the story is told as a kind of diary. And for another, the "dead paper" on which it is written is so strikingly analogized to the "inanimate thing" (7) that is the wallpaper itself, with its "lame uncertain curves" (5), which, violating "every principle of design" (9), may come to seem unreadable as a decorative "pattern" precisely to the extent that they come to seem readable as a kind of writing—or, if that seems too strong, as a kind of marking. For the narrator's two main activities in "The

Yellow Wallpaper" are both forms of marking: she makes marks on paper when she writes, and she also makes "a very funny mark" on the wall when she creeps around the room, "a long, straight, even *smooch*, as if it had been rubbed over and over" (15). Marks may be produced either by covering paper or by uncovering it. And in the course of this marking, the "dead paper," "inanimate thing," comes alive; it begins to move, it begins to smell, it begins to mark back—the "smooch" the narrator makes on the wallpaper is doubled by the "yellow smooches" (14) the wallpaper makes on the narrator. Her own body thus takes its place in the chain of writing surfaces, and she herself comes to seem an animated effect of writing; for not only does her body bear the trace of writing but also it is described as having literally emerged from the wallpaper, so that she can end by wondering if those other "creeping women" "come out of the wallpaper as I did" (18). It is as if she has written herself into her body or, more precisely perhaps, written herself into existence. " 'I want to mark!' " says the child in *Women and Economics*: "He is not seeking to get something into himself but to put something out of himself" (117). Beginning with the child's desire to put something out of herself, the narrator of "The Yellow Wallpaper" ends by writing herself into herself.

I suggest, then, that the work of writing in "The Yellow Wallpaper" is the work of something like self-generation and that, far from being a story about a woman driven crazy by Weir Mitchell's refusal to allow her to produce, it is about a woman driven crazy (if she is crazy) by a commitment to production so complete that it requires her to begin by producing herself. Weir Mitchell recommended the infantilization of nervous women; sufferers from "hysterical motor ataxia" were given kneepads and taught to balance themselves on all fours before learning to "creep." After creeping came walking: "following nature's lessons with docile mind, we have treated the woman as nature treats an infant."[1] "The Yellow Wallpaper" repeats and extends this treatment—not only does the narrator creep, but she also ties herself to the bed with an umbilical cord ("I am securely fastened now by my well-hidden rope" [18])—while reimagining the return to infancy as a moment of willed self-begetting.

[. . .]

For Gilman, then, the work of writing is the work simultaneously of production and consumption, a work in which woman's body is rewritten as the utopian body of the market economy, imagined as a scene of circulation so efficient that exchange is instantaneous: products not only exist to be consumed, but coming into existence they already are consumed. My point here is not to insist on the utopian character of this description (although given the prolonged crisis of what in the eighties and nineties was universally understood as "overproduction," the term *utopian* is hardly inappropriate) but to emphasize the importance for Gilman of the feminine body, understood not only as an object to be exchanged—

---

1 [Benn Michaels's note.] Mitchell, *Lectures on Diseases of the Nervous System* (Philadelphia, 1885), 47.

as when the newly professionalized mothers of *Women and Economics* sell their maternal skills—but as the very site of exchange. In "The Yellow Wallpaper," being oneself depends on owning oneself, and owning oneself depends on producing oneself. Producing is thus a kind of buying—it gives you title to yourself—and a kind of selling too—your labor in making yourself is sold for the self you have made. There can be no question, then, of the self entering into exchange; exchange is the condition of its existence. Producer and consumer, buyer and seller, the narrator of "The Yellow Wallpaper" need not leave her nursery to follow the other creeping women out into the market; her nursery already is the market. Her nervous breakdown marks for Gilman the triumphant omnipresence of market relations.

To read "The Yellow Wallpaper" in this way, then, is to read it as narrating the genesis of the marketplace or, more specifically, the birth of what historians have come to call (with varying degrees of disapproval) the "culture of consumption." [. . .]

From **Catherine J. Golden, "The Writing of 'The Yellow Wallpaper': A Double Palimpsest"** (1989), revised for Denise D. Knight, ed. *Charlotte Perkins Gilman: A Study of the Short Fiction* (New York: Twayne, 1997), 155–65

Style, word choice, and grammar function as agents of meaning in "The Yellow Wall-Paper," Gilman's best-written tale. Catherine Golden argues that while the narrator's actions of crawling on the floor and tearing the wallpaper speak to her descent into madness, the writing of "The Yellow Wall-Paper" tells a different story. Building upon the work of Judith Fetterley (see Further Reading, **pp. 158–9**), Golden suggests that we read this tale as a double "palimpsest," a term that describes, for example, a piece of parchment written upon, erased, and then written on again so that the original faded writing emerges as a second muted or background pattern. The yellow wallpaper has a front or dominant pattern of bars and a back or muted pattern of a figure trapped behind them. Likewise, the narrator's dramatic actions—tearing the wallpaper and creeping—function as the dominant text of the story while the narrator's language, particularly her pronoun usage and references to John, form a second muted text. Linguistic and syntactic features, such as the first-person narration, reveal a dramatic change in the narrator's identity and self-awareness at the point when the dominant text of her actions compromises her sanity and dooms her to madness.

The excerpts that follow offer a close linguistic and syntactic reading to demonstrate how in Gilman's carefully crafted tale, form conveys meaning. Highlighting a syntactical and linguistic reversal in gender dynamics, Golden challenges an interpretation of defeat and insanity (see, for example, Hedges, **pp. 88–90**). The narrator has a qualified victory: she gains a defiant voice as she creeps into madness and banishes John—whom she now calls "that man" and "him"—to the outskirts of her own "sentence."

The first-person narrative of "The Yellow Wallpaper" unfolds as a diary written by a woman undergoing a three month rest cure for a postpartum depression. Judith Fetterley has argued that the wallpaper functions as a text through which the narrator expresses herself; its pattern becomes the dominant text and the woman behind the pattern the subtext with which the narrator identifies.[1] To recall the terminology of *The Madwoman in the Attic*, the yellow wallpaper thus can be perceived as a "palimpsest." Similarly, Charlotte Perkins Gilman's story itself can be read as a palimpsest. The hallucinations and dramatic actions of tearing the wallpaper and creeping on the floor comprise the dominant text, but the writing comprises the second muted text, informing the narrator's final characterization. This muted text shows how the narrator fictionalizes herself as the audience of her story. Forbidden to write but continuing to do so in secret, the narrator comes to express herself by writing her own text. As she comes to see the wallpaper as a palimpsest, she presents herself on paper in a way that suggests that, although mad, she is not completely "destroyed"[2] by her patriarchal society. As the story unfolds, the narrator's writing ceases to match her thoughts and actions or to convey a cohesive characterization of a timid oppressed figure. The increased use of "I" and her syntactical placement of the nominative case pronoun within her own sentences demonstrate a positive change in self-presentation precisely at the point when her actions dramatically compromise her sanity and condemn her to madness.[3]

The narrator records her stay in a country ancestral hall through twelve diary-like entries, each undated and separated only by several lines of blank space. The separateness of these units can be seen as a spatial indication of the narrator's own fragmented sense of self. As Walter Ong notes, the audience of a diarist is oneself "encased in fictions. . . . The diarist pretending to be talking to himself has also, since he is writing, to pretend he is somehow not there. And to what self is he talking? To the self he imagines he is? Or would like to be?"[4] Although the narrator may in fact be writing for a fictional self, the way she imagines this self to be changes as the entries continue. [. . .]

---

1   [Golden's note.] Judith Fetterley, "Reading About Reading: 'A Jury of Her Peers,' 'The Murders in the Rue Morgue,' and 'The Yellow Wallpaper,'" in *Gender and Reading: Essays on Readers, Texts, and Contexts*, ed. Elizabeth A. Flynn and Patrocinio P. Schweikart (Baltimore: Johns Hopkins University Press, 1986), pp. 147—64. Fetterley advances that "blocked from expressing herself *on* paper, she seeks to express herself through paper" (p. 162). Although my reading concurs with and draws upon Fetterley's analysis, I would argue that the narrator does not experience writer's "block." While writing less and less frequently, she, in fact, writes more forcefully as she expresses herself through the paper and gets in to the subtext.

2   [Golden's note.] Elaine R. Hedges, "Afterword," *The Yellow Wallpaper* (New York: The Feminist Press, 1973), p. 55. Hedges praises the late nineteenth-century work because it authenticates the experience of women restricted by a patriarchal society, but she concludes that the narrator's final actions confirm her destruction.

3   [Golden's note.] The relationship between language and the mental and social condition of the narrator has not gone undetected in previous literary and biographical criticism. See Hedges, pp. 48–49, on paragraphing and mental state; Annette Kolodny, "A Map for Rereading: Or, Gender and the Interpretation of Literary Texts," *New Literary History*, 11 (1980), 458–59, on pronouns and identity; and Treichler, *Tulsa Studies in Women's Literature* 3 (1984) p. 75, on the narrator as language user. These observations suggest a need for a systematic examination of the way the narrator writes to herself and for herself in her patriarchal society. Verb usage, discussed only briefly in this article, remains a rich field for systematic examination.

4   [Golden's note.] Walter Ong, "A Writer's Audience Is Always a Fiction," *PMLA*, 90 (1975), 20.

[. . .]

More than the tone of writing or pronoun usage, the placement of pronouns in this closing paragraph reveals the narrator's growing sense of awareness of her former submissive state and a reversal of the power dynamics of gender. Relegating John to a modifying phrase following an intransitive verb, the narrator assumes the subject position within the final clause. This sentence, in fact, exchanges the grammatical positions the narrator originally elected for each to occupy in a grammatically similar sentence on the opening page of "The Yellow Wallpaper": "John laughs at me, of course, but one expects that in marriage" (p. 9). In selecting an intransitive verb to convey John's abuse, the narrator in her early writing undeniably isolates herself from his emotional cruelty. The verb "to laugh" can only function intransitively and thus cannot possess or envelop the narrator, "me," as its object. But, in doing so, the narrator relegates herself (and later John) to a weak position within the formal bounds of the sentence. Not a basic or essential sentence part, the prepositional phrase "at me" functions as a modifier embellishing the sentence (in this case adverbially). Governed only by the preposition "at," the narrator in the first entry can be dropped from her sentence, which would thus read grammatically: "John laughs . . ., of course, but one expects that in marriage." With such a revision her presence would remain only through a disguised reference to self ("one"). However, by changing positions with John in the grammatically similar sentence in the twelfth entry, the narrator now sends John—who has fainted to the floor—to a non-essential, powerless, syntactical place. Governed only by the preposition "over," John can be dropped from her final clause, which would thus read grammatically: "I had to creep . . . every time!" (p. 36). The narrator's actions are outside the realm of sanity, but the syntactic position she comes to occupy conveys her emerging sense of defiance against one of the forces in her patriarchal society that has fragmented her.

Other examples, particularly in the final four paragraphs of the twelfth entry, join with this exchange of grammatical positions to affirm the narrator's newly imagined self:

> "What is the matter?" he cried. "For God's sake, what are you doing!"
> I kept on creeping just the same, but I looked at him over my shoulder.
> "I've got out at last," said I, "in spite of you and Jane. And I've pulled off most of the paper, so you can't put me back!"
> Now why should that man have fainted? But he did, and right across my path by the wall, so that I had to creep over him every time!
> (p. 36)

John's name seems conspicuously absent from these paragraphs. Four times the narrator substitutes the nominative case for John's name ("he cried" and "he did" within her narration and "you" twice in her dialogue). Within these paragraphs she thrice substitutes the objective case for John and further reduces his status by making each pronoun an object of a preposition ("at him," "of you," and "over him"). In the final paragraph she also uses the demonstrative pronoun "that" in "that man," a detached and generic reference to John. Unlike the demonstrative "this," "that" points the reader to something or someone who is respectively farther away in a spatial sense and thus works to distance the reader and the narrator from John and his authority, to which she once readily adhered. Used to direct the reader to a preceding rather than a subsequent reference, "that man" also orients the reader to the previous rather than the two future references to him, occurring in the final sentence; the wording anticipates John's disappearance from the final dramatic clause and close of "The Yellow Wallpaper," which leaves the narrator creeping flamboyantly in the daylight as she desires.

The narrator presents herself as "I" six times in the final four paragraphs, twice forcefully beginning her own paragraphs. She displays her growing sense of self, power, and confidence at the point at which she has uncoded the text of the yellow wallpaper and liberated its muted side. In addition, an exclamation point at the end of both the last and the penultimate paragraphs gives emphasis to her final sentences, in which she moves into the subject place initially reserved for John. When referring to self, she uses the possessive case twice and the objective case once, but she no longer positions the objective case reference for self in a precarious place. Importantly, in the sentence "can't put me back," "me" functions as a direct object of the transitive verb "put." Securely positioned, "me" becomes essentially connected to the action verb. The use of negation in this sentence subtly undermines the contents of earlier sentences containing transitive verbs, such as "John gathered me up in his arms, and just carried me upstairs and laid me on the bed" (p. 21); while in both sentences "me" carries the force of her male oppressor, the negation in the later sentence equally negates his force and matches the writing in the finale, where the narrator is able to write a sentence that can function grammatically without "John."

Examining the muted text of the narrator's writing within this palimpsest in relation to the dominant text of her delusional actions permits the narrator a dubious victory. Her widening use of "I" and grammatical repositioning of "I" and "John" hint at a degree of personal liberation for her fictionalized self recorded within this tale of a woman's breakdown. The muted text of her writing comes to reflect her growing self-awareness as she moves beyond the prescription of healthy eating, moderate exercise, and abundant rest and chooses literal madness over John's prescription for sanity. As the narrator tears the paper to free the woman and that part of herself trapped within the story's mirrored palimpsest and creeps over her husband, she acts in a way that implies a cogent madness, rid of the timidity and fear that punctuate her earlier entries. Only at the point at which she acts out of madness does she find a place within the patriarchal language she uses, although not yet within her larger social reality. Creeping deeper into madness and her fictionalized self, the narrator writes in a defiant voice, circumvents John's force, and banishes "him" to the outer boundaries of her own sentence.

From **Susan Lanser, "Feminist Criticism, 'The Yellow Wallpaper,'
and the Politics of Color in America,"** Feminist Studies 15:3 (Fall 1989):
415–41

Critic Susan Lanser recognizes Gilman's darker side—her racism, ethnocentrism, and classicism as well as her belief in eugenics. The story's feminist
thrust becomes secondary when Lanser sets the tale in its political and ideological contexts of racial anxiety and nativism. "The Yellow Wall-Paper"
emerges as a product of a late nineteenth-century American culture obsessed
with issues of race due to the mass immigration of peoples from Asia and
southern and eastern Europe. Lanser challenges the canonical status of "The
Yellow Wall-Paper" established by feminist critics of the 1970s and 1980s. She
criticizes the practice of white academics searching the story for support of
their own interpretations of the wallpaper as a text of patriarchy or as a woman's text. To Lanser, rather, the wallpaper is culture's text and, particularly, a
reflection of the Yellow Peril.
    The central symbol of the story, with its distinctive yellow color and odor,
comes to signify uncleanness, inferiority, and the racial "Other." The wallpaper
functions as a repository for problems of race, class, and ethnicity rooted in the
psychic geography of turn-of-the-twentieth-century America obsessed with the
Yellow Peril; in fact, these nativist tendencies, disturbing to readers today,
become particularly evident in Gilman's post-1900 writings. As Lanser notes,
"For if anxieties about race, class, and ethnicity have inscribed themselves as a
political unconscious upon the yellow wallpaper, they were conscious and
indeed obsessive problems for Gilman herself." Lanser importantly initiates
discussion of the limitations and biases of Gilman's life and legacy, the subject of
The Mixed Legacy of Charlotte Perkins Gilman (2000), edited by Catherine J.
Golden and Joanna Schneider Zangrando and published by University of Delaware Press. Gilman's persistent presentation of racial, ethnic, religious, and class
stereotypes remains a topic for further development in Gilman studies.

[. . .]

[. . .] If we locate Gilman's story within the "psychic geography" of Anglo-
America at the turn of the century, we locate it in a culture obsessively pre-
occupied with race as the foundation of character, a culture desperate to maintain
Aryan superiority in the face of massive immigrations from Southern and Eastern
Europe, a culture openly anti-Semitic, anti-Asian, anti-Catholic, and Jim Crow. In
New England, where Gilman was born and raised, agricultural decline, native
emigration, and soaring immigrant birth rates had generated "a distrust of the
immigrant [that] reached the proportions of a movement in the 1880's and
1890's."[1] In California, where Gilman lived while writing "The Yellow
Wallpaper," mass anxiety about the "Yellow Peril" had already yielded such

---

1 [Lanser's note.] Thomas F. Gossett, *Race: The History of an Idea in America* (Dallas: Southern
Methodist University Press, 1975), 299.

legislation as the Chinese Exclusion Act of 1882.[2] Across the United States, newly formed groups were calling for selective breeding, restricted entry, and "American Protection" of various kinds. White, Christian, American-born intellectuals – novelists, political scientists, economists, sociologists, crusaders for social reform – not only shared this racial anxiety but, as John Higham puts it, "blazed the way for ordinary nativists" by giving popular racism an "intellectual respectability."[3]

[. . .]

Implicit or explicit in these descriptions is a new racial ideology through which "newcomers from Europe could seem a fundamentally different order" from what were then called "native Americans." The common nineteenth-century belief in three races – black, white, yellow – each linked to a specific continent, was reconstituted so that "white" came to mean only "Nordic" or Northern European, while "yellow" applied not only to the Chinese, Japanese, and light-skinned African-Americans but also to Jews, Poles, Hungarians, Italians, and even the Irish. Crusaders warned of "yellow inundation." The California chapter of the Protestant white supremacist Junior Order of United American Mechanics teamed up with the Asiatic Exclusion League to proclaim that Southern Europeans were "semi-Mongolian" and should be excluded from immigration and citizenship on the same basis as the Chinese; Madison Grant declared Jews to be "a Mongrel admixture ... of Slavs and of Asiatic invaders of Russia"; and a member of Congress announced that " 'the color of thousands' " of the new immigrants " 'differs materially from that of the Anglo-Saxon.' " The greatest dangers were almost always traced back to Asia; in a dazzling conflation of enemies, for example, Grant warned that " 'in the guise of Bolshevism with Semitic leadership and Chinese executioners, [Asia] is organizing an assault upon Western Europe.' " Lothrop Stoddard predicted that " 'colored migration' " was yielding the " 'very immediate danger that the white stocks may be swamped by Asiatic blood.' " Again and again, nativists announced that democracy "simply will not work among Asiatics," that "non-Aryans," especially Slavs, Italians, and Jews, were "impossible to Americanize." The threat of "Yellow Peril" thus had "racial implications" much broader than anxiety about a takeover of Chinese or Japanese: "in every section, the Negro, the Oriental, and the Southern European appeared more and more in a common light."[4] In such a cultural moment, "yellow" readily connoted inferiority, strangeness, cowardice, ugliness, and backwardness. "Yellow-belly" and "yellow dog" were common slurs, the former

---

2   The 1882 Chinese Exclusion Act was a treaty banning Chinese immigration for ten years. In a new treaty of 1894, China accepted immigration exclusion for another ten years; this policy continued until 1924 when Congress enacted an immigration law excluding all Asians.

3   [Lanser's note.] John Higham, *Strangers in the Land: Patterns of American Nativism, 1860–1925*, 2nd ed. (New York: Atheneum, 1975), 133, 39.

4   [Lanser's note.] Roger Daniels and Harry Kitano, *American Racism: Exploration of the Nature of Prejudice* (Englewood Cliffs, N.J.: Prentice-Hall, 1970), 44; Higham, 174; Madison Grant, *The Conquest of a Continent* (New York: Scribners, 1933), 255; Higham, 168; Madison Grant, *The Passing of the Great Race* (1916), cited in Daniels and Kitano, 55; Lothrop Stoddard, cited in Daniels and Kitano, 55; Grant, *The Conquest of a Continent*, 356; and Higham, 166, 173.

applied to groups as diverse as the Irish and the Mexicans. Associations of "yellow" with disease, cowardice, worthlessness, uncleanliness, and decay may also have become implicit associations of race and class.

If "The Yellow Wallpaper" is read within this discourse of racial anxiety, certain of its tropes take on an obvious political charge. [. . .]

[. . .]

Is the wallpaper, then, the political unconscious of a culture in which an Aryan woman's madness, desire, and anger, repressed by the imperatives of "reason," "duty" (p. 14), and "proper self-control" (p. 11), are projected onto the "yellow" woman who is, however, also the feared alien? When the narrator tries to liberate the woman from the wall, is she trying to purge her of her color, to peel her from the yellow paper, so that she can accept this woman as herself? If, as I suggested earlier, the wallpaper is at once the text of patriarchy and the woman's text, then perhaps the narrator is both resisting and embracing the woman of color who is self and not-self, a woman who might need to be rescued from the text of patriarchy but cannot yet be allowed to go free. Might we explain the narrator's pervasive horror of a yellow color and smell that threaten to take over the "ancestral halls," "stain-[ing] everything it touched," as the British-American fear of a takeover by "aliens"? In a cultural moment when immigrant peoples and African Americans were being widely caricatured in the popular press through distorted facial and bodily images, might the "interminable grotesques" (p. 20) of "The Yellow Wallpaper" – with their lolling necks and "bulbous eyes" "staring everywhere," with their "peculiar odor" and "yellow smell" (p. 29), their colors "repellent, almost revolting," "smouldering" and "unclean" (p. 13), "sickly" and "particularly irritating" (p. 18), their "new shades of yellow" (p. 28) erupting constantly – figure the Asians and Jews, the Italians and Poles, the long list of "aliens" whom the narrator (and perhaps Gilman herself) might want at once to rescue and to flee?

For if anxieties about race, class, and ethnicity have inscribed themselves as a political unconscious upon the yellow wallpaper, they were conscious and indeed obsessive problems for Gilman herself, as I discovered when, disturbed by my own reading of "The Yellow Wallpaper," I turned to Gilman's later work. Despite her socialist values, her active participation in movements for reform, her strong theoretical commitment to racial harmony, her unconventional support of interracial marriages, and her frequent condemnation of America's racist history,[5] Gilman upheld white Protestant supremacy; belonged for a time to eugenics and nationalist organizations; opposed open immigration; and inscribed racism, Nationalism, and classism into her proposals for social change. In *Concerning Children* (1900), she maintains that "a sturdy English baby would be worth more than an equally vigorous young Fuegian. With the same training and care, you could develop higher faculties in the English specimen than in the Fuegian

5   [Lanser's note.] See, for example, Gilman's "My Ancestors," *Forerunner* 4 (March 1913): 73–75, in which the narrator represents all humans as one family; "Race Pride," *Forerunner* 4 (April 1913): 88–89, in which she explicitly criticizes Owen Wister's *The Virginian* for white supremacy; and *With Her in Ourland, Forerunner* 7 (1916): passim, in which America is chastized for its abuse of Negroes, Mexicans, and Indians.

specimen, because it was better bred." In the same book, she argues that American children made "better citizens" than "the more submissive races" and in particular that "the Chinese and the Hindu, where parents are fairly worshipped and blindly obeyed," were "not races of free and progressive thought and healthy activity." Gilman advocated virtually compulsory enlistment of Blacks in a militaristic industrial corps, even as she opposed such regimentation for whites. In *The Forerunner*, the journal she produced single-handedly for seven years, "yellow" groups are singled out frequently and gratuitously: Gilman chides the "lazy old orientals" who consider work a curse, singles out Chinatown for "criminal conditions," and uses China as an example of various unhealthy social practices. And she all but justifies anti-Semitism by arguing, both in her "own" voice and more boldly through her Herlandian mouthpiece Ellador, that Jews have not yet " 'passed the tribal stage' " of human development, that they practice an " 'unethical' " and " 'morally degrading' " religion of " 'race egotism' " and " 'concentrated pride,' " which has unfortunately found its way through the Bible into Western literature, and that in refusing to intermarry they " 'artificially maintain characteristics which the whole world dislikes, and then complain of race prejudice.' "[6]

Like many other "nativist" intellectuals, Gilman was especially disturbed by the influx of poor immigrants to American cities and argued on both race and class grounds that these "undesirables" would destroy America. [. . .]

[. . .]

From **Tom Lutz,** *American Nervousness, 1903: An Anecdotal History*
(Ithaca and London: Cornell University Press, 1991), 229–31

> This excerpt forms part of a chapter on Gilman and Wharton from Tom Lutz's socio-historical and cultural study of George Beard, the recognized father of neurasthenia and author of *American Nervousness*. Lutz argues that Gilman believed in neurasthenia as a disease and bought into notions of women's limited energy, evident in the writings of Dr. S. Weir Mitchell and Dr. Edward H. Clarke (see **pp. 61–8** and **pp. 57–9**). To Lutz, Gilman was criticizing not a

---

6   [Lanser's note.] Gilman, *Concerning Children*, 89 and 55; Gilman, in the *American Journal of Sociology* (July 1908), 78–85, both cited in Scharnhorst, 66, 127. See Gilman, "Why We Honestly Fear Socialism," *The Forerunner* 1 (December 1909): 9. This charge is also made of the Jews in Gilman's *The Man-Made World: or, Our Androcentric Culture* (New York: Charlton, 1911), 231. See Gilman, review of "The Woman Voter," *Forerunner* 3 (August 1912): 224; and see, for example, *Forerunner* 4 (February 1913): 47, and 3 (March 1912): 66. Gilman, *With Her in Ourland*, *Forerunner* 7 (October 1916): 266–67. See similar statements in "Growth and Combat," *Forerunner* 7 (April 1916): 108; and the following example from "Race Pride," *Forerunner* 4 (April 1913): 89: "Perhaps the most pronounced instance of this absurdity [of race superiority] is in the historic pride of the Hebrews, firmly believing themselves to be the only people God cared about, and despising all the other races of the earth for thousands upon thousands of years, while all those other races unanimously return the compliment." In at least one earlier text, however, Gilman does note without blaming the victim that "the hideous Injustice of Christianity to the Jew attracted no attention through many centuries." See *Women and Economics* (1898; rpt. New York: Harper & Row, 1966), 78.

disease increasing in epidemic proportions in turn-of-the-twentieth-century America, but the rest cure designed to treat it. Specifically, a doctor's mandate to rest compounded the symptoms of nervous women devoid of significant employment in which to channel their energy. Gilman's plans for kitchenless homes and house service, an essential part of her legacy, would enable women to perform meaningful work outside the home to create a more human world.

Lutz argues further that in writing "The Yellow Wall-Paper," Gilman also revealed her belief in another popular medical theory of the time associated with colored and patterned wallpaper. Gilman places her narrator undergoing a rest cure in a room patterned with a yellow paper that manifests two major nineteenth-century medical concerns: monotony in patterning and poisonous dyes. Aside from failing to meet aesthetic standards (see Eastlake, **pp. 55–6**), monotony in patterning was believed to lead to nervous irritability, sickness, insomnia, and nightmarish responses, which the narrator experiences in the horrors of the wallpaper pattern, repeated by "breadths." Dyes, particularly yellow and red, often contained arsenic. As Lutz argues, the narrator's efforts to liberate herself from sanctioned domesticity becomes a form of "self-poisoning." As Lutz powerfully concludes, Gilman ultimately invalidated neurasthenia as a role option for leisured late nineteenth-century women.

[. . .]

[. . .] Gilman knew the discourse of neurasthenia well and knew how to manipulate it rhetorically, and . . . she also maintained a fully skeptical attitude toward its standard deployment. But it is also clear that Gilman still accepted many of the basic tenets of the neurasthenic understanding of the world. In 1903 Orison Swett Marden's *Success Magazine* asked a group of successful women what they would do differently if they had their lives to live over, and the results of these interviews were published in a series of articles titled "If I Were a Girl Again." Gilman, by then famous for her economic writings, replied: "The only line of conduct pursued in girlhood which I now consider injudicious lay in a too lavish expenditure of nerve force, and on that point I may give useful warning." She then relates this view to her own philosophy of work: "Nerve force is capital. Use the interest carefully, saving some to increase the principal for your heirs; [and here she even seems to accept the notion of the necessity of women to conserve their energy for the purposes of childbearing] but never break into the principal unless some issue of life and death compels. The world needs helping and we all want to help it; but the best service is in a lifetime's strong and steady work, rather than a few years of feverish struggles."[1]

And so Gilman, like Henry James and Edith Wharton, a writer with an ability to see the discourse inside and out and to deconstruct it forcefully in her fiction, turns out to believe quite firmly in the disease after all. In "Why I Wrote the Yellow Wallpaper" Gilman claims that she wrote the story in the hopes that other

---

1   [Lutz's note.] "If I Were a Girl Again: Advice from a Thinker," *Success Magazine* (1903): 5372.

women would not be driven "to the borderline of mental ruin" by doctors' advice, especially by advice not to work, which as we have seen was part of the process and purpose of the rest cure. What Gilman wanted to argue was that women's work as it existed, since it was wasteful, led to neurasthenia, but when women's work would become the same as men's work, it would be a reinvestment of nervous energy and lead away from nervousness. Completely involved in the medical discourse and its moral and economic correlatives, Gilman used it to make her political points, and what seems to be a criticism of the disease is actually a criticism of aspects of its deployment made from a ground constructed of the same materials. The argument's lack of cogency, given the high incidence of neurasthenia among men in the professions, also points to its polemic rather than mimetic function.

There is other evidence of Gilman's belief in the allied medical theories of her time. For one, patterned wallpaper (and Gilman claims this motif in "The Yellow Wallpaper" has no strictly autobiographical basis), had its medical detractors, and the critique of domesticity many readers find implied in this central metaphor turns out itself to have had a medical history. Citing medical opinion in 1883, Robert W. Edis wrote, "The endless multiplication and monotony of strongly-marked patterns . . . [is] a source of infinite torture and annoyance in times of sickness and sleeplessness." Not only did patterned wallpapers fail all aesthetic tests, but they "could materially add to our discomfort and nervous irritability, and after a time have a ghastly and nightmarish effect upon the brain."[2] And at the same time, John Harvey Kellogg, who also treated neurasthenics, warned readers of his *Household Manual of Domestic Hygiene, Food, and Diet* (1882) to stay away from certain kinds of wallpaper because of the use of poisonous dyes, many containing arsenic. The two worst culprits, Kellogg wrote, were red and yellow wallpapers. Children had died scratching at pieces of wallpaper and ingesting fatal amounts of arsenic. Not only is the narrator's abnormal response to the wallpaper a normal process according to medical opinion, but she is poisoning herself in her attempt to tear the wallpaper from the walls: this strongest image of the woman's attempts to break free from the constraints of domesticity is also an image of self-poisoning.

Gilman claimed that S. Weir Mitchell changed the regimen of his cure after reading "The Yellow Wallpaper." Whether he did or not, the cure and the disease changed radically, eventually changing right out of existence. And it is clear that although Gilman had no interest in changing the neurasthenic understanding of sickness and health, this well-known and controversial story had an effect. Gilman's appropriation bought more than she had bargained for, as her use of the disease to make her own points helped undermine the position of neurasthenia and the neurasthenic. Patricia Meyer Spacks claims that Gilman's adoption of sickness as an alternative to the roles of wife and mother "exemplifies the remarkably devious relationship possible between a woman and her work," in which she "achieves greatly as a mysterious corollary to self-deprecation."[3] In outlining the

2   [Lutz's note.] Robert W. Edis, "Internal Decoration." in *Our Homes*, ed. Shirley F. Murphy (London, 1883), 313, 321.
3   [Lutz's note.] Patricia Meyer Spacks, *The Female Imagination* (New York, 1975), 214, 208. This interpretation is seconded by Sheryl L. Meyering in her introduction to the volume of criticism she collected, *Charlotte Perkins Gilman: The Woman and Her Work* (Ann Arbor, Mich., 1989), 1–10.

relationship between women, work, and ill health, Gilman validated her own decision to write, validated women's intellectual labor in general, and helped, finally, to invalidate neurasthenia as a role option. She represented neurasthenia as poisonous, as a mark of leisured affluence and what was poisonously wrong with such affluence.

[. . .]

From **Jonathan Crewe, "Queering The Yellow Wallpaper?
Charlotte Perkins Gilman and the Politics of Form,"** *Tulsa Studies
in Women's Literature* 14: 2 (1995): 273–94

Burgeoning feminist discourse on "The Yellow Wall-Paper" places the story in the socio-political context of the 1970s; queer theory, rather, sets it amidst the rising gay and lesbian movements of the 1990s. Queer theory appropriates the epithet "queer" as a strategically useful term. While cutting-edge queer theory deconstructs the notion of identity as rooted in sexual orientation, Jonathan Crewe offers a more moderate approach. He uses the tools of "queer theory" not only to read the homoerotic subtext of repressed desire in "The Yellow Wall-Paper" but to make visible numerous instabilities of normative hetero-sexuality, produced by the threat of queerness; in essence, heterosexuality is itself queer.

The question mark in the title makes a conscious attempt to "avoid begging the question whether Gilman's text can or should be 'queered.' " Crewe calls upon the work of Eve Kosofsky Sedgwick, who, in *Tendencies* (Durham, North Carolina: Duke University Press, 1993), considers the time period of the story a "queer" one in the marketplace of images in American culture. The recurrence of the term "queer" and variations of it in the story (e.g. "strange" and "pecu-liar") invite a "queering" of the text. In fact, the word "queer," which deepens and shifts as the story develops, first appears in the third short paragraph in the opening entry when the narrator assumes the house must be odd since it is let so inexpensively. Crewe maintains that in 1890s America, sentences such as "Jennie wanted to sleep with me" can be read as having lesbian intent: "Even the narrator's prissy 'I don't like it a bit' leaves open the possibility of liking it far too much, hence the need for outside male intervention." Focusing on "the para-doxical queerness of the norms under which queerness is suppressed," Crewe explores not only same-sex desire but also energies within a culture that sup-presses what is deemed "queer."

The narrator's sister-in-law, Jennie, identifies with her brother, Dr. John, and male patriarchy at large. Jennie appears as a jailor figure, treating the narrator as a "patient," not as a potential bedfellow or even a sister. Same-sex bonding occurs, rather, between the narrator and the "strange" figure of a woman locked behind the barred pattern of the wallpaper, whom the narrator frees. The narrator first notices "a strange, provoking, formless sort of figure" (**p. 135**) lurking behind the conspicuous front or top pattern. As the story con-tinues, the figure "is like a woman stooping" (**p. 138**), and in the sixth entry, the narrator confirms, "now I am quite sure it is a woman" (**p. 139**) For the

narrator, the trapped woman shifts from subtext to main text of the wallpaper.
The sentence "I pulled and she shook, I shook and she pulled, and before
morning we had peeled off yards of that paper" (p. 143) in the twelfth and final
diary entry shows the narrator merging with the object of her obsession and
actually "becoming her own same-sex partner," to quote Crewe.

The narrator has no outlet for sisterly bonding beyond deadened wallpaper,
so same-sex desire remains active only in her imagination. Nonetheless, the
once-muted pattern of the wallpaper becomes dominant in the narrator's eyes,
leading Crewe to conclude the story has the elements of a "decidedly queer
experience," so threatening to 1890s America that Gilman recalls John, who
functions as "censor and heterosexual rescuer." To many feminist critics who
variously pronounce the narrator "destroyed" (Hedges, see **pp. 88–90**) or
liberated (Gilbert and Gubar, see **pp. 91–2**), John is a repressor who represents
patriarchy. To Crewe, however, John censors the narrator's dawning awareness of same-sex kinship with the woman in the wallpaper, reestablishing
heterosexuality as the norm.

In the close of his article, Crewe makes apparent the interface between
feminist theory and queer theory. The nameless narrator emerges as a "queer-
female 'patient,' " a wife under control of her all-knowing husband/physician
and decidedly "Other." Being a woman or being queer does not make one sick
or insane even if the socio-political context of late nineteenth-century America
dictates it so. This is a point, Crewe suggests, that still remains "hardly trivial to
establish."

[. . .]

Following Sedgwick, then, queering *The Yellow Wallpaper* or any other text
would mean more than identifying a definitively homoerotic subtext or mode of
repressed desire in it. It would at least include the continuing process of tracking
the "gravity . . . the *gravitas*, the meaning, but also the center of gravity [as] the
term 'queer' itself [historically] deepens and shifts."[1] Conceivably, it could
prompt more widespread queer self-recognition on the part of readers, inasmuch
as even straight readers would be called upon to recognize same-sex desire as
repressed, not absent, in normative heterosexuality. Further, if Michael Warner is
correct, a heavy investment in the text is one of the defining features of queer
theory: "Almost everything that would be called queer theory is about ways in
which texts—either literature or mass culture or language—shape sexuality . . .
you can't eliminate queerness, says queer theory, or screen it out."[2] What might

---

1 [Crewe's note.] Sedgwick, "Queer and Now," *Tendencies*, p. 9.
2 [Crewe's note.] Michael Warner, "From Queer to Eternity," *Voice Literary Supplement*, 106 (June
   1992), 19, cited in Doty, p. xiii. Richard Feldstein, in "Reader, Text, and Ambiguous Referentiality
   in 'The Yellow Wall-Paper,' " in *The Captive Imagination*, p. 308, notes that editors have regular-
   ized the spelling of "wallpaper" from the first publication of Gilman's text up through The Feminist Press edition. In Gilman's manuscript, spellings include wallpaper, wall paper, and wall-paper,
   this hyphenation sometimes being rendered ambiguous by a line-break between "wall-" and
   "paper." The signification of textuality allowed by these variations is hardly inconsequential, as
   Feldstein argues.

logically follow is that "a heavy investment in the text"—that is, any intense, prolonged commitment to textual interpretation—renders or reveals as "queer" all who make that investment. Such an investment may be enough of a cultural anomaly, especially in the late twentieth century, to be queer in and of itself, while the willingness to make the investment may logically imply the existence of some equally anomalous form of desire. Yet these broader prospects neither can nor should take precedence over the narrower, more "literal" construction of queerness as same-sex desire and/or avowal. If queerness is not reducible to same-sex desire or identification, it is also not discontinuous with them. Both this continuity and irreducibility are apparent, I believe, in *The Yellow Wallpaper*, for which reason above all Gilman's text qualifies as an exemplary queer one.

As if by uncanny coincidence or anticipation, the term "queer" and such cognates as "strange" and "peculiar" (both of which have done duty as socially stigmatizing euphemisms for the homosexual) begin to circulate early on in *The Yellow Wallpaper*. While I know of no evidence to suggest that the term "queer" could be used as a pejorative colloquialism for persons or forms of behavior identified as homosexual in the 1890s—as is now fairly well known, the first OED citation for "queer" in the sense of (male) homosexual dates from 1922—the narrator's "queer" experience, including her obsessive-projective-defensive relation to the wallpaper, gets implicitly connected to a scenario of repressed desire in the text. This desire might be called "lesbian," implying an inadmissible positive orientation, but might equally be recognized as a desire constitutively repressed under what Adrienne Rich has called the regime of compulsory heterosexuality. The narrator's disaffection from her husband and phobic relation to her child, as well as her partial transfer of affect to the "sister" Jennie—the husband's sibling-surrogate, other woman, sister-in-law, nursing-sister, keeper—is consistent with this oppressive regime. So is the narrator's hermeneutic eliciting of abjected yet sexualized "woman," first as subtext then as text of the wallpaper:

> There are things in that paper that nobody knows but me, or ever will.
> Behind that outside pattern the dim shapes get clearer every day.
> It is always the same shape, only very numerous.
> And it is like a woman stooping down and creeping about behind that pattern. I don't like it a bit. I wonder—I begin to think—I wish John would take me away from here! (pp. 32–33)

Knowledge experienced as wholly secret and unshareable; dimly apprehended "things"; an outline growing clearer every day; the "shape" of a woman yet perhaps of all women; wondering; beginning to think: such are the components of a decidedly queer experience, yet one so immediately threatening to this self-styled ordinary person (p. 24) that the repudiated husband has to be recalled as censor and heterosexual rescuer.

However "innocent" this situation may appear—and however unknowing the narrator may in fact be—it would be historically false to suppose that, in 1890, there could be no lesbian implication in sentences like "Jennie wanted to sleep with me" or "she wouldn't mind doing it herself." [. . .] Even the narrator's prissy "I don't like it a bit" leaves open the possibility of liking it far too much, hence the need for outside male intervention. Yet without any conscious recourse, let alone political recourse, to same-sex desire or "sisterly" bonding,, the narrator's queerness is mainly doomed to manifest itself perversely, symptomatically, self-destructively.

[. . .]

[. . .] The transformation of the schoolroom and gymnasium in *The Yellow Wall-paper* into a ward in which the queer-female "patient" is confined—"wife" being reconstituted as "patient" while "husband" is reconstituted as "doctor"—could hardly be more pointed, while the emergence of psychoanalytic discourse as broad cultural discourse could hardly be more telling. It is under precisely these conditions that depathologization becomes an especially important common enterprise of feminism and queer theory. Yet if it remains important to establish that being a woman or being queer is not tantamount to being sick or insane, it is hardly trivial to establish that being so is not tantamount, either, to exhibiting bad form.

From **Ann Heilmann, "Overwriting Decadence: Charlotte Perkins Gilman, Oscar Wilde, and the Feminization of Art in 'The Yellow Wall-Paper,' "** in *The Mixed Legacy of Charlotte Perkins Gilman*, eds. Catherine J. Golden and Joanna Schneider Zangrando (Newark: University of Delaware Press; London: Associated University Presses, 2000), 175–88

Ann Heilmann offers a new historicist reading of "The Yellow Wall-Paper." Setting the story in the context of the Yellow Nineties, she explores an association between wallpaper and fin-de-siècle decadence associated with Oscar Wilde, the color yellow, and a male-dominated aesthetic. Heilmann cites the earlier work of Mary Jacobus and Susan Lanser (see **pp. 94–6** and **pp. 105–8**), who raise the social and racial fears surrounding the color yellow. But most important to her argument, yellow invokes a decidedly male late nineteenth-century aesthetic movement. "Yellow" decadence—linked with images of, for example, Oscar Wilde and the floral tapestry of William Morris—became a visible manifestation not of female subversion (as critics beginning with Hedges have previously claimed), but of patriarchy itself. In making the yellow wallpaper the controlling metaphor of her story, "Gilman," Heilmann argues, "was visualizing her emerging feminist opposition to the 'pointless pattern' of male thought and cultural production."

Heilmann's reference to wallpaper as cultural production recalls, with a feminist twist, the work of Walter Benn Michaels, who connects the story to the capitalistic processes of production and consumption (see **pp. 99–101**). Set in this cultural context, the narrator's ripping of the wallpaper "constitutes a metaphorical 'overwriting' of the male patterns inscribed into the text: marriage, medicine, and art." This excerpt concludes with Heilmann's assertion that the narrator, in moving into the open as Sandra Gilbert and Susan Gubar also claim (see **p. 92**), gains more than freedom. The narrator replaces decadent yellow with vibrant green, symbolic of life. In allowing her narrator literally to free herself from the color of patriarchy, Gilman launches a new female aestheticism.

[. . .]

If "The Yellow Wall-Paper" was written to teach Silas Weir Mitchell and, by implication, other wielders of patriarchal authority, "the error of [their] ways" (*Living* 121), Gilman also responded to the dominant artistic discourse of her time by "translating her vision" of political art. In the context of the 1890s, the color and strange floral pattern of the wallpaper literally and literarily take on a specific cultural meaning. Why yellow? As Mary Jacobus and Susan Lanser have noted, yellow, the "color of sickness," would at that time have been associated with racial fears of national invasion (the "Yellow Peril") and with social fears of the invasion of privacy (the sensationalist "Yellow Press").[1] Most significantly, of course, it stood for the aesthetic and decadent movement. Morris's fashionable designs in which [. . .] yellow featured significantly, Van Gogh's sunflowers, Whistler's blue-and-yellow room, the French yellowback novel, *The Yellow Book*, and indeed, the Yellow Nineties.[2] Above all, the color yellow evokes the image of Oscar Wilde, self-styled "Professor of Aesthetics," carrying sunflowers and a yellow silk handkerchief in lieu of aestheticism to the America of the 1880s, and responding to hostile newspaper reports by quipping, "If you survive yellow journalism, you need not be afraid of yellow fever"; Wilde who put a novel bound in yellow, mistakenly thought to be *The Yellow Book*, under his arm when he was arrested and whose *A Woman of No Importance* (1893) features a young American woman with a purpose, teaching the higher morality to decadent English aristocrats in a "Yellow Drawing-room."[3]

Wilde's poems "In the Gold Room: A Harmony" (1882), "Symphony in Yellow" (1889), "Remorse (A Study in Saffron)" (1889) and "La Dame Jaune" (undated) established yellow as the color of decadence, conjuring up an atmosphere where the erotic connoted decay and the rotting "flowers of evil" (falling hair in "Remorse" and "In the Gold Room," falling clothes in "La Dame Jaune," falling leaves in "Symphony in Yellow") (Wilde, *Complete Works* 862, 872–73; Ellmann, *Oscar Wilde* 196). Decadent eroticism was similarly visualized in painting, for instance in Albert Moore's "Yellow Marguerites" (ca. 1880), which encoded female "solitary vice" by depicting a languid young woman reclining on a sofa against a background of flowery yellow wallpaper. Sexual perversion was made explicit in *The Yellow Room*, an anonymous sado-masochistic text published a year before "The Yellow Wall-Paper," in which the title room is the site of the heroine's flagellation by her uncle.[4]

By turning the two signifiers of aestheticism (the color yellow and the flower tapestry made so famous by William Morris) into the central metaphor of her

---

1   Both Lanser's and Jacobus's essays are included in this sourcebook (see **pp. 105–8 and 94–6**).
2   The term yellowback refers to cheap mid-to-late-nineteenth-century sensational popular novels typically printed with yellow enamelled paper covers. *The Yellow Book* was an 1890s quarterly of fiction, poetry, essays, and illustrations whose contributors include Oscar Wilde and William Butler Yeats; Aubrey Beardsley was the first art editor. The "Yellow Nineties" refers to the nativist tendencies of the decade.
3   [Heilmann's note.] For references on Wilde see William Gaunt, *The Aesthetic Adventure* (London: Cape, 1945), 105; Martin Fido, *Oscar Wilde* (Leicester: Galley Press, 1988), 41; Richard Ellmann, *Oscar Wilde* (London: Penguin, 1987), 166, 168, 170; H. Montgomery Hyde, *Oscar Wilde* (London: Mandarin, 1990), 510; Fraser Harrison, "Introduction" to *The Yellow Book. An Anthology* (Woodbridge: Boydell Press, 1982), 10–11; Oscar Wilde, *A Woman of No Importance* (1893), in *The Complete Works of Oscar Wilde* (London: Harper Collins, 1996), 477.
4   [Heilmann's note.] Anon., *The New Epicurean and The Yellow Room* (Ware, Hertfordshire: Wordsworth Classics, 1996), 69–127.

story on women's sociocultural oppression, Gilman was visualizing her emerging feminist opposition to the "pointless pattern" of male thought and cultural production (31), juxtaposing these with a woman-centered politics and perspective, the central female consciousness of her text. Judging by a lecture she gave in 1894, "Art for Art's Sake" was, as she noted in her diary, bound to have "evil results" (*Diaries* 2: 583). Like so many feminists of the time, in particular the British New Woman writers, Gilman constructed decadence not as subversion, but merely as a different expression of patriarchy. If, on a symbolic level, the yellow wallpaper denotes the phallocentric structures of science and the patriarchal family, it quite literally reflects contemporary male art and also [. . .] male consumer culture. [. . .]

[. . .]

[. . .] To impress on his audience "what a great effect might be realised with a little and simple colour," Wilde gave a detailed description of Whistler's blue-and-yellow room:

> The walls are distempered in blue, the ceiling is a light and warm yellow; the floor is laid with a richly painted matting in light yellow, with a light line or leaf here and there of blue. The woodwork is all cane-yellow, and the shelves are filled with blue and white china; the curtains of white serge have a yellow border tastefully worked in, and hang in careless but graceful folds. When the breakfast-table is laid in this apartment, with its light cloth and its dainty blue and white china, with a cluster of red and yellow chrysanthemums in an old Nankin[5] vase in the centre, it is a charming room, catching all the warm light and taking on of all surrounding beauty, and giving to the guest a sense of joyousness, comfort, and rest (*Complete Works* 916–17, 922)

No doubt this room, significantly also one singled out for providing "rest," sounds incomparably more habitable and peaceful to the mind than Gilman's nursery. In fact, Wilde stressed the importance of congruence and symmetry, advising against compiling a "collection of a great many things individually pretty but which do not combine to make a harmonious whole" (*Complete Works* 915). In principle Gilman shared Wilde's notion of beauty; in *The Man-Made World* she declared the highest form of art, that is, "human" (as opposed to sex-specific) art, to be characterized by "regularity, symmetry, repetition, and alteration" (75)—the very opposite, that is, of her wallpaper, which, as she notes in her story, is "not arranged on any laws of radiation, or alteration, or repetition, or symmetry" (31). The point that Gilman makes is that "human" art and, therefore, true beauty and aesthetic expression are not possible in an androcentric culture; as long as women are oppressed, Whistler's vision of peaceful symmetry must inevitably turn into the nightmare of the nursery.

---

5   Nanking is a type of porcelain that has a blue-and-white pattern and derives its name from Nanking, China.

Taken by itself, or in conjunction with different furnishings and in a more positive context, the wallpaper would not be as "horrid" as it must appear to the narrator (32). What makes the nursery so disturbing is the violent clash between the wallpaper's pretense to aestheticism and the room's function as a prison. [. . .]

[. . .]

While the narrator herself remains suspended between absolute psychological freedom and physical confinement to a room in the "ancestral halls" of patriarchy (24), death (of her former self: the "Jane" she names on the last page) and rebirth (into a state unnamed and undefined by any man), the process of writing about the ripping of the wallpaper constitutes a metaphorical "overwriting" of the male patterns inscribed into the text: marriage, medicine, and art. Placed in the cultural context of the Yellow Nineties, the journey Gilman takes the reader on is thus one that leads from male aestheticism to the vision of a feminized future. As yet the Other self of the artist that the narrator has released is creeping, but she is creeping out in the open; she is moving fast, and has replaced the yellow of decadence and decay with the green color of life (41).

[. . .]

From **Marty Roth, "Gilman's Arabesque Wallpaper,"** *Mosaic* 34: 4 (2001): 1145–62

Marty Roth, like Susan Lanser, calls attention to the darker side of Charlotte Perkins Gilman, now criticized for white supremacist attitudes evident in her essays written after "The Yellow Wall-Paper," such as "A Study of the Negro Problem" (1908). Roth suggests that the beginnings of Gilman's repugnant ethnocentrism and racial and ethnic biases emerge in her presentation of the dominant symbol of the story, the wallpaper. While Lanser highlights the politics of the color yellow, Roth—also reading "The Yellow Wall-Paper" along socio-political lines—explores the culture of nineteenth-century imperialism dominant in the arabesque pattern of the wallpaper. Roth specifically exposes the imperialist anxiety surrounding the Oriental "fluid arabesque," haunting the room in which John requires the narrator to reside.

Having studied at Rhode Island School of Design, Gilman would have been familiar with the arabesque pattern, a twisting and turning eastern design that originated in Baghdad, noted for its disturbing hallucinatory associations. Roth explores the paradigm of the arabesque as an eastern motif in western music and literature and links the narcotic associations of the arabesque pattern to a tradition of Poe-esque fiction. He also connects Gilman's landmark story to traditional Anglo-American tales of haunted houses and captivity narratives. The woman caught behind the arabesque pattern, to Roth, seems trapped by a sphere "where imperialist and feminist anxiety meet."

Charlotte Perkins Gilman is one of the few American women writers of the late nineteenth century to be included in discussions of cultural imperialism—because of her white supremacist attitudes at home and her utopian fiction set abroad. Her most notable fiction is *Herland*, which describes a lost colony of white women discovered in the secret heart of South America. By contrast, studies of the culture of American empire tend to observe male priority in obedience to a doctrine of separate spheres. As Amy Kaplan observes, the "binary opposition of the foreign and the domestic is itself imbued with the rhetoric of gender hierarchies that implicitly elevate the international to a male, public realm, and relegate the national to a female, private sphere" (Kaplan and Pease 16).

In a recent volume, *Utopia and Cosmopolis: Globalization in the Era of American Literary Realism*, Thomas Peyser discusses how Gilman's utopian novels and essays "fit the emerging discourse of globalization" (74). I want to extend this application to include Gilman's literary masterpiece, "The Yellow Wallpaper." This is not to imply that mine is the only reading of the tale along socio-political lines. There is an excellent article by Susan Lanser, written in 1989 and entitled "Feminist Criticism, 'The Yellow Wallpaper,' and the Politics of Color in America," that very successfully explores the situation of Asian-American and other racial minorities in *fin-de-siècle* America and relates this to the universalising white reading that Gilman's tale has received at the hands of her feminist critics. In a sense, Lanser's article reads "Yellow"; mine reads "Wallpaper."

As an immediate earnest of imperialist anxiety, the tale is haunted by an "Oriental" fantasy (i.e., the yellow wallpaper), and this functions as an environment or surround for the dominant American subjectivity represented by the narrator of the tale. There is no question about the Oriental identity of the art: Gilman calls it "florid arabesque," and since she trained briefly at the Rhode Island School of Design, she would have known what the term implied. Domestic ornament in the nineteenth century contained sign systems that articulate a complex of attitudes about the imaginary East.

This essay, then, is devoted to the uncovering and recovery of contexts that are held in place by a central allusion to arabesque. Oriental art was aesthetically repulsive to some because it was indeterminate and saturated by a drug culture presumed to be rampant in the East. The most immediate context, however, is the work of Edgar Allan Poe and an Anglo-American tradition of haunted house fiction that provide the imperialist implications of Gilman's tale with a lineage.

Gilman's tale is dominated by the wallpaper in her narrator's bedroom which, this middle-class wife and mother insists, is aesthetically disgusting: "repellent, almost revolting; a smouldering unclean yellow. [. . .] I never saw a worse paper in my life. One of those sprawling flamboyant patterns committing every artistic sin" (13); "by daylight, there is a lack of sequence, a defiance of law, that is a constant irritant to a normal mind. [. . .] the color is hideous enough, and unreliable enough, and infuriating enough, but the pattern is torturing. You think you have mastered it, but just as you get well underway in following, it turns a back-somersault and there you are. It slaps you in the face, knocks you down, and tramples upon you. It is like a bad dream" (25). The tale intones a litany of repulsive worlds and phrases for this design item: "bloated," "waddling," "fungus," "lolls," "bulbous," "wallowing": shapeless and floppy words (16, 20). The wallpaper is not simply shapeless, however, but potentially terrifying: "the sprawling outlines run off in great slanting waves of optic horror" (25). [. . .]

Arabesque was widely accepted and appreciated in Western art. Why, then, does Gilman's narrator find it so intolerable? Several nineteenth-century critics of art and design, with John Ruskin at their head, resisted the appeal of this figure for architectural or interior design because it was Islamic or, more generally, "eastern": Ruskin "execrated the decoration of the Alhambra as an abomination" (qtd. in Gombrich 53). He regarded arabesque as an "Oriental" writing that "proved" that eastern races were inherently superficial, fanciful, and cruel: "The fancy and delicacy of eye," he wrote, "in interweaving lines and arranging colors—mere line and color, observe, without natural form—seems to be somehow an inheritance of ignorance and cruelty, belonging to men as spots to the tiger or hues to the snake" (qtd. in Crinson 60). Edward A. Freeman, a nineteenth-century historian of Islamic architecture, claimed that arabesque was "the exuberance of fancy, vivid and fertile to the last degree, but uncontrolled by any law of taste or consistency" (qtd. in Crinson 42).

Wallpaper itself came under general attack about the time of Gilman's tale, and this was, partly at least, a reaction to certain unsettling implications of Oriental aesthetics. According to Jan Jennings, wallpaper became an object of contention between two groups who competed for the female consumer: "Wallpaper manufacturers perpetuated the ornamental aesthetic that home economists and other progressives attempted to eradicate" (254). Reformers spoke of wallpaper as "the invention of laziness and filth," concealing "dirt and noisomeness of every description" (256). They objected to wallpaper for its colours and its inappropriate patterns, while Jane Addams opposed it because it tended to harbour vermin (255). Edith Wharton, who shared with Gilman the privilege of undergoing S. Weir Mitchell's rest cure (the biographical experience behind Gilman's tale), also disliked wallpaper: "It was well for the future of house-decoration when medical science declared itself against the use of wall-papers. These hangings have, in fact, little to recommend them" (Wharton and Codman 44). [. . .]

As infinite, arabesque is dangerous, a "perceptual confusion" that can lead to a loss of limits, even insanity (Gordon, *Ornament* 89), the drift of one of Christian Morgenstern's gallow songs (1905):

Wallpaper flower, that is I,
in May I do not bloom;
but endlessly I multiply
throughout the four-walled room.
Your eyes that search unceasingly
look for the end in vain;
and if they hopscotch after me,
my love, you go insane.
(213)

[. . .]

In the course of the tale, the wallpaper is transformed from a two- to a three-dimensional form: the figure of a creeping woman emerges from behind the florid arabesque. That is the fantastic plot of "The Yellow Wallpaper." [. . .]

[. . .] And what is "The Yellow Wallpaper" but a wallpaper hallucination of a woman imprisoned behind a two-dimensional arabesque plane, struggling to break free? [. . .]

Arabesque, an aesthetic of unreadability, and narcotic associations all point back to Edgar Allan Poe, the early American Orientalist writer of horror tales and the author with whom Gilman was regularly crossed and confused in the first readings of her work. Elaine Hedges reports, "In its time the story was read essentially as a Poe-esque tale of chilling horror," (qtd. in Owens 67) and Walter Stetson informed Gilman that he found the story "utterly ghastly, more horrifying than even Poe's tales of terror" (qtd. in Haney-Peritz 95). Even though a recent generation of critics has warned us away from such readings (Annette Kolodny claims that there has been great difficulty in comprehending the story because it was located "not as any deviation from a previous tradition of women's fiction but, instead, as a continuation of a genre popularized by Poe" [455]), I plan to travel this path again. [. . .]

Poe's works give wide play to the concept and image of the arabesque (there are at least two critical articles and a book on the subject): this includes proposing it as the name for one of his two types of signature tale in *Tales of the Grotesque and Arabesque*. In Prospero's masquerade in "The Masque of the Red Death," there "were arabesque figures with unsuited limbs and appointments, [. . .] delirious fancies such as the madman fashions" (673), while in "The Fall of the House of Usher," to cite one more of many references, Roderick Usher's face is said to wear an "Arabesque expression" which the narrator cannot connect "with any idea of simple humanity" (402). Poe occupies both evaluative positions in respect to arabesque: he treats it in the tales as a most praiseworthy ornament but he denounces it in "The Philosophy of Furniture," echoing Ruskin's position that it is a product of the "warm but inappropriate fancy" of the "Chinese and most of the eastern races" (495). [. . .]

"The Yellow Wallpaper" was originally read as a particular type of gothic tale, a haunted house fiction. Popular during the *fin-de-siècle* period, one line of these tales betrays an obvious Orientalist horizon: stories set within the larger safety of a metropolis where one dwelling was disturbed by an alien sensibility, often a curse brought back from the colonies, as in W.W. Jacobs's "Monkey's Paw." Edith Wharton's "Kerfol" is a haunted house story about an imprisoned wife, comforted by the gift of a "little brown dog from the East" (286). Henry James's "The Turn of the Screw" is a ghost story linked to the Orient. The children need a governess because they have had to be sent back to England from India where they had been living: "He had been left, by the death of their parents in India, guardian to a small nephew and a small niece, children of a younger, a military brother, whom he had lost two years before" (11–12). *Jane Eyre* also fits this paradigm and Lanser does a good job of linking the Gilman tale back to the Brontë novel (428).

Real houses of the period had "haunted" rooms where the domestic interior played out an Orientalist fantasy, for example, the "Turkish" corner or "Moorish" smoking room. [. . .] And in "The Man With the Twisted Lip," Holmes makes his own Turkish corner: He "wandered about the room collecting pillows from his bed, and cushions from the sofas and armchairs. With these he constructed a sort of Eastern divan, upon which he perched himself cross-legged, with an ounce of shag tobacco and a box of matches laid out in front of him" (140–41). As John Maass points out, "Even middle-class Americans could afford a 'Turkish corner', where a few hangings, a rug, a divan, and a water pipe lent an exotic touch to the parlor" (101). [. . .]

A second line of haunted house stories, it is true, took a feminist turn and thus led us back to the more common readings of "The Yellow Wallpaper." There are a number of studies and collections devoted to the many ghost stories produced by women at the turn of the century and the meaning this might have for an understanding of the genre (see Bendixen; Dyman; Moody; Patrick; Salmonson). Jenni Dyman argues for the existence of a "buried" feminist text and a female aesthetic "made possible by the subversive nature and odd conventions of supernatural fiction" (6), and Barbara Patrick writes: "Again and again, women writers found in the supernatural tale metaphors for the unredressed wrongs women have suffered, for the invisibility of women's work, and for women's emotional, social, and political oppression" (74). [. . .]

As a haunted house tale, Gilman's "The Yellow Wallpaper" offers a unique terrain on which to examine turn-of-the-century American fiction as a place where imperialist and feminist anxiety meet, where the abjection of the woman and the abjection of the Eastern other collide and negotiate a release of terrifying energy.

From **Guiyou Huang, "The Use of Audiovisual Material as an Aid in Teaching 'The Yellow Wall-Paper,'"** in *Approaches to Teaching Gilman's "The Yellow Wall-Paper" and Herland,"* eds. Denise D. Knight and Cynthia J. Davis (New York: The Modern Language Association of America, 2003), 67–74

Guiyou Huang's essay responds to the growing interest in media studies and the current trend of film adaptations of eighteenth- and nineteenth-century fiction, such as by Jane Austen and Charles Dickens. Huang makes a persuasive argument that audiovisual materials—specifically film adaptations and period photographs—aid understanding of the social and cultural dimensions of "The Yellow Wall-Paper." Such materials also offset Gilman's choppy style and diary-like format, which prove to be stumbling blocks for some readers. Huang's focus on the audiovisual encompasses film versions as well as period photographs of Gilman and first husband Charles Walter Stetson, nineteenth-century women's fashion, and period insane asylums.

Although Huang writes for an audience of teachers, he offers a general reader a valuable summary and critique of three film versions: *The Yellow Wall-Paper.* Director John Clive. 90 minutes. Performances by Julia Watson and Stephen Dillon. WGBH Education Foundation and BBC Education and Training, 1989; *The Yellow Wall-Paper.* Director John Robbins. 15 minutes. Performance by Eda Seasongood. Internat. Instructional Television, 1977; *The Yellow Wall-Paper.* Director Tony Romain. 26 minutes. Performances by Rachael Lillis and Michael Slayton. Tony Romain/Vision Films, 1996. Taking the place of a "work in performance" section, Huang's article guides readers to make effective choices about which film version to view or study.[1]

---

1   I would also mention a fourth short film—*The Yellow Wall-Paper.* Director Marie Ashton. 14 minutes. Women Make Movies, 1977. The narrator, an aspiring writer, is called Elizabeth. Undergoing a rest cure administered by her doctor-husband, she is completely isolated in a room with barred windows, and she creates a world within the wallpaper from which she is unable to escape.

In his larger essay, Huang also emphasizes the importance of showing students a range of images from the period. Nineteenth-century insane asylums show real and possible consequences of the narrator's madness. Period wallpaper designs allow readers to glimpse the pattern that initially plagues but then completely fascinates the narrator. Photographs of Gilman and her first husband—also included in this sourcebook—bring vividly to life the people upon whom Gilman based her story.

The narrator of "The Yellow Wall-Paper" suffers a nervous breakdown that results in her inability to control both the environment and her mental condition; she is thus considered a mental patient by medical professionals such as Dr. S. Weir Mitchell (by implication), by her brother, and by her husband, John. In writing this autobiographically inspired story challenging biased medical views, Gilman uses visual, olfactory, and tactile imagery in a masterly manner throughout the narrative: the narrator imagines the existence of a woman struggling behind the pattern of the wallpaper in the room (visual); she claims that she smells the smoldering yellow color (olfactory); and in the end she literally tears down the hideous wallpaper (tactile), accomplishing the act of self-liberation from an asylum-like house.

The story spans a period of three months, during which time the reader witnesses the protagonist's gradual descent into madness. The narrator characterized the wallpaper as possessing two salient properties: patterns that resemble iron bars on prison windows that trap and suppress whatever is behind them (in this case an imaginary woman) and the odor of the paper that the narrator describes as "yellow" (13). Despite questions about the state of the narrator's mind, the story is truly poetic because of the use of metaphoric language to express feelings and emotions. Yet the structure of the story, largely reflecting the narrator's unstable mental health, poses difficulty to students who may find it hard to follow the choppy style that the narrator employs. It therefore follows that in teaching this short masterpiece the instructor and students will both be well served by the use of audio and visual materials to enhance students' understanding of the social and cultural dynamics in the story.

This essay considers the following materials: three film versions of the story; pictures and drawings of asylums for the insane; illustrations and photographs of women's fashions; pictures of nineteenth-century wallpaper; and photographs of Gilman and her first husband, the artist Charles Walter Stetson.

Like the narrative itself, the International Instructional Television production of "The Yellow Wall-Paper," directed by John Robbins, utilizes the protagonist to narrate her story to a presumed audience. For most of the film's fifteen-minute duration, the narrator delivers a monologue commenting on her predicament in confinement, on other characters, and on her immediate physical surroundings: the room and its yellow wallpaper and the outside world represented by the seeable but unreachable green garden. Because students may look for differences between the written text and film representations—for instance, changes or alterations in the plot or the characters' appearances—the instructor may emphasize the film as one of many interpretations of the story. For example, two important visual suspects that the film depicts effectively are the layout of the room, for-merly a nursery, in which the narrator is confined and the design and surface appearance of its wallpaper.

The woman in the Robbins film cries a lot from hysteria, caused by what we would now call postpartum depression (one might remind students that the word *hysteria* originates from the Latin word for "uterus"). The wallpaper and the path in the garden are two things she obsesses over during the three-month rental of the colonial mansion. She also alludes to "some legal trouble [. . .] about the heirs and co-heirs" (11), which suggests male dominance both in the ancestral house and in history. The tedium of a confined stay in a room with a bolted down bed—symbolizing the narrator's immovable and inflexible situation—contrasts sharply with the variety of the wallpaper patterns in yellow and orange that the narrator despises. The principle of wallpaper design, about which the narrator claims to "know a little" (19), does not seem relevant, because the pattern is pointless, an observation the narrator makes repeatedly in both the film and the story. This pointlessness is perceivable, however, only to the obsessed narrator. Her husband, John, and his sister, Jennie, do not seem to be bothered by the alleged lack of design principle. It is only the narrator who casts it as pointless, just as she views Dr. Mitchell's rest cure as pointless, and more important, male dominance as pointless.

Male dominance manifests itself symbolically, and specifically, in the bars sur-rounding the narrator: bars on the windows, bars created by the moonlight on the wallpaper, and bars on the banister. These visual images clearly work more con-cretely and immediately on the film viewer than their textual descriptions do on the reader; the instructor would thus point them out while screening the film for the students, in order to stress their symbolic significance. I recommend connect-ing these images to the oppressive power of male-dominated social and familial structures that not only severely limit someone's physical freedom but also restrict the exercising of their imaginative faculty. The narrator is prohibited from writ-ing by her husband, a restrictive rule implemented with the help, ironically, of another woman, Jennie, who in the film is represented as a tall, serious, and stern figure.

John Clive's film, often used in the classroom, has three distinct characteristics: it is a full-length film that runs ninety minutes, longer than any other film adapta-tions of "The Yellow Wall-Paper"; it relocates the story to England, to a village outside London, with characters who speak British English; and it changes the personages or names of several characters and adds new ones. For example, the protagonist is called Charlotte (Lotta), which reflects the autobiographical nature of the original story; and taking the place of the actual historical figure, Dr. Mitchell, is a Dr. Charles Stark, who is depicted as a condescending man. Among the other new characters are the couple's son, James, and a little girl (the garden-er's daughter) riding a bicycle. Jennie's characterization is also noteworthy: unlike her counterpart in the story, who is content with her role in life, Jennie in the end of the Clive film begins to question her brother's treatment of her sister-in-law and seems on the verge of a rebellion.[2]

---

2   Also, in the Clive version, Doctor John shows a desire for a physical relationship with the narrator not explicitly addressed in the story.

Using this film, the instructor may want to point out that unlike other film versions and the story itself, Clive does not overemphasize the function of the wallpaper. Instead, special attention is given to a golden yellow dress that John bought for Charlotte in Rome and that Charlotte believes was worn by a woman who is now somewhere in hiding. Also highlighted is the recurring sound of rustling, to suggest the creepiness and perhaps Gothic aspects of the haunted house. The rustling, caused either by someone tearing at the wallpaper or someone crawling on the leafy ground, taps Charlotte's imaginative faculties. John is presented largely along the lines of the original story, though in the movie he appears to be very ambitious and is more concerned with his professional success than with his wife's mental health. Because of his frequent absences, Charlotte suffers intense boredom, which contributes to her descent into madness. Contrasting her boredom is the freedom that the gardener's daughter enjoys riding her bicycle on the garden path: her freedom emphasizes Charlotte's lack of it, signified by the barred windows of the nursery on the top floor, by the repetitive patterns of the yellow wallpaper, and by the yellow dress worn by the woman behind the wallpaper, who emerges to meet and merge with Charlotte, who now appears insane.

The third film, Tony Romain's, is considerably different from the previous two in a number of ways. First, this twenty-six-minute film juxtaposes the story of a woman writing the narrative with images from the actual story of the nineteenth-century character she is creating. It also endows the principal characters with full names; the original unnamed woman narrator becomes Kathy Parker, her husband is called John Parker, and Kathryn is the name given her fictional creation. Another difference is that it emphasizes the abusive relationship that Kathy has with John (she is seen with a large bruise on the side of her face). Jennie is presented as a vibrant small woman in her twenties, conspicuously different from Robbins's much older, taller, and sterner counterpart or Clive's artistic and questioning figure. Also noteworthy are Dr. Mitchell's brief visit and appearances of the couple's child, who is not featured in Robbins's film. While Robbins's film seems to follow the original story more closely, Romain's seems to capture its spirit.

[. . .]

3

Text

Introduction

Of the several published versions of "The Yellow Wall-Paper"—namely, the manuscript or copy-text located at the Schlesinger Library (Radcliffe College), the 1892 *New England Magazine* version, and the 1899 chapbook edition published by Small, Maynard & Co.—I have chosen to reproduce the original illustrated magazine version, which appeared in *New England Magazine* (5 [January 1892]: 647–56) under the name Charlotte Perkins Stetson (the author's name when she published the tale).[1] "The Yellow Wall-Paper" originally appeared as a dual columned text of twelve sections, each separated by a row of six asterisks centred in a column. The form of the story is important to its interpretation: it unfolds as a diary that the narrator is keeping. I direct the reader to the syntax and style in these entries. In this tale—commonly considered the best written of Gilman's short stories—form conveys meaning. The entries grow shorter as the story continues. The short, taut sentences and proclivity of one- and two-sentence paragraphs reflect the narrator's changing mental state and can be read as an outward sign of the narrator's deteriorating mental condition. While the separation of the diary entries speaks to the reader's increasing fragmentation of self, as critics note (see Hedges, **pp. 88–90** and Golden **pp. 101–4**), the diary genre urges us to question how the narrator imagines the self to whom she is writing. Shifts in pronouns ("one" and "myself" versus "I") reveal growth in self-expression. Increased definition of the figure trapped behind the wallpaper pattern reflects the narrator's psychological state (madness or liberation).

This sourcebook aims to recreate the story as closely as possible to how period readers first encountered it. This reprinting includes many of the original textual features. For example, columns and original page numbers appear parenthetically in bold. The asterisks between sections indicate the twelve diary-like entries that make up the story. A layout of the opening page (Fig. 6) reveals the first of three illustrations by Jo. H. Hatfield, forming a headpiece to the story, and a decorative pictorial capital, as was customary for stories published in *New England Magazine*.[2]

---

1   Following the social constructionist school of textual studies associated with Jerome McGann, I have given priority to the first printing.
2   Jerome McGann calls these features "bibliographical codes."

"I am sitting by the Window in this Atrocious Nursery."

THE YELLOW WALL-PAPER.

By Charlotte Perkins Stetson.

T is very seldom that mere ordinary people like John and myself secure ancestral halls for the summer.

A colonial mansion, a hereditary estate, I would say a haunted house, and reach the height of romantic felicity — but that would be asking too much of fate !

Still I will proudly declare that there is something queer about it.

Else, why should it be let so cheaply? And why have stood so long untenanted?

John laughs at me, of course, but one expects that in marriage.

John is practical in the extreme. He has no patience with faith, an intense horror of superstition, and he scoffs openly at any talk of things not to be felt and seen and put down in figures.

John is a physician, and *perhaps* — (I would not say it to a living soul, of course, but this is dead paper and a great relief to my mind —) *perhaps* that is one reason I do not get well faster.

You see he does not believe I am sick ! And what can one do?

Figure 6 **Opening page of "The Yellow Wall-Paper,"** *New England Magazine,* **1892. Illustration by Jo. H. Hatfield, "I am sitting by the Window in this Atrocious Nursery." Courtesy of Special Collections, Schaffer Library, Union College.**

Illustrations are part of the text and thus integral to the interpretive process. Jo. H. Hatfield, a staff illustrator for *New England Magazine*, was Joseph Henry Hatfield (1863–1928), a Boston area painter skilled in portraiture and genre and landscape painting. Although little information exists on Hatfield, dates, location, and signature confirm the match (see John Castagno's *American Artists: Signatures and Monograms, 1800–1989*, published by Scarecrow Press in 1990). Born in Kingston, Ontario, Canada, Hatfield studied in the Parisian ateliers before moving to the Boston area where he earned his reputation. In the 1890s, he exhibited at the Boston Art Club and the Paris salons. In 1892, he earned a silver medal from the Massachusetts Charitable Mechanics Association, and in 1896 he won second prize at the National Academy of Design. Along with many talented nineteenth-century British and American artists, Hatfield turned to the lucrative field of book and magazine publication. Hatfield's illustrations for "The Yellow Wall-Paper" showcase his talent in genre painting and portraiture. Gilman apparently never saw Hatfield's illustrations prior to publication of "The Yellow Wall-Paper," nor did she comment on them subsequently. Nonetheless, they seem to have influenced some of the original interpretations of the story as a horror tale (see reviews, **pp. 81–6**).

A Note on the Text

My approach to the linguistic text is not to improve it but to preserve it. I have reprinted inconsistencies in the spelling of wallpaper in the 1892 version (wall-paper, wallpaper, wall paper, and paper), a subject of lively scholarly debate. To some critics, these variations are but a mark of Gilman's notoriously inconsistent spelling. To others, they are a means of highlighting the narrator's shifting relationship with the major symbol of the story.[3] However, I have emended obvious typographical errors to improve the readability of the text,[4] as follows: page 134, line 28: *breaths* was changed to *breadths*; page 134, line 48: unneeded quotation marks were deleted before *But*; page 135, line 38: *it it* was changed to *it is*; page 135, line 39: *nos* was changed to *not*; page 136, line 12, *grotesque* was changed to *grotesques*; page 141, line 22, *furnitnre* was changed to *furniture*; page 144, line 15, *plaintain* was changed to *plantain*. Conferring with other Gilman scholars after analyzing the copy-text, I have emended additional typographical errors according to the manuscript, as follows: page 134, line 2, *an airy and comfortable room* was changed to *as airy and comfortable a room*; page 142, lines 35–6, *John to stay in town* was changed to *John had to stay in town*; page 143, line 46, *come out* was changed to *came out*; and page 144, line 25 *"in spite of you and Jane?"* was changed to *"in spite of you and Jane!"*[5] The manuscript version, which Denise D. Knight skillfully transcribed for *"The Yellow Wall-Paper" and Selected Stories of Charlotte Perkins Gilman* (1994), holds authority as a text. Thus, I have added notes to indicate significant linguistic differences between the copy-text and the 1892 version, which regrettably increases the number of paragraph breaks; such a change is significant as Shawn St. Jean indicates in his 2002 article in *Feminist Studies* entitled "Hanging 'The Yellow Wall-Paper': Feminism and Textual Studies": "the manuscript crafts a more subtle situation: the protagonist, originally quite coherent, at least providing a well-paragraphed narrative, gradually degenerates as a *result* of her confinement" (402, see Further Reading, **p. 159**). Though this change may be more dramatic in the manuscript version, as

---

3 A quick glance at the Contents of this sourcebook reveals that this same variety in hyphenation also appears in criticism about the story, although the preferred spelling is now "The Yellow Wall-Paper."

4 In this respect, I am nodding to the "Greg-Bowers" school of textual studies.

5 Gilman's exclamation point in the MS had a slight curling, leading the printer to misread it as a question mark, which changes the meaning of the sentence.

St. Jean observes, readers can still trace this progression in the narrator's mental state in the *New England Magazine* version.

Glosses, numbered and placed in tinted boxes at the end of the unbroken text, illuminate the psychological, linguistic, feminist, historical, and socio-political dimensions of the story. While thorough, the glosses are intended to spark original investigations and alternative readings, not to preclude them. Glosses serve several functions. The language of the text remains an under-utilized source for student analysis. Accordingly, glosses direct particular attention to paragraphing, sentence structure, word choice, pronoun usage and placement, and repetition to encourage readers to trace the changes in the wallpaper pattern; shifts between diary entries in regard to style, theme, and plot also provide indications of the narrator's mental state. Of particular importance are the transformations in the dominant symbol of the wallpaper and the increased definition of the figure trapped behind the yellow wallpaper. To set the story in its historical and literary context, glosses direct attention to the illustrations and include numerous cross-references to material in the Contemporary Documents, Interpretations, and Modern Criticism sections (these appear in bold). Finally, glosses ask readers to question their first assumptions of this story and to read entries again to gain a deeper appreciation not only of this story, but of the multi-faceted process of reading itself.

The Yellow Wall-Paper

1 [page 647, column 1:]IT is very seldom that mere ordinary people like John and myself[6] secure ancestral halls for the summer.

A colonial mansion, a hereditary estate, I would say a haunted house, and reach the height of romantic felicity — but that would be asking too much of fate!

Still I will proudly declare that there is something queer about it.

[page 647, column 2:]Else, why should it be let so cheaply? And why have stood so long untenanted?

John laughs at me, of course, but one expects that in marriage.

John is practical in the extreme. He has no patience with faith, an intense horror of superstition, and he scoffs openly at any talk of things not to be felt and seen and put down in figures.

— John is a physician, and *perhaps* — (I would not say it to a living soul, of course, but this is dead paper and a great relief to my mind —) *perhaps* that is one reason I do not get well faster.

You see he does not believe I am sick!

And what can one do?

[page 648, column 1:]If a physician of high standing, and one's own husband, assures friends and relatives that there is really nothing the matter with one but temporary nervous depression — a slight hysterical tendency — what is one to do?

My brother is also a physician, and also of high standing, and he says the same thing.

So I take phosphates or phosphites — whichever it is,[7] and tonics, and journeys, and air, and exercise, and am absolutely forbidden to "work" until I am well again.

Personally, I disagree with their ideas.

Personally, I believe that congenial work, with excitement and change, would do me good.

But what is one to do?

I did write for a while in spite of them; but it *does* exhaust me a good deal — having to be so sly about it, or else meet with heavy opposition.

I sometimes fancy that in my condition if I had less opposition and more society

---

6 Interestingly, in the manuscript version of "The Yellow Wall-Paper," Gilman uses the nominative case pronoun "I," which, though more forceful than the revision, is grammatically incorrect.

7 Diet was an important part of the rest cure treatment. Likely the narrator takes phosphates, a carbonated, flavoured beverage containing a small amount of phosphoric acid; a phosphite is a phosphorous acid salt. See **pp. 61–6** in this sourcebook.

and stimulus —but John says the very worst thing I can do is to think about my condition, and I confess it always makes me feel bad.

So I will let it alone and talk[8] about the house.

The most beautiful place! It is quite alone, standing well back from the road, quite three miles from the village. It makes me think of English places that you read about, for there are hedges and walls and gates that lock, and lots of separate little houses for the gardeners and people.

There is a *delicious* garden! I never saw such a garden — large and shady, full of box-bordered paths, and lined with long grape-covered arbors with seats under them.

There were greenhouses, too, but they are all broken now.

There was some legal trouble, I believe, something about the heirs and co-heirs; anyhow, the place[9] has been empty for years.

That spoils my ghostliness, I am afraid, but I don't care — there is something strange about the house — I can feel it.

I even said so to John one moonlight evening, but he said what I felt was a *draught*, and shut the window.

[page 648, column 2:]I get unreasonably angry with John sometimes. I'm sure I never used to be so sensitive. I think it is due to this nervous condition.

But John says if I feel so, I shall neglect proper self-control; so I take pains to control myself — before him, at least, and that makes me very tired.

I don't like our room a bit. I wanted one downstairs that opened on the piazza and had roses all over the window, and such pretty old-fashioned chintz hangings! but John would not hear of it.

He said there was only one window and not room for two beds, and no near room for him if he took another.

He is very careful and loving, and hardly lets me stir without special direction.

I have a schedule prescription for each hour in the day; he takes all care from me,[10] and so I feel basely ungrateful not to value it more.

He said we came here solely on my account, that I was to have perfect rest and all the air I could get. "Your exercise depends on your strength, my dear," said he, "and your food somewhat on your appetite; but air you can absorb all the time." So we took the nursery at the top of the house.

It is a big, airy room, the whole floor nearly, with windows that look all ways, and air and sunshine galore. It was nursery first and then playroom and gymnasium, I should judge; for the windows are barred for little children, and there are rings and things in the walls.

The paint and paper look as if a boys' school had used it. It is stripped off — the paper — in great patches all around the head of my bed, about as far as I can reach, and in a great place on the other side of the room low down. I never saw a worse paper in my life.

One of those sprawling flamboyant patterns committing every artistic sin.

It is dull enough to confuse the eye in following, pronounced enough to con-

---

8 The manuscript reads "write" about the house, giving more emphasis to the narrator as a writer.
9 The manuscript states "it" instead of "the place."
10 Here the manuscript reads more awkwardly, "he takes every care."

stantly irritate and provoke study, and when you follow the lame uncertain curves for a little distance they suddenly commit suicide — plunge off at outrageous angles, destroy themselves in unheard of contradictions.

[page 649, column 1:]The color is repellant, almost revolting; a smouldering unclean yellow, strangely faded by the slow-turning sunlight.

It is a dull yet lurid orange in some places, a sickly sulphur tint[11] in others.

No wonder the children hated it! I should hate it myself if I had to live in this room long.

— There comes John, and I must put this away, — he hates to have me write a word.

* * * * * *

2 [page 649, column 1:]We have been here two weeks, and I haven't felt like writing before, since that first day.

I am sitting by the window now, up in this atrocious nursery, and there is nothing to hinder my writing as much as I please, save lack of strength.

John is away all day, and even some nights when his cases are serious.

I am glad my case is not serious!

But these nervous troubles are dreadfully depressing.

— John does not know how much I really suffer. He knows there is no *reason* to suffer, and that satisfies him.

Of course it is only nervousness. It does weigh on me so not to do my duty in any way!

I meant to be such a help to John, such a real rest and comfort, and here I am a comparative burden already!

Nobody would believe what an effort it is to do what little I am able, — to dress and entertain, and order things.

It is fortunate Mary is so good with the baby. Such a dear baby!

And yet I *cannot* be with him, it makes me so nervous.

I suppose John never was nervous in his life. He laughs at me so about this wall-paper!

At first he meant to repaper the room, but afterwards he said that I was letting it get the better of me, and that nothing was worse for a nervous patient than to give way to such fancies.

He said that after the wall-paper was changed it would be the heavy bedstead, and then the barred windows, and then that gate at the head of the stairs, and so on.

"You know the place is doing you [page 649, column 2:] good," he said, "and really, dear, I don't care to renovate the house just for a three months' rental."

"Then do let us go downstairs," I said, "there are such pretty rooms there."

Then he took me in his arms[12] and called me a blessed little goose, and said he would go down cellar, if I wished, and have it whitewashed into the bargain.

---

11 This reference recalls the discussion of arsenic in period wallpapers. See Tom Lutz, **pp. 108–11.**
12 The manuscript inserts the adjective "strong" before arms, giving John both a manly and protective image.

But he is right enough about the beds and windows and things.

It is as airy and comfortable a room as any one need wish, and, of course, I would not be so silly as to make him uncomfortable just for a whim.

I'm really getting quite fond of the big room, all but that horrid paper.

Out of one window I can see the garden, those mysterious deep-shaded arbors, the riotous old-fashioned flowers, and bushes and gnarly trees.

Out of another I get a lovely view of the bay and a little private wharf belonging to the estate. There is a beautiful shaded lane that runs down there from the house. I always fancy I see people walking in these numerous paths and arbors, but John has cautioned me not to give way to fancy in the least. He says that with my imaginative power and habit of story-making, a nervous weakness like mine is sure to lead to all manner of excited fancies, and that I ought to use my will and good sense to check the tendency. So I try.

I think sometimes that if I were only well enough to write a little it would relieve the press of ideas and rest me.

But I find I get pretty tired when I try.

It is so discouraging not to have any advice and companionship about my work. When I get really well, John says we will ask Cousin Henry and Julia down for a long visit; but he says he would as soon put fireworks in my pillow-case as to let me have those stimulating people about now.

I wish I could get well faster.

But I must not think about that. This paper looks to me as if it *knew* what a vicious influence it had!

There is a recurrent spot where the pattern lolls like a broken neck and two bulbous eyes stare at you upside down.

I get positively angry with the imperti-[**page 650, column 1:**]nence of it and the everlastingness. Up and down and sideways they crawl, and those absurd, unblinking eyes are everywhere. There is one place where two breadths didn't match, and the eyes go all up and down the line, one a little higher than the other.

I never saw so much expression in an inanimate thing before, and we all know how much expression they have! I used to lie awake as a child and get more entertainment and terror out of blank walls and plain furniture than most children could find in a toy-store.

I remember what a kindly wink the knobs of our big, old bureau used to have, and there was one chair that always seemed like a strong friend.

I used to feel that if any of the other things looked too fierce I could always hop into that chair and be safe.

The furniture in this room is no worse than inharmonious, however, for we had to bring it all from downstairs. I suppose when this was used as a playroom they had to take the nursery things out, and no wonder! I never saw such ravages as the children have made here.

The wall-paper, as I said before, is torn off in spots, and it sticketh closer than a brother — they must have had perseverance as well as hatred.

Then the floor is scratched and gouged and splintered, the plaster itself is dug out here and there, and this great heavy bed which is all we found in the room, looks as if it had been through the wars.

But I don't mind it a bit — only the paper.

There comes John's sister. Such a dear girl as she is, and so careful of me! I must not let her find me writing.

She is a perfect and enthusiastic housekeeper, and hopes for no better profession. I verily believe she thinks it is the writing which made me sick!

But I can write when she is out, and see her a long way off from these windows.

There is one that commands the road, a lovely shaded winding road, and one that just looks off over the country. A lovely country, too, full of great elms and velvet meadows.

This wallpaper has a kind of sub-pattern in a different shade, a particularly [page 650, column 2:]irritating one, for you can only see it in certain lights, and not clearly then.

But in the places where it isn't faded and where the sun is just so — I can see a strange, provoking, formless sort of figure, that seems to skulk about behind that silly and conspicuous front design.

There's sister on the stairs!

* * * * * *

3 [page 650, column 2:]Well, the Fourth of July is over! The people are all gone and I am tired out. John thought it might do me good to see a little company, so we just had mother and Nellie and the children down for a week.

Of course I didn't do a thing. Jennie sees to everything now.

But it tired me all the same.

John says if I don't pick up faster he shall send me to Weir Mitchell in the fall.

But I don't want to go there at all. I had a friend who was in his hands once, and she says he is just like John and my brother, only more so!

Besides, it is such an undertaking to go so far.

I don't feel as if it was worth while to turn my hand over for anything, and I'm getting dreadfully fretful and querulous.

I cry at nothing, and cry most of the time.

Of course I don't when John is here, or anybody else, but when I am alone.

And I am alone a good deal just now. John is kept in town very often by serious cases, and Jennie is good and lets me alone when I want her to.

So I walk a little in the garden or down that lovely lane, sit on the porch under the roses, and lie down up here a good deal.

I'm getting really fond of the room in spite of the wallpaper. Perhaps *because* of the wallpaper.

It dwells in my mind so!

I lie here on this great immovable bed — it is nailed down, I believe — and follow that pattern about by the hour. It is as good as gymnastics, I assure you. I start, we'll say, at the bottom, down in the corner over there where it has not been touched, and I determine for the thousandth time that I *will* follow that pointless pattern to some sort of a conclusion.

[page 651, column1:]I know a little of the principle of design, and I know this thing was not arranged on any laws of radiation, or alternation, or repetition, or symmetry, or anything else that I ever heard of.

It is repeated, of course, by the breadths, but not otherwise.

Looked at in one way each breadth stands alone, the bloated curves and flourishes — a kind of "debased Romanesque" with *delirium tremens*[13] — go waddling up and down in isolated columns of fatuity.

But, on the other hand, they connect diagonally, and the sprawling outlines run off in great slanting waves of optic horror, like a lot of wallowing seaweeds in full chase.

The whole thing goes horizontally, too, at least it seems so, and I exhaust myself in trying to distinguish the order of its going in that direction.

They have used a horizontal breadth for a frieze,[14] and that adds wonderfully to the confusion.

There is one end of the room where it is almost intact, and there, when the crosslights fade and the low sun shines directly upon it, I can almost fancy radiation after all, — the interminable grotesques seem to form around a common centre and rush off in headlong plunges of equal distraction.

It makes me tired to follow it. I will take a nap I guess.

* * * * * *

4 [page 651, column 1:]I don't know why I should write this.

I don't want to.

I don't feel able.

And I know John would think it [page 651, column 2:]absurd. But I *must* say what I feel and think in some way — it is such a relief!

But the effort is getting to be greater than the relief.

Half the time now I am awfully lazy, and lie down ever so much.

John says I mustn't lose my strength, and has me take cod liver oil and lots of tonics and things, to say nothing of ale and wine and rare meat.

Dear John! He loves me very dearly, and hates to have me sick. I tried to have a real earnest reasonable talk with him the other day, and tell him how I wish he would let me go and make a visit to Cousin Henry and Julia.

But he said I wasn't able to go, nor able to stand it after I got there; and I did not make out a very good case for myself, for I was crying before I had finished.

[page 652, column 1:]It is getting to be a great effort for me to think straight. Just this nervous weakness I suppose.

And dear John gathered me up in his arms,[15] and just carried me upstairs and laid me on the bed, and sat by me and read to me till it tired my head.

He said I was his darling and his comfort and all he had, and that I must take care of myself for his sake, and keep well.

He says no one but myself can help me out of it, that I must use my will and self-control and not let any silly fancies run away with me.

---

13 This phrasing is often cited in Gilman criticism. Gilman here describes the wallpaper as a debased or lesser quality Romanesque architecture, a transitional style of design common in painting and sculpture from the ninth to the twelfth centuries. The already inferior Romanesque design is then personified with a human ailment, delirium tremens: an acute state of mental confusion marked by sweating, hallucinations, tremors, delusions, etc. The term delirium tremens, abbreviated as the "dts," describes a state of shaking and incoherence induced by alcohol poisoning.

14 Here the manuscript reads "border."

15 Here the manuscript reads: "And dear John gathered me up in his strong arms." Again John gains strength.

"She didn't know I was in the Room."

Figure 7 Jo. H. Hatfield, "She didn't know I was in the Room" for "The Yellow Wall-Paper," *New England Magazine*, 1892. Courtesy of Special Collections, Schaffer Library, Union College.

There's one comfort, the baby is well and happy, and does not have to occupy this nursery with the horrid wallpaper.

If we had not used it,[16] that blessed child would have! What a fortunate escape! Why, I wouldn't have a child of mine, an impressionable little thing, live in such a room for worlds.

---

16 The manuscript states, "If I had not used it that blessed child would have!"

I never thought of it before, but it is lucky that John kept me here after all, I can stand it so much easier than a baby, you see.

Of course I never mention it to them any more — I am too wise, — but I keep watch of it all the same.

There are things in that paper that nobody knows but me, or ever will.

Behind that outside pattern the dim shapes get clearer every day.

It is always the same shape, only very numerous.

And it is like a woman stooping down and creeping about behind that pattern. I don't like it a bit. I wonder — I begin to think — I wish John would take me away from here!

* * * * * *

5 [page 652, column 1:]It is so hard to talk with John about my case, because he is so wise, and because he loves me so.

But I tried it last night.

It was moonlight. The moon shines in all around just as the sun does.

I hate to see it sometimes, it creeps so slowly, and always comes in by one window or another.

John was asleep and I hated to waken him, so I kept still and watched the moonlight on that undulating wallpaper till I felt creepy.[17]

[page 652, column 2:]The faint figure behind seemed to shake the pattern, just as if she wanted to get out.

I got up softly and went to feel and see if the paper *did* move, and when I came back John was awake.

"What is it, little girl?" he said. "Don't go walking about like that — you'll get cold."

I thought it was a good time to talk, so I told him that I really was not gaining here, and that I wished he would take me away.

"Why, darling!" said he, "our lease will be up in three weeks, and I can't see how to leave before.

"The repairs are not done at home, and I cannot possibly leave town just now. Of course if you were in any danger, I could and would, but you really are better, dear, whether you can see it or not. I am a doctor, dear, and I know. You are gaining flesh and color, your appetite is better, I feel really much easier about you."

"I don't weigh a bit more," said I, "nor as much; and my appetite may be better in the evening when you are here, but it is worse in the morning when you are away!"

"Bless her little heart!" said he with a big hug, "she shall be as sick as she pleases! But now let's improve the shining hours[18] by going to sleep, and talk about it in the morning."

---

17 The line reads in the ms., "till it made me creepy."
18 John paraphrases the second line of the first stanza of Isaac Watts's didactic poem "Against Idleness and Mischief" included in Watts's devotional treatise *Divine and Moral Songs for Children* (1715). The opening lines read, "How doth the little busy bee/ Improve each shining hour". The line from one of Watts's decidedly mild poems invokes the glory of the daytime made glowing by the busy bee's industry. A fan of Lewis Carroll, Gilman was likely familiar with Carroll's parody in *The Adventures of Alice in Wonderland* wherein he transforms the industrious bee into a lazy crocodile. When viewed in its original context, the reference is ironic in that the narrator is undergoing a rest cure requiring absolute inactivity.

"And you won't go away?" I asked gloomily.

"Why, how can I, dear? It is only three weeks more and then we will take a nice little trip of a few days while Jennie is getting the house ready. Really dear you are better!"

"Better in body perhaps — " I began, and stopped short, for he sat up straight and looked at me with such a stern, reproachful look that I could not say another word.

"My darling," said he, "I beg of you, for my sake and for our child's sake, as well as for your own, that you will never for one instant let that idea enter your mind! There is nothing so dangerous, so fascinating, to a temperament like yours. It is a false and foolish fancy. Can you not trust me as a physician when I tell you so?"

[page 653, column 1:]So of course I said no more on that score, and we went to sleep before long. He thought I was asleep at first, but I wasn't, and lay there for hours trying to decide whether that front pattern and the back pattern really did move together or separately.

* * * * * *

6 [page 653, column 1:]On a pattern like this, by daylight, there is a lack[19] of sequence, a defiance of law, that is a constant irritant to a normal mind.

The color is hideous enough, and unreliable enough, and infuriating enough, but the pattern is torturing.

You think you have mastered it, but just as you get well underway in following, it turns a back-somersault and there you are. It slaps you in the face, knocks you down, and tramples upon you. It is like a bad dream.

The outside pattern is a florid arabesque,[20] reminding one of a fungus. If you can imagine a toadstool in joints, an interminable string of toadstools, budding and sprouting in endless convolutions — why, that is something like it.

That is, sometimes!

There is one marked peculiarity about this paper, a thing nobody seems to notice but myself, and that is that it changes as the light changes.

When the sun shoots in through the east window — I always watch for that first long, straight ray — it changes so quickly that I never can quite believe it.

That is why I watch it always.

By moonlight — the moon shines in all night when there is a moon — I wouldn't know it was the same paper.

At night in any kind of light, in twilight, candlelight, lamplight, and worst of all by moonlight, it becomes bars! The outside pattern I mean, and the woman behind it is as plain as can be.

I didn't realize for a long time what the thing was that showed behind, that dim sub-pattern, but now I am quite sure it is a woman.

By daylight she is subdued, quiet. I fancy it is the pattern that keeps her so still. It is so puzzling. It keeps me quiet by the hour.

---

19 The word "certain" precedes "lack" in the ms.
20 The term "arabesque" describes a heavily ornate and complex eastern design of, for example, flowers, foliage, and geometrical figures that has narcotic associations.

I lie down ever so much now. John says it is good for me, and to sleep all I can.
[page 653, column 2:]Indeed he started the habit by making me lie down for an hour after each meal.

It is a very bad habit I am convinced, for you see I don't sleep.

And that cultivates deceit, for I don't tell them I'm awake — O no!

The fact is I am getting a little afraid of John.

He seems very queer sometimes, and even Jennie has an inexplicable look.

It strikes me occasionally, just as a scientific hypothesis, — that perhaps it is the paper!

I have watched John when he did not know I was looking, and come into the room suddenly on the most innocent excuses, and I've caught him several times *looking at the paper!* And Jennie too. I caught Jennie with her hand on it once.

She didn't know I was in the room, and when I asked her in a quiet, a very quiet voice, with the most restrained manner possible, what she was doing with the paper — she turned around as if she had been caught stealing, and looked quite angry — asked me why I should frighten her so!

Then she said that the paper stained everything it touched, that she had found yellow smooches on all my clothes and John's, and she wished we would be more careful!

Did not that sound innocent? But I know she was studying that pattern, and I am determined that nobody shall find it out but myself!

* * * * * *

7 [page 653, column 2:]Life is very much more exciting now than it used to be. You see I have something more to expect, to look forward to, to watch. I really do eat better, and am more quiet than I was.[21]

John is so pleased to see me improve! He laughed a little the other day, and said I seemed to be flourishing in spite of my wall-paper.

I turned it off with a laugh. I had no intention of telling him it was *because* of the wall-paper — he would make fun of me. He might even want to take me away.

I don't want to leave now until I have found it out. There is a week more, and I think that will be enough.

* * * * * *

8 [page 653, column 2:]I'm feeling ever so much better! I [page 654, column 1:] don't sleep much at night, for it is so interesting to watch developments; but I sleep a good deal in the daytime.

In the daytime it is tiresome and perplexing.

There are always new shoots on the fungus, and new shades of yellow all over it. I cannot keep count of them, though I have tried conscientiously.

It is the strangest yellow, that wall-paper![22] It makes me think of all the yellow things I ever saw — not beautiful ones like buttercups, but old foul, bad yellow things.

---

21 In the ms. this reads, "am much more quiet than I was."
22 The manuscript uses "paper" instead of "wall-paper." Then a line is inserted in the manuscript that says, "A sickly penetrating suggestive yellow."

But there is something else[23] about that paper — the smell! I noticed it the moment we came into the room, but with so much air and sun it was not bad.

Now we have had a week of fog and rain, and whether the windows are open or not, the smell is here.

It creeps all over the house.

I find it hovering in the dining-room, skulking in the parlor, hiding in the hall, lying in wait for me on the stairs.

It gets into my hair.

Even when I go to ride, if I turn my head suddenly and surprise it — there is that smell!

Such a peculiar odor, too! I have spent hours in trying to analyze it, to find what it smelled like.

It is not bad — at first, and very gentle, but quite the subtlest, most enduring odor I ever met.

In this damp weather it is awful, I wake up in the night and find it hanging over me.

It used to disturb me at first. I thought seriously of burning the house — to reach the smell.

But now I am used to it. The only thing I can think of that it is like is the *color* of the paper! A yellow smell.

There is a very funny mark on this wall, low down, near the mopboard. A streak that runs round the room. It goes behind every piece of furniture, except the bed, a long, straight, even *smooch*, as if it had been rubbed over and over.

I wonder how it was done and who did it, and what they did it for. Round and round and round — round and round and round — it makes me dizzy!

* * * * * *

9 [page 654, column 2:]I really have discovered something at last.

Through watching so much at night, when it changes so, I have finally found out.

The front pattern *does* move — and no wonder! The woman behind shakes it!

Sometimes I think there are a great many women behind, and sometimes only one, and she crawls around fast, and her crawling shakes it all over.

Then in the very bright spots she keeps still, and in the very shady spots she just takes hold of the bars and shakes them hard.

And she is all the time trying to climb through. But nobody could climb through that pattern — it strangles so; I think that is why it has so many heads.

They get through, and then the pattern strangles them off and turns them upside down, and makes their eyes white!

If those heads were covered or taken off it would not be half so bad.

* * * * * *

10 [page 654, column 2:]I think that woman gets out in the daytime!

And I'll tell you why — privately — I've seen her!

I can see her out of every one of my windows!

---

23 The ms. reads, "But there is another thing about that paper—the smell!"

It is the same woman, I know, for she is always creeping, and most women do not creep by daylight.

I see her in that long shaded lane, creeping up and down. I see her in those dark grape arbors, creeping all around the garden.

I see her on that long road under the trees, creeping along, and when a carriage comes she hides under the blackberry vines.

I don't blame her a bit. It must be very humiliating to be caught creeping by daylight!

I always lock the door when I creep by daylight. I can't do it at night, for I know John would suspect something at once.

And John is so queer now, that I don't want to irritate him. I wish he would take another room! Besides, I don't want anybody to get that woman out at night but myself.

I often wonder if I could see her out of all the windows at once.

[page 655, column 1:]But, turn as fast as I can, I can only see out of one at one time.

And though I always see her, she *may* be able to creep faster than I can turn!

I have watched her sometimes away off in the open country, creeping as fast as a cloud shadow in a high wind.

* * * * * *

11 [page 655, column 1:]If only that top pattern could be gotten off from the under one! I mean to try it,[24] little by little.

I have found out another funny thing, but I shan't tell it this time! It does not do to trust people too much.

There are only two more days to get this paper off, and I believe John is beginning to notice. I don't like the look in his eyes.

And I heard him ask Jennie a lot of professional questions about me. She had a very good report to give.

She said I slept a good deal in the daytime.

John knows I don't sleep very well at night, for all I'm so quiet!

He asked me all sorts of questions, too, and pretended to be very loving and kind.

As if I couldn't see through him!

Still, I don't wonder he acts so, sleeping under this paper for three months.

It only interests me, but I feel sure John and Jennie are secretly affected by it.

* * * * * *

12 [page 655, column 1:]Hurrah! This is the last day, but it is enough. John had to stay in town over night, and won't be out until this evening.

Jennie wanted to sleep with me — the sly thing! but I told her I should undoubtedly rest better for a night all alone.

That was clever, for really I wasn't alone a bit! As soon as it was moonlight and that poor thing began to crawl and shake the pattern, I got up and ran to help her.

24 This line reads in the ms., "I mean to try tearing it, little by little."

__ I pulled and she shook, I shook and she pulled, and before morning we had peeled off yards of that paper.

A strip about as high as my head and half around the room.

And then when the sun came and that awful pattern began to laugh at me, I declared I would finish it to-day!

We go away to-morrow, and they are [page 655, column 2:]moving all my furniture down again to leave things as they were before.

Jennie looked at the wall in amazement, but I told her merrily that I did it out of pure spite at the vicious thing.

She laughed and said she wouldn't mind doing it herself, but I must not get tired.

How she betrayed herself that time!

But I am here, and no person touches this paper but me, — not *alive!*

She tried to get me out of the room — it was too patent! But I said it was so quiet and empty and clean now that I believed I would lie down again and sleep all I could; and not to wake me even for dinner — I would call when I woke.

So now she is gone, and the servants are gone, and the things are gone, and there is nothing left but that great bedstead nailed down, with the canvas mattress we found on it.

We shall sleep downstairs to-night, and take the boat home to-morrow.

I quite enjoy the room, now it is bare again.

How those children did tear about here!

This bedstead is fairly gnawed!

But I must get to work.

I have locked the door and thrown the key down into the front path.

I don't want to go out, and I don't want to have anybody come in, till John comes.

I want to astonish him.

I've got a rope up here that even Jennie did not find. If that woman does get out, and tries to get away, I can tie her!

But I forgot I could not reach far without anything to stand on!

This bed will *not* move!

I tried to lift and push it until I was lame, and then I got so angry I bit off a little piece at one corner — but it hurt my teeth.

Then I peeled off all the paper I could reach standing on the floor. It sticks horribly and the pattern just enjoys it! All those strangled heads and bulbous eyes and waddling fungus growths just shriek with derision!

I am getting angry enough to do something desperate. To jump out of the [page 656, column 1:]window would be admirable exercise, but the bars are too strong even to try.

Besides I wouldn't do it. Of course not. I know well enough that a step like that is improper and might be misconstrued.

I don't like to *look* out of the windows even — there are so many of those creeping women, and they creep so fast.

I wonder if they all came out of that wall-paper as I did?

But I am securely fastened now by my well-hidden rope — you don't get *me* out in the road there!

I suppose I shall have to get back behind the pattern when it comes night, and that is hard!

It is so pleasant to be out in this great room and creep around as I please!

I don't want to go outside. I won't, even if Jennie asks me to.

For outside you have to creep on the ground, and everything is green instead of yellow.

But here I can creep smoothly on the floor, and my shoulder just fits in that long smooch around the wall, so I cannot lose my way.

Why there's John at the door!

[page 656, column 2:]It is no use, young man, you can't open it!

How he does call and pound!

Now he's crying for an axe.

It would be a shame to break down that beautiful door![25]

"John dear!" said I in the gentlest voice, "the key is down by the front steps, under a plantain leaf!"

That silenced him for a few moments.

Then he said — very quietly indeed, "Open the door, my darling!"

"I can't," said I. "The key is down by the front door under a plantain leaf!"

And then I said it again, several times, very gently and slowly, and said it so often that he had to go and see, and he got it of course, and came in. He stopped short by the door.

"What is the matter?" he cried. "For God's sake, what are you doing!"

I kept on creeping just the same, but I looked at him over my shoulder.

"I've got out at last," said I, "in spite of you and Jane! And I've pulled off most of the paper, so you can't put me back!"

Now why should that man have fainted? But he did, and right across my path by the wall, so that I had to creep over him every time![26]

Entry 1
Gilman establishes the setting for the story and the gender dynamics between the nameless narrator and her doctor-husband, John. The narrator, who has an active imagination, clashes with rational John, a man of science in an age of industry and industrialization; such a dichotomy reflects the dual tendencies of Romanticism and realism characteristic of the nineteenth century in England and America. In a nod to the transatlantic debate over women's reading,[27] Gilman also reveals the narrator has a penchant for British fiction: she is a reader as well as a writer, who finds writing therapeutic. Her diary writing

---

25 The adjective "strong" again appears in the ms., this time before "door": "It would be a shame to break that beautiful strong door!" Repeatedly, the copy-text magnifies John's strength.
26 The concluding line of the ms. reads, "so that I had to creep over him!" The addition of "every time" to the NEM version compounds the narrator's insanity, suggesting the narrator's circling is ongoing.
27 For more information on the fiery transatlantic debate over women's reading, I recommend Catherine Golden's *Images of the Woman Reader in Victorian British and American Fiction*, published by University Press of Florida in 2003.

Figure 8 Jo. H. Hatfield, tailpiece for "The Yellow Wall-Paper," *New England Magazine*, 1892. Courtesy of Special Collections, Schaffer Library, Union College.

provides an outlet for her nervous condition even if her doctor-husband forbids it (see also Alice James, **pp. 32–4**).

Critics also have made much of how the narrator describes the ancestral hall as a "strange" "haunted house" with an air of "ghostliness." Early critics established these Gothic references in likening "The Yellow Wall-Paper" to a horror tale in the tradition of Edgar Allan Poe (see **pp. 28–32**). Twentieth-century critics use these same "ghostly" references to various ends: for example, Janice Haney-Peritz invokes the work of Lacan to argue that the narrator firmly encrypts herself in the realm of the imaginary (see **pp. 96–9**). Jonathan Crewe uses these terms as an invitation to apply queer theory as a gloss to read the story (see **pp. 111–14**).

Gilman makes no mention of the narrator's appearance in the text, but the first illustration renders her according to Victorian convention. Hatfield shows her to be a respectable and sane woman wearing conventional period dress—high collar, long sleeves, full-length bodice; her hair sweeps into a bun in accordance with the coiffure of the day. However, she is writing, a subversive act. Limited intellectual activity—along with enforced rest, seclusion, diet, and various types of electrical stimulation and massage—were essential components of the rest cure that American physician and author S. Weir Mitchell pioneered and Gilman experienced firsthand in the spring of 1887 (see Mitchell, **pp. 61–8** and Gilman, **pp. 47–52**). Serving as headpiece to the entire story, the illustration gives prominence to the narrator's commitment to write at a time when women's intellectual pursuits were a topic of grave concern and thought to sabotage women's health (see Clarke, **pp. 57–9** and Beecher and Beecher Stowe, **pp. 52–5**).

While the caption accompanying this illustration labels the narrator's room an "atrocious nursery," Gilman also refers to it as a playroom and gymnasium. For what reasons might John insist the narrator reside in a room that invites associations of infantilization? Hatfield features the bars on the windows, mentioned in this entry. The bars, nailed down bed, and gate at the top of the stairs can be interpreted, alternatively, as symbols of patriarchal repression. How might these interpretations of infantilization and repression intersect?

The opening entry also calls attention to the dominant symbol of the wallpaper, which grows increasingly animated as the story continues. Even here Gilman singles out its provocative yet irritating pattern, its repellent colors, and its noxious smell. Many critics have scrutinized the color of the dominant symbol of the story, offering various interpretations to consider. To Susan Lanser, yellow signifies Gilman's nativist tendencies heightened in response to the influx of immigrants from Asia and southern Europe during a period commonly referred to as the Yellow Peril (see Lanser, **pp. 105–8**). To Mary Jacobus, yellow embodies man's fears of woman's sexuality during a time of sexual repression in Victorian America (see Jacobus, **pp. 94–6**). To Ann Heilmann, yellow reeks of a dominant male aestheticism against which the narrator rebels (see Heilmann, **pp. 114–17**).

This entry also establishes issues of gender and power embedded in the language of the text—a prime source of evidence that readers often overlook. That the narrator remains nameless offers a prime topic for exploration. She refers to herself as "myself" in the opening entry; this weak reflexive case pronoun reads more cumbersomely than the objective case "me," which more commonly follows a preposition. The narrator also frequently refers to herself as "one," a pronoun linguist Otto Jespersen calls "a kind of disguised *I*" (150) in *The Essentials of English Grammar* (published by Alabama University Press in 1981). In contrast, throughout the opening entry, the narrator continually refers to John by name. In fact, his name thrice prominently appears as the first word in a series of one- and two-sentence paragraphs in this entry (**p. 131**), conveying the narrator's deference to John as well as her agitated state. Readers might profitably consider if the narrator's namelessness contributes to her sense of fragmentation while her reliance on vague self-references ("one"), qualifiers (e.g. "personally", "perhaps"), and rhetorical questions ("what is one to do?") indicates her perceived social inferiority to her physician-husband from whom she hides her writing.

Entry 2

After a two-week period of abstinence, the narrator resumes her writing of the very story we are reading. She maintains in the second entry that writing is therapeutic, but her previous insistence on this point gives way to fatigue. The opening illustration positioned as headpiece to the story actually accompanies a line in this entry. With the opening image of a sane and respectable-looking narrator placed outside this section in the *New England Magazine* version, the narrator's habit of story making and the fervency of her imagination dominate as themes of Entry 2.

The narrator admits to lying awake as a child, staring at her walls and furniture, turning inanimate objects into terrors and friends. How might the narrator's penchant for fancies, of which John disapproves, inform her perception of the "formless sort of figure" whom the narrator ultimately frees in the twelfth and final entry? As Catherine Golden argues in "The Writing of 'The Yellow Wallpaper': A Double Palimpsest," the wallpaper functions as a "palimpsest" with two perceptible patterns—the dominant front pattern of bars and the muted figure behind it (see **pp. 101–4**).

This entry introduces the narrator's baby, a son who makes her uncontrollably nervous, and a key secondary character, John's sister. Jennie embodies society's construction of domestic femininity and embraces her domestic role absolutely. In superintending the housekeeping of a home that rightfully falls under the jurisdiction of her brother's wife, Jennie becomes a "lineal descendant of Jane Murdstone" (198), the odious housekeeper in Charles Dickens's *David Copperfield* (1850), as John Sutherland argues in his artful essay on Gilman's story in *Can Jane Eyre be Happy?* (Oxford University Press, 1997; see Further Reading, **p. 159**). Unlike Gilman's later fiction where women unite against a patriarch (e.g. see "Turned" [1911] and *Unpunished* [*ca.*1929]), Jennie buys into the traditional male medical model that the writing makes the narrator mad, and she monitors her sister-in-law's rest cure for her brother.

John's language in this entry appears indicative of the way many Victorian men saw women as infantile "Gooseys" to help them build an opposing case for masculine rationality. The term "blessed little goose" may well have been meant as a term of endearment. The epithet "little" here, which recurs when John calls the narrator his "little girl" (**p. 138**), makes the narrator seem child-like and diminutive in accordance with contemporary feminine ideals. The term speaks to a bourgeois consciousness that imprisoned women like Henrik Ibsen's Nora Helmer of *A Doll's House* (1879). Likewise, another man of science, Elizabeth Gaskell's Doctor Gibson in *Wives and Daughters* (1866), repeatedly calls his bright and dutiful daughter "my little Molly" and uses the term "Goosey" as a pet name for her. These terms not only render a woman endearingly brainless but deny her sexuality and responsibility. In her oeuvre, Gilman rejected the notion of woman as a small, passive being in favor of a stronger brand of womanhood, as evident in her creation of the liberated Amazonian women populating her all-female community in her utopian novel *Herland* (1915). Moreover, as in other late nineteenth-century literature that treats the "woman question" (e.g. Ibsen's *A Doll's House*, Kate Chopin's *The Awakening*

[1899] and "The Story of an Hour" [1894, see **pp. 37–9**], and Mona Caird's *The Daughters of Danaus* [1894]), the female protagonist calls on her inner resources to attempt to free herself from patriarchal oppression.

This entry also calls attention to changes in the dominant symbol of the story. Gilman personifies the wallpaper, which gains emotion and movement. It glares at her with features that seem like disconnected human parts—two bulging eyes and a broken neck. Eventually, it looks like "a formless sort of figure." The paper, as the narrator sometimes calls it, still allegedly repels her, though it fascinates the narrator more and more as she identifies a sub-pattern, and it takes on human characteristics.

Entry 3

The entire text contains short, choppy paragraphs, lending a sense of fragmentation to the story. However, from this third entry, which begins with a reference to "Independence Day" in the United States, the narrator does not refer to her act of writing. Has the story turned into an interior monologue (see Sutherland, Further Reading, **p. 159**)? Rather, does it read as a stream of consciousness narrative like Gilman's "Through This" (see **pp. 34–7**)?

The entry includes Gilman's oft-cited reference to her famous neurologist, Dr. Silas Weir Mitchell, who went by his middle name, Weir. In 1887, Charlotte Perkins Stetson underwent Mitchell's rest cure in his Philadelphia sanatorium. Gilman claims in her 1913 *Forerunner* article "Why I Wrote 'The Yellow Wallpaper'?" (see **pp. 45–7**) that she wrote her story to show Mitchell the debilitating consequences of his rest cure, particularly his final mandate never to write for the rest of her life. Blurring the lines between fiction and reality, this section has invited an autobiographical reading, evident in early criticism about "The Yellow Wall-Paper." For example, Elaine R. Hedges argues that where the narrator "fails," Gilman succeeded in real life and went on to write this story (see **pp. 88–90**). Sandra Gilbert and Susan Gubar, however, argue that the narrator follows the same steps as Gilman herself, moving from "dis-ease into health" (see **pp. 91–2**).

Gilman followed a two-year course at the Rhode Island School of Design in Providence, RI and was a freelance commercial artist in the years prior to her marriage. In this entry, she endows her narrator with a knowledge of design. The narrator calls attention to bloated curves of the paper, its "optic horror," transferring the ghostliness of the place onto the dominant theme of the story itself. The narrator changes her opinion of the wallpaper, which lacks the principles of symmetry and alternation common to period wallpapers (see Eastlake, **pp. 55–6**). Terms "in spite of" and "*because*"—hint how the wallpaper transforms from a source of repulsion to attraction, fascination, and eventually obsession. Interested readers might examine the work of Tom Lutz, who reads "The Yellow Wall-Paper" in relation to period concerns surrounding wallpaper (see **pp. 108–11**). Ann Heilmann calls attention to the dominant male aesthetic of the paper, which the narrator attempts to revise (see **pp. 114–17**).

Entry 4
This fourth entry also invites a reading of the wallpaper as a palimpsest with dominant and muted sides that warrant investigation. In what ways do the narrator's actions—the dominant text—show a characterization of the narrator different from her language of self-expression? The narrator's uncontrollable and frequent crying, extreme fatigue, and hallucination, all signs of the onset of madness, occur just when the narrator's language—the muted text—reveals a more forceful sense of self. The frequent use of "I" at the beginning of the fourth entry contrasts forcefully to the language of the first entry where the narrator defers to John and weakly refers to herself as "myself" and "one" (see pp. 131–3 and Golden, pp. 101–4). Each sentence in this "I" sequence forms a one-sentence paragraph, engendering a sense of fragmentation that critics interpret as psychic degeneration.

Simultaneously in this entry, the figure in the wallpaper gains definition: now she is "like a woman stooping down and creeping about behind that pattern" (p. 138). The narrator will adopt this movement of "creeping," or crawling slowly and stealthily. Do the narrator's hallucinations and avowal that she alone sees things in the wallpaper suggest her ultimate defeat in madness? Conversely, how might her recognition that the trapped woman graphically represents her own condition in her patriarchal world be interpreted as a victory?

The second illustration, positioned within this entry in the New England Magazine version, actually refers to the sixth entry where the narrator exhibits paranoia surrounding her preoccupation with the wallpaper. She fears John and Jennie are monitoring her behavior as she studies the wallpaper and vows that she alone can figure out the pattern. Paranoia was a common symptom of puerperal mania, a nervous disease similar to the one from which the narrator suffers (see Barker, pp. 59–61). Although the narrator still appears sane in this illustration—she wears the same conventional dress and coiffure—her face exhibits a clouded look, suggesting the beginning stages of madness. Hatfield indicates a flamboyant design in the section of wallpaper surrounding Jennie; of note, the design seems visible to the reader and to the narrator, but invisible to Jennie. Gilman develops the narrator's paranoia in the sixth entry. However, by placing this illustration in the fourth entry, the New England Magazine version arguably emphasizes two key symptoms of the narrator's madness—hallucinations and paranoia, also evident in the narrator of Poe's "The Tell-Tale Heart" narrator (see pp. 28–32).

Entry 5
In the fifth entry, Gilman linguistically exhibits the patriarchal domination of women. Patronizing language is also evident in the fourth entry where the narrator describes how John carries her upstairs and reads to her in bed. In this entry, he calls her his "little girl," scolds her for getting out of bed at night, and implies her nervous depression is a child's ploy for attention: " 'Bless her little heart!' . . . 'she shall be as sick as she pleases!' " (p. 138) Through John's

language, Gilman intensifies the notion of infantilization embedded in the rest cure, which put women to bed and left them dependent on a doctor's sage council.

The narrator alarms her physician-husband when she states that she is better in body, though not in mind. Gilman here taps into concerns of the nineteenth-century medical community. In his treatise on the related disease of puerperal mania, Fordyce Barker advances that if the condition persists, the result is prolonged insanity. John's "stern, reproachful look" (p. 139) and insistence that the narrator squelch this idea from her vivid imagination validates not only the seriousness of the narrator's mental condition but Gilman's knowledge of and belief in neurasthenia, if not the proposed cure for it (see Lutz, pp. 108–11).

Entry 6

This entry continues many salient themes: the personification of the paper (here it stains the narrator's clothes, changes with the light, and forcefully "slaps," "knocks down," and "tramples" the narrator); the peculiarities of the wallpaper pattern (e.g. burgeoning toadstools and heavily decorated arabesques; see Roth, pp. 117–21; Heather Kirk Thomas in Golden and Zangrando's The Mixed Legacy of Charlotte Perkins Gilman, Further Reading, p. 161); the narrator's obsession with "reading" the pattern of the paper (see Barbara Hochman, Further Reading, p. 159; Catherine Golden, Chapter 7 in Images of the Woman Reader in Victorian British and American Fiction); and the notion of wallpaper as palimpsest (see Golden, pp. 101–4). The figure trapped behind the dominant pattern of bars gains definition. The metaphorical qualification, "like a woman," expressed in the fourth entry (p. 138) gives way to certainty: "now I am quite sure it is a woman" (p. 139). The wallpaper marks a smooch on the narrator, crawling in circles. From a Derridean perspective, is the narrator producing the self she wishes to be through writing her body and thus becoming part of a chain of production within the capitalist marketplace (see Benn Michaels, pp. 99–101)?

The second of the three illustrations, positioned in the fourth entry, comes from a line in this sixth entry, which reveals the narrator's suspicion and fear of John, whom she calls "queer." She admits a new habit of deceit, feigning sleep after a meal, thus subverting the rest cure that John oversees. Gilman's critique extends to the prevailing medical model, particularly J. Patrick Geddes's (and his pupil J. Arthur Thomson's) belief in different habits of body between the sexes—men have a katabolic constitution providing unlimited energy whereas women with an anabolic constitution have limited energy that they must conserve for reproduction. However, the narrator cannot rest because of her determination to read the wallpaper and decipher its pattern.

Entry 7
Worthy of comment in this four-paragraph entry is the role of the wallpaper. John believes the narrator is getting better "in spite" of the wallpaper; the narrator knows she is allegedly "improving" "*because*" of the wallpaper, but "turned it [John's comment] off with a laugh." John laughs at the narrator in the first entry—Gilman suggests that is expected in a patriarchal marriage. Who is laughing now? And why does the narrator consciously refrain from telling John why she believes she is getting better? Is she again cultivating deceit? Also noteworthy is the narrator's sense of purpose in vowing to remain in the room she once detested to figure out how to read the text on the wall.

Entry 8
Readers might profitably explore the development of the wallpaper in tandem with the narrator's increasing preoccupation with reading its pattern. The paper gains increasing definition in odor, color, and movement. It "creeps"— moves stealthily—and "gets into my hair." The shade of yellow now connotes badness and foulness, and the smell is a "yellow smell," leading Susan Lanser to argue that Gilman projects onto the color of the wallpaper her nativist fears of immigrant populations "creeping" into America and overtaking its Puritan origins (see **pp. 105–8**). Gilman also gives attention to the yellow smooch that encircles the room. Previously, the wallpaper marks the narrator; here she is marking the paper. Is she writing into existence her own body as she wishes it to be, thus birthing herself? To adopt a Derridean perspective, is she becoming part of the capitalist chain of production (see Benn Michaels, **pp. 99–101**)?

Entry 9
Feminist critics of the 1970s emphasize the sexual politics of the story, which appear vivid in entry nine. The trapped woman functions as the narrator's double. More globally, she represents a Victorian woman's place in a patriarchal world. The dominant front or top pattern of bars, in turn, symbolizes the restrictions of the domestic sphere against which the narrator rebels. The narrator's double shakes the bars hard with determination to liberate herself from patriarchy.

The multiplicity of women whom the narrator imagines emerging from the wallpaper supports the notion that the muted pattern symbolizes woman's plight. Infantilized women are reduced to creeping and crawling; such slow but often stealthy movements require keeping the body close to the ground much as a baby does when moving on hands and knees. The narrator connects the dislocated images of strangled heads from the earlier entries to the trapped creeping women attempting to climb/crawl/creep through the front pattern, becoming strangled in the process. To gain further insight into the Victorian ideals of womanhood and Gilman's charges against them, readers might profitably compare this entry to excerpts from Catharine Beecher and Harriet Beecher Stowe and Sylvanus Stall (see **pp. 52–5** and **p. 57**) in conjunction with Gilman's poetry (see "To the Young Wife," **pp. 43–4** and "In Duty Bound," **pp. 42–3**) and short fiction (see "Through This," **pp. 34–7**).

Entry 10
Creeping gains complexity in the tenth entry. The narrator sees a woman creeping outside in the daylight; she seems puzzled that the trapped woman, her double, can creep out of doors and "as fast as a cloud shadow in a high wind" (see **p. 142**). The narrator sympathizes with her double, who risks public humiliation by creeping in daylight; simultaneously, she envies her since she can creep so fast. Creeping, we learn here, is something women typically only do at night. The narrator locks her door when she creeps by daylight; she cannot creep at night because John will object. She acts surreptitiously around John, whom she calls "so queer now" (see **p. 142**). Is her mania deepening? Alternately, is she gaining power in allowing herself to creep in the daytime? In locking John out of the room, is the narrator, who very much longs to write, gaining a room of her own or losing touch with reality?

Critics included in the Modern Criticism section variously interpret Gilman's reference to the narrator's double creeping in "open country." Sandra Gilbert and Susan Gubar connect this image to the progress of nineteenth-century women writers who defy the "texts defined by patriarchal poetics" to move "into the open spaces of their own authority" (see **p. 92**). Janice Haney-Peritz paraphrases Gilbert and Gubar's view to argue just the opposite: the narrator "does not move out into open country" but installs herself firmly in the realm of the imaginary by encrypting herself in a haunted house (see **p. 98**). Thus, critics readily engage in conversation with each other as they read "The Yellow Wall-Paper." Curiously, the term "creeping" recurs in "Through This" where the narrator describes shades of color "creeping" up or down her bedroom wall (see **p. 35** and **p. 37**).

Entry 11
In the penultimate entry, the narrator's paranoia noticeably mounts. The narrator reveals a distrust of John and Jennie, of "people" in general, and even of writing in her diary. She even fears confiding on "dead paper" though she attests this relieves her mind in the opening entry (see **p. 131**). John's and Jennie's professional roles as doctor and caretaker subsume their personal roles as husband and sister-in-law. Gilman also authenticates period beliefs that chemicals in wallpapers cause dementia. While some period critics suggest dyes affect the narrator's mental state, the narrator believes John and Jennie may be affected by the wallpaper. Interested readers might profitably examine 1899 reviews (see **pp. 81–7**) and Tom Lutz's reading of the effects

of poisonous dyes in late nineteenth-century American wallpapers (see **pp. 108–11**).

Entry 12

Although the entries grow shorter as the diary continues (particularly after the fourth entry), this final entry is long and complex. It includes a provocative final illustration of the narrator crawling over John, and an ambiguous ending— the narrator presumes John has fainted, but will he awake? What will happen if and when he does? The dramatic denouement of the story invariably prompts spirited debate. Is the narrator liberated (see Gilbert and Gubar, **pp. 91–2**), dubiously victorious (see Golden, **pp. 101–4**), defeated (see Hedges, **pp. 88–90**), or encrypted in a realm of the imaginary (see Haney-Peritz, **pp. 96–9**)? Since the narrator has locked John out, does she, in madness, gain a room of her own? Rather, does the room trap her in her madness? Does the narrator's crawling symbolize infantilization or rebirth? If the narrator does, in fact, descend into madness, who is writing this story?

More complexities invite consideration. As Catherine Golden argues (see **pp. 101–4**), just at the point where the dominant text of the narrator's actions (e.g. ripping wallpaper from the walls and crawling in circles) accentuates her madness, the muted text suggests that the narrator gains a more powerful sense of self. Pronoun usage and placement in the final entry reveal a reversal in the dynamics of gender and power: the narrator rejects patriarchy and her former passive state. The narrator, who initially defers to her doctor-husband, John, now calls John "he," "him," and "that man." In particular, the demonstrative pronoun "that" distances the narrator from John, and she eventually banishes "him" to a prepositional phrase in the final sentence ("over him"), a non-essential sentence part. The narrator, who disguises her own views as "one" in the first entry (see **pp. 131–3**), forcefully presents her opinions as "I" in this final entry. Beginning and ending sentences with "I" (e.g. " 'I can't,' said I"), the narrator assumes the two most important parts of a sentence in rebelling against patriarchy. Readers contending that the narrator achieves some degree of liberation might profitably contrast her language of self-expression between the first and final entries, noting her powerful language even as she acts out of madness in the twelfth entry. Readers who argue the opposite—that the narrator loses her grip on sanity—might beneficially focus on the proclivity of one-sentence paragraphs that riddle this final entry, the multiplicity of creeping women, and the narrator's avowal that she came out of the wallpaper just like these skulking women.

Of note is the linguistic fusion that occurs between the narrator and the woman trapped behind the bars of the wallpaper. Do the narrator ("I") and the narrator's double ("she") fuse ("we") (**p. 143**)? Such a step invites another question: in becoming one with her double, does the narrator intensify her madness or, alternately, gain power and/or freedom? To compound the complexity, why does the narrator have a rope to tie her double (who may now be one with herself)? She considers suicide, but rejects it since it might look "improper" or be "misconstrued." Does she commit suicide all the same, leading John to faint—a not uncommon student perspective? While my students have effectively linked the narrator's decline to the act of fusing with the woman behind the wallpaper, a puzzle remains with this interpretation: who, in effect, continues the narrative if the narrator, in fusing with her double, has committed suicide and is, in fact, dead? Rather, does the narrator's regard for her larger social reality serve as an indication that she has not lost touch with her proper Victorian American world, another commonly held view?

Readers might beneficially compare Hatfield's first and final depictions of the narrator, paying attention to pose, expression, dress, and hairstyle. How do the postures in the third illustration influence a reading of Doctor John, now in a fetal position, and the narrator, creeping in endless circles over him? How do we read the angle of the narrator's hands and arms as she creeps over John, an obstacle in her path (see "An Obstacle," **pp. 41–2**)? In the NEM magazine version, the words "every time" appear in the final sentence, suggesting this graphic depiction of the narrator's creeping is ongoing. Do this image and the supporting text support a case of full-blown insanity? Her disheveled dress and wild hair prove significant at a time when fashion and coiffure marked a woman's social class and temperament; her pose and frizzled mane depict her as a stereotypical madwoman in the attic, of whom Bertha Mason was a prime example. To readers today, might the narrator's wild and free hair, conversely, symbolize empowerment? If her hair and figure suggest she is free from tight constraints, from whom is she liberated—patriarchy, John, Jennie, and/or Jane?

Who is Jane? The narrator makes but one reference to Jane when she asserts her independence: "I've got out at last, . . . in spite of you and Jane!" (**p. 144**). This reference could conceivably be a printer's error, though this interpretation seems unlikely since Gilman had many opportunities to correct it in subsequent reprintings during her lifetime (e.g. 1899, 1920). The narrator previously mentions two other women characters whose names begin with "J": cousin Julia and Jennie. In the nineteenth century, Jennie was a nickname for Jane and may well refer to her sister-in-law, called Jennie throughout the story. Arguably, Jane may be the narrator's hitherto unmentioned name, a representation of herself as John and traditional nineteenth-century society define her. Such an interpretation grants the narrator a degree of liberation from her traditional roles of wife and mother within a bourgeois domestic sphere that Gilman considered prison bondage; interested readers might also examine the repressive homes in Mona Caird's The Daughters of Danaus (1894), Henrik Ibsen's A Doll's House (1879), as well as Kate Chopin's The Awakening (1899) and "The Story of an Hour" (1894) (see **pp. 37–9**). Finally, what does it mean that the narrator is "out at last" (**p. 144**)? In other words, how do we interpret the narrator's final state—defeat, liberation, or a qualified victory?

4

Further Reading

Further Reading

Recent years have witnessed an explosion of books and articles about "The Yellow Wall-Paper." Not comprehensive, this list guides readers to the most helpful, illuminating, and, in some cases, affordable works that concentrate on "The Yellow Wall-Paper" (or offer significant attention to it) and/or illuminate Gilman's life and legacy. It does not include articles already excerpted in this sourcebook since their inclusion makes implicit my endorsement of them. Fiction by Gilman that complements "The Yellow Wall-Paper" appears in Companion Pieces.

Story Collections

Gilman, Charlotte Perkins. *The Yellow Wall-Paper*. Second Edition. Afterword by Elaine R. Hedges. New York: The Feminist Press, 1996, 8th printing. This revised Feminist Press edition presents the January 1892 version of the story printed in *New England Magazine* (without the original illustrations). Reasonably priced and attractive, the 1996 paperback corrects errors that crept into the first (1973) Feminist Press edition, but retains Hedges's original 1973 afterword; though dated, Hedges's pioneering "Afterword" reintroduced Gilman's story to the academic community and sparked numerous interpretations.

Knight, Denise D., ed. *"The Yellow Wall-Paper" and Selected Stories of Charlotte Perkins Gilman*. Newark, Del.: University of Delaware Press, 1994. Knight includes a substantial, informative introduction, Gilman's original manuscript version of "The Yellow Wall-Paper," its companion tale "Through This," and an ample selection of stories about social consciousness (e.g. "The Vintage"), women's empowerment (e.g. "The Chair of English"), and female bonding (e.g. "Dr. Clair's Place") as well as Gilman's fables, parables, and studies in style (largely originally published in *Forerunner*).

Lane, Ann J., ed. *The Charlotte Perkins Gilman Reader*. 2nd edition. Charlottesville, Va.: University Press of Virginia, 1999. Originally published by Pantheon (1980), this revised paperback edition contains an updated and informative introduction by Gilman biographer Ann J. Lane, the 1892 version of "The Yellow Wall-Paper" (without illustrations), and ten other stories including "Turned,"

"Making a Change," and "The Unnatural Mother." Less effective is Lane's inclusion of representative chapters from seven Gilman novels, most of which are now readily available in their entirety.

Shulman, Robert, ed. *"The Yellow Wall-Paper" and Other Stories*. Oxford: Oxford University Press, 1995. This affordable paperback edition has much to offer: thirty-nine short stories spanning a period of twenty-four years taken from their original magazine publications, such as *New England Magazine* (it reprints the 1892 version of "The Yellow Wall-Paper" without illustrations), *Forerunner, Kate Field's Washington, Woman's Journal*, and the *Impress*. It offers a chronology of Gilman's life, selections from Gilman's story studies, and "Why I Wrote 'The Yellow Wallpaper'?"

Editions with Story and Criticism

Bauer, Dale, ed. *The Yellow Wallpaper*. Boston: Bedford, 1998. Bauer offers a rich presentation of historical information, setting the story in a social and cultural context. A fine volume, it reprints the 1892 version with illustrations as well as helpful selections from, among others, S. Weir Mitchell, Alice James, Jane Addams, Edward Bellamy, John Harvey Kellogg, George M. Beard, Kate Chopin, and Gilman. It includes a comprehensive chronology of Gilman's life and times. The cover art is mistakenly attributed to Josephine H. Hatfield, not the real artist, Joseph Henry Hatfield.

Erskine, Thomas L., and Connie Richards. *The Yellow Wallpaper*. New Brunswick, NJ: Rutgers University Press, 1993. Although the contents are similar to *The Captive Imagination* that appeared the previous year, this edition includes the January 1892 version (without illustrations or bibliographical codes), two Gilman short stories ("Through This" and "Making a Change"), and nine works of criticism on "The Yellow Wall-Paper," notably one by Lanser not included in *The Captive Imagination*.

Golden, Catherine J. *The Captive Imagination: A Casebook on "The Yellow Wallpaper."* New York: The Feminist Press, 1992. This edition, which includes the original 1892 illustrations by Jo. H. Hatfield, regrettably inherited errors that crept into the 1973 Feminist Press edition. Effective for classroom teaching, it contains an informative introductory essay, a substantial background section, fourteen previously published critical essays, and a retrospective essay by Elaine R. Hedges specially commissioned for this volume.

Articles

Fetterley, Judith. "Reading About Reading: 'A Jury of Her Peers,' 'The Murders in the Rue Morgue,' and 'The Yellow Wallpaper." In *Gender and Reading: Essays on Readers, Texts, and Contexts*. Eds. Elizabeth A. Flynn and Patrocinio P. Schweikhert. Baltimore, Md.: Johns Hopkins University Press, 1986, 147–64.

Fetterley reads the wallpaper as a text through which the narrator expresses herself in this essay, which analyzes "The Yellow Wall-Paper" alongside works by Susan Glaspell and Edgar Allan Poe.

Hedges, Elaine R. " 'Out at Last?': 'The Yellow Wallpaper' after Two Decades of Feminist Criticism." In *The Captive Imagination*. Ed. Catherine Golden. New York: The Feminist Press, 1992, 319–33. Analyzing the pioneering 1970s feminist essays through to new historicist and cultural studies approaches in the 1980s and early 1990s, Hedges offers an important overview of ways critics within and beyond this volume have explored Gilman's landmark tale.

Hochman, Barbara. "The Reading Habit and 'The Yellow Wallpaper.' " *American Literature* 74: 1 (2002): 89–110. Hochman presents the narrator's obsession with the wallpaper in relation to period concerns with reading addiction, commonly referred to as the "reading habit."

Scharnhorst, Gary. "A Note on Gilman's 'M. D.' " *Charlotte Perkins Gilman Newsletter* IX: 1 (Spring 2004: 5). Scharnhorst provides evidence that one of Gilman's first and harshest reviewers, who she suspected was a male doctor—and whose identity pioneering critics assumed as well—was, in fact, a male Medicinae Doctor.

Shumaker, Conrad. " 'Too Terribly Good to Be Printed': Charlotte Perkins Gilman's 'The Yellow Wallpaper.' " *American Literature* 4 (1985): 588–99. Shumaker analyzes Gilman's tale in relation to central concerns within the dominant tradition of American literature represented by Henry James, Mark Twain, Edith Wharton, and, in particular, Nathaniel Hawthorne.

Smith-Rosenberg, Carroll. "The Hysterical Woman: Sex Roles and Role Conflict in Nineteenth-Century America" *Social Research* 39 (Winter 1972): 652–78. In the late 1960s and early 1970s, nineteenth-century women's health emerged as an area of importance in social history and literature. Carroll Smith-Rosenberg offers a complex analysis of multiple factors in the history of women's health. It also provides insight into the pervasive medical model against which Gilman positioned her tale.

St. Jean, Shawn. "Hanging 'The Yellow Wall-Paper': Feminism and Textual Studies." *Feminist Studies* 28: 2 (Summer 2002): 397–415. St. Jean raises the notion of an "authoritative" text and examines various versions of "The Yellow Wall-Paper" from the vantage point of textual studies.

Sutherland, John. "What Cure for the Madwoman in the Attic? Charlotte Perkins Gilman's The Yellow Wall-Paper, 1892" In *Can Jane Eyre Be Happy?* Oxford: Oxford University Press, 1997, 192–9. Sutherland's piercing analysis of "The Yellow Wall-Paper" in his book on literary puzzles from classic fiction explores some of the many ambiguities of the story, giving particular attention to the rest cure and the narration of the tale.

Biographical Reading

Gilman, Charlotte Perkins. *The Living of Charlotte Perkins Gilman*. With an introduction by Ann J. Lane, foreword by Zona Gale. Madison, Wis.: The University of Wisconsin Press, 1990. This is an engaging autobiography with an introduction by a leading Gilman biographer and a foreword by the noted author Zona Gale. If not always accurate about details regarding Gilman's life and work, the autobiography makes for interesting reading and sheds insight into the creation of "The Yellow Wall-Paper."

Hill, Mary A. *The Making of a Radical Feminist, 1860–96*. Philadelphia, Pa.: Temple University Press, 1980. An important early study, Hill focuses on Gilman's life until the age of thirty-six.

Knight, Denise D. *The Diaries of Charlotte Perkins Gilman*. 2 vols. Charlottesville, Va.: University of Virginia Press, 1994. Thoroughly researched, the diaries offer an abundance of biographical information and astute introductions by Knight.

Lane, Ann J. *To Herland and Beyond*. New York: Pantheon Books, 1990. In this personal biography, Lane illuminates important relationships in Gilman's life—e.g. Charles Walter Stetson, Grace Ellery Channing, Houghton Gilman, and S. Weir Mitchell—and includes discussion of "The Yellow Wall-Paper."

Scharnhorst, Gary. *Charlotte Perkins Gilman*. Boston: Twayne, 1985. A Gilman bibliographer and biographer, Scharnhorst offers a literary biography that is meticulously researched and includes a section on "The Yellow Wall-Paper."

Bibliographical Approaches

Dock, Julie Bates. *"The Yellow Wall-paper" and the History of its Publication and Reception. A Critical Edition and Documentary Casebook*. University Park, PA: Penn State University Press, 1998. A work of thorough scholarship, it reprints the 1892 version of "The Yellow Wall-Paper" (without illustrations), makes available early appraisals of the story (notably sixteen reviews following publication of the 1899 chapbook by Small, Maynard & Company), and corrects publication "legends" that turned Gilman into "Saint Charlotte" and Dr. Mitchell into a villain.

Scharnhorst, Gary. *Charlotte Perkins Gilman: A Bibliography*. Metuchen, NJ: The Scarecrow Press, 1985. This bibliography serves as an invaluable resource for students and scholars of Gilman alike. Scharnhorst provides an accurate, comprehensive listing of Gilman's fiction and non-fiction. Chronologically arranged, it groups Gilman's work according to type.

Pedagogical Approaches

Knight, Denise D. and Cynthia J. Davis, eds. *Approaches to Teaching Gilman's "The Yellow Wall-Paper" and Herland*. New York: The Modern Language Association of America, 2003. This long-awaited volume in the MLA teaching series offers a wide range of approaches to teaching "The Yellow Wall-Paper" and *Herland* in varying course contexts. The editors, both noted Gilman scholars, offer insightful discussion of editions of "The Yellow Wall-Paper," film adaptations, historical documents, teaching aids, and paper assignments based on an MLA survey they conducted.

Books on Gilman's Oeuvre

Golden, Catherine J. and Joanna Schneider Zangrando, eds. *The Mixed Legacy of Charlotte Perkins Gilman*. Newark: University of Delaware Press, 2000. A timely addition to Gilman studies, this collection of fourteen new essays by leading Gilman biographers and scholars gives attention to Gilman's prejudice—her racism, ethnocentrism, and classism—and promise for a more "human world," integral parts of her legacy. It includes two new essays on "The Yellow Wall-Paper" by Ann Heilmann and Heather Kirk Thomas.

Karpinski, Joanne, ed. *Critical Essays on Charlotte Perkins Gilman*. New York: G. K. Hall, 1992. Karpinski offers criticism from Gilman's contemporaries and leading scholars, who explore Gilman's theoretical work, poetry, and fiction and compare her contributions to her contemporaries, including William Dean Howells, Olive Schreiner, and S. Weir Mitchell.

Knight, Denise D. *Charlotte Perkins Gilman: A Study of the Short Fiction*. New York, Twayne, 1997. Knight provides an effective overview in which she analyzes Gilman's didactic and utopian short fiction. She sets "The Yellow Wall-Paper" in context of Gilman's oeuvre of short fiction, often neglected in favor of "The Yellow Wall-Paper," while offering autobiographical material and critical essays by Gilman scholars (e.g. Hedges, Golden, Scharnhorst, Kessler) to advance study of Gilman's landmark tale.

Rudd, Jill and Val Gough, eds. *Charlotte Perkins Gilman: Optimist Reformer*. Iowa City: University of Iowa Press, 1999. Rudd and Gough present a collection of thirteen new essays on a range of topics including feminism, women and work, motherhood and reproduction, and poetry. The collection showcases the wide scope of Gilman's writing and her persistent optimism, making her legacy for reform relevant to feminists today.

Companion Pieces by Gilman

The Crux. Edited and with an introduction by Jennifer S. Tuttle. Newark: University of Delaware Press, 2002. *The Crux*, a social hygiene novel originally serialized in *Forerunner* in 1911, lambastes the secrecy surrounding venereal disease and advocates woman's growth and fulfillment through economic independence. Tuttle offers an engaging and informative introduction addressing turn-of-the-century views on sexually transmitted diseases, the American frontier, and the implications of gender ideology for social welfare.

Mag-Marjorie and Won Over. Introduction by Denise D. Knight. New York: Ironweed Press, 1999. This edition brings together two works originally serialized in *Forerunner: Mag-Marjorie*, a work of seduction, betrayal, and redemption; *Won Over*, a critique of the domestic sphere. Knight provides an introduction.

Unpunished. Edited and with an "Afterword" by Catherine J. Golden and Denise D. Knight. New York: The Feminist Press, 1997. Golden and Knight, both leading Gilman scholars, edited and secured publication of Gilman's heretofore unpublished feminist detective novel (written *ca.*1929). Beginning with the death of a misogynist who is killed five, possibly six, ways, Gilman's engaging novel argues against domestic abuse and champions women's empowerment. The "Afterword" analyzes the novel in context of Gilman's oeuvre, discusses its ethnic and racial biases, and foregrounds Gilman's message, relevant to the twenty-first-century legal system.

Index

23, 52, 86–7; "Similar Cases" and 1, 19,
27, 27n1, 71; "The Yellow Wall-Paper"
and 26–27, 28, 50n1, 71, 86–7, 93–4, 96
Howells, Winifred 61
Huang, Guiyou 79, 121–4
hysteria 4, 19, 32–4, 45, 64, 77, 94–6 *see
also* neurasthenia

Ibsen, Henrik 13, 18, 147, 154
Impress 14, 20, 28, 158
Industrial Revolution (industrialism) 9, 144
In This Our World (Gilman) 13, 14, 20,
39–45
infertility 13, 58–9
insanity 13, 35, 48, 58, 60–1, 85, 91–2, 94

Jacobus, Mary 77, 94–6, 114, 115, 115n1,
146
James, Alice 4, 23, 32–4, 61, 145, 158
James, Henry 32, 76, 86, 109, 159
James, William 20, 32, 33, 33n1
Jane Eyre (C. Brontë) 3, 35, 91, 92, 95, 120,
154, 159

Karpinski, Joanne 63, 79, 87, 161
Kellogg, John Harvey 110, 158
Kennard, Jean 74, 76–77, 96
Kessler, Carol Farley 161
Key, Ellen 9
Knapp, Adeline 20
Knight, Denise D. 25, 28, 34, 40, 79–80,
157, 160, 161, 162
Kolodny, Annette 74, 76–7, 92–4, 96,
102n3

Lane, Ann J. 25, 47, 77, 157–8, 160
Lane, Martha Luther 18, 26–7
Lanser, Susan 5, 75, 77, 105–8, 114, 115,
115n1, 117, 118, 120, 146, 151, 158
Lincoln, Abraham 17, 81
Living of Charlotte Perkins Gilman, The
(Gilman) 1, 10–12, 23, 24, 47–52, 159
Lowell, James Russell 1, 50n1
Lutz, Thomas 56, 108–11, 133n11, 152–3

McGann, Jerome 4, 4n1, 127, 127n2
MacPike, Loralee 76
Madwoman in the Attic, The (Gilbert and
Gubar) 74, 77, 88, 91–2, 96–7, 102, 114
Man-Made World, The (Gilman) 22
Mag-Marjorie (Gilman) 162
marriage 13, 34–5, 37–8, 40, 57, 77, 85

Mead, Edwin 71–2, 87
medical model/establishment: 59–61, 61–4,
108–11, 122, 147, 150, 159, 161–2;
Clarke and 18, 57–9; cult of female frailty
and invalidism 4, 12, 13, 32–4, 37–8, 53,
60–1, 64–8, 108–11, 147, 159; death of
22; *Doctor and Patient* and 19; *Fat and
Blood* and 10, 18, 61–8; Freud and 10,
12, 63, 95; Mitchell and 10, 12, 19, 61–8
incl. Fig 4, 115, 122, 123
Mitchell, Dr. Silas Weir 10, 12, 19, 22, 47,
53, 60, 61–4 incl. Fig. 4, 122, 145–6,
148, 160, 161; novels and 18, 19, 20, 21;
"The Yellow Wall-Paper" and 45–52,
100, 114–15, 122, 123; *Wear and Tear*
and 12, 18
*Mixed Legacy of Charlotte Perkins Gilman,
The* (Golden and Zangrando) 78, 79,
105, 114, 150, 161
Morris, William 55–6, 78, 83, 114, 115
motherhood 13, 14–16, 34–5, 57, 77
mother-woman 13, 34–5, 57
Moving the Mountain 22

Neely, Carol 76
neurasthenia (nervous disorders) 4, 10, 13,
32–4, 45, 47, 48, 58, 59–68, 82, 108–11,
149, 150 *see also* hysteria
New England Magazine: 20, 71–2, 84, 85,
87, 158; Jo. H. Hatfield and 4, 60,
127–29; "The Yellow Wall-Paper" and 4,
20, 46, 51, 51n1, 71, 72, 94, 127–8, 149

Ong, Walter 102, 102n4

palimpsest 76, 102, 149
Parker, Gail 76
Perkins, Frederick Beecher 9, 10, 17
Perkins, Mary Fitch Westcott 9–10, 17, 19,
20
Perkins, Thomas 10
Poe, Edgar Allan 4, 10, 28, 74, 118, 159;
Gilman compared to 26, 37, 51, 71, 72,
85, 86, 90, 92–4, 117, 120–1, 145; "The
Tell-Tale Heart" and 28–32, 149

Reform Darwinism 16
rest cure 10, 32–4, 53, 60, 61–8, 108–9,
123, 145–6, 150, 159; Gilman taking the
cure and 6, 10, 12–13, 46, 49, 108–11,
146, 150
Rich, Adrienne 113

eBooks – at www.eBookstore.tandf.co.uk

A library at your fingertips!

eBooks are electronic versions of printed books. You can store them on your PC/laptop or browse them online.

They have advantages for anyone needing rapid access to a wide variety of published, copyright information.

eBooks can help your research by enabling you to bookmark chapters, annotate text and use instant searches to find specific words or phrases. Several eBook files would fit on even a small laptop or PDA.

NEW: Save money by eSubscribing: cheap, online access to any eBook for as long as you need it.

Annual subscription packages

We now offer special low-cost bulk subscriptions to packages of eBooks in certain subject areas. These are available to libraries or to individuals.

For more information please contact webmaster.ebooks@tandf.co.uk

We're continually developing the eBook concept, so keep up to date by visiting the website.

www.eBookstore.tandf.co.uk